SCANDINAVIAN CLASSICS
VOLUME XXVII
∴
NORSE MYTHOLOGY

ESTABLISHED BY

NIELS POULSON

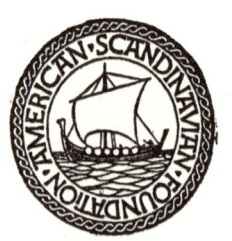

NORSE MYTHOLOGY
LEGENDS OF GODS AND HEROES

By

PETER ANDREAS MUNCH

In the Revision of
MAGNUS OLSEN

Translated from the Norwegian by
SIGURD BERNHARD HUSTVEDT

WILDSIDE PRESS

The Rumford Press, Concord, New Hampshire, U. S. A.

CONTENTS

Contents

II. THE HEROIC LEGENDS

Contents

TRANSLATOR'S PREFACE

THE Norwegian original on which the present translation is based was written by Peter Andreas Munch, the founder of the Norwegian school of history. Munch's scholarly interests embraced also many related subjects, such as general history, archaeology, geography, ethnography, linguistics, and jurisprudence. His varied labors have in large part stood the test of time. His most important work, the "History of the Norwegian People" (*Det norske folks historie*, 8 vols. 1851–63) covering the period of Norway's ancient independence ending with the Kalmar Union of 1397, still remains a source book and a point of departure for historians. The great significance of Munch's scholarship lies in its influence upon the modern renascence of Norwegian culture. In the middle of the nineteenth century he was the most conspicuous intellectual force in the country, as Wergeland had been before him and as Bjørnson came to be after him. The national spirit in Norway, which has steadily gained strength, owes a heavy debt to the gifted leaders of an earlier generation, not least among whom was Munch. As an historian, as an editor of Old Norse poetry and saga, as a recorder of the venerable myths and legends of the race, he did yeoman service in establishing a sense of historical continuity between the Norway of the past and the Norway of the present. Since his day, Norwegians have labored in the fields of history, folklore, and related subjects, deepening and strengthening that fruitful sense of national consciousness which he did so much to awaken.

Translator's Preface

Munch's handbook of Norse Mythology, which first appeared in 1840, was originally written as a supplementary volume to a school text on the history of Norway, Sweden, and Denmark. As a book for students and as a work of general reference it has maintained its popularity. The third edition (1922) from which the translation is made, was prepared by Professor Magnus Olsen of the University of Oslo, in response to the demand for an up-to-date treatment of the entire subject. He found it advisable, however, to revise Munch's work rather than to attempt a wholly original book, since he was thus able to incorporate the results of later research in a volume which had long enjoyed both popular and scholarly approval. The value of Munch's work has been greatly increased through Professor Olsen's revision.

The English translation is intended as a companion volume to two other books published in the SCANDINAVIAN CLASSICS series, *The Prose Edda*, translated by Arthur Gilchrist Brodeur, and *The Poetic Edda*, translated by Henry Adams Bellows. *Norse Mythology* will serve alike the student of Old Norse literature, and the general reader who seeks an authoritative guide through the world of Northern myth and legend.

My thanks are due to Professor Magnus Olsen for permission to translate the work, and to Professor William Witherle Lawrence, of Columbia University, Chairman of the Publications Committee of the American-Scandinavian Foundation, for many valuable suggestions.

S. B. H.

INTRODUCTION

THE mythology of our forefathers, as we know it from
Norse mythical poems and from the records of ancient
writers, has not come down to us in its genuine pagan
form. It is extant only in a later form, dating from a
period when its devotees had begun to lose their absolute faith in the older divinities, had begun to harbor
doubts and to catch intimations of a consolation
nobler and better than that which the ancient divinities had been able to give them. We learn to know it,
furthermore, in the sources designated, as it mani-
fested itself in Norway during the centuries just preceding the introduction of Christianity and as it
appeared, something more than a hundred years
earlier, upon its transference into Iceland by the Norwegian emigrants. In its main outlines it was at that
time common to all the so-called Germanic tribes: on
the one hand, to Norwegians, Swedes, and Danes; and
on the other hand, to Goths, Franks, Saxons, Swabians,
Frisians, Anglo-Saxons, and other peoples. Yet in
the nature of the case, as the Germanic tribes gradually
diverged with respect to language, customs, and modes
of living, and each thus entered upon a separate development, it followed of necessity that mythology
and cult took on a distinct character in each of these
tribes; even in early prehistoric times, moreover,
external influences proceeding from the more cultivated of neighboring non-Germanic peoples must
have been at work, and also mutually operative in-

Introduction

fluences as between the Germanic tribes themselves. The ancient Norse religion was thus far from being identical with the mythology and worship of the other Northern or Germanic peoples. Evidence to this effect is to be discovered even in a cursory comparison with the few available accounts of religious conditions among the various German tribes during the pagan era. The pagan beliefs of the Swedes and the Danes, of which little is known through direct tradition, must also have differed in many particulars from those prevailing in Norway and Iceland as paganism drew toward its end. According to the plan of the present work, the Norwegian-Icelandic myths will have the most prominent place; it is these which particularly concern us, and only by means of these is it possible to reconstruct anything like a complete mythology. So far as it is practicable, nevertheless, reference will be made to the religious survivals of the other Germanic peoples.

Among the various Germanic tribes the pagan mythology was gradually driven back as Christianity spread abroad: first of all in France, about five centuries after the birth of Christ; thereafter in England, a century or two later; and still later in Germany, where the Saxons, who received the new faith at the hands of Charlemagne about the year 800, stood last of the pagan tribes. In the North paganism held its ground more stubbornly; in Iceland it did not loose its hold before the beginning of the eleventh century, in Norway and Denmark thirty years later, and in Sweden probably not before the year 1150.

Introduction

Farther to the south the ancient faith was so thoroughly uprooted that scarcely a reminiscence survived. Only a small number of the early writers have set down so much as an occasional comment on the pagan divinities; their references lack fulness and exactitude and bear the clear stamp of prejudice and contempt. In more southerly lands, even those occupied by German tribes, there existed no such deep need and desire for the preservation of ancestral traditions as marked the North; or, if these tendencies had once prevailed, they had been smothered by the growing influence of the Catholic clergy. Furthermore, such writers as took any interest in recording the memories of the past were almost without exception ecclesiastics, who held it sinful to mention the ancient gods more than was strictly necessary. The situation was different in the North; there the pagan faith maintained a firmer footing, the general interest in searching out old traditions and listening to tales of ancestral prowess had struck deeper roots, and, what is more important, the clergy had never gained so complete an ascendency as in the South. The chief reason for these conditions, at any rate in Norway and Iceland, was that the people held fast both in writing and in speech to the mother tongue, so that Latin, the language of the church, never became well established. The Norse historian would have found little profit in using Latin after the manner of the southern clergy, since few would have been able to read what he might write. Historical composition thus came to be the province of the laity rather than of the clergy. Moreover, our

Introduction

forefathers were inordinately fond of skaldic poetry and song. The skalds made their verses in the vernacular; and since they drew most of their figures and similes from the old mythology, study of the myths was necessary both for the poets and for those who listened to their lays. The skald Hallfred, for example, upon his baptism made the unequivocal statement to king Olaf Tryggvason that he would neither deride the ancient gods nor refrain from naming them in his verse.

Through these various means a knowledge of the older mythology was maintained in Norway and Iceland; and for a long time nothing more than a visit to the neighboring kingdom of Sweden was required to discover a land still wholly pagan. In Iceland the common interest in poetry and history remained so vigorous that, even after medieval Christianity had run a good part of its course, two comprehensive and otherwise remarkable source books of Norse mythology made their appearance, namely Snorri's *Edda* and the so-called *Sæmund's Edda*. Snorri's *Edda* is a veritable handbook for skaldic poets, written about the year 1220 by the illustrious Snorri Sturluson; the first part of the work contains a full account of the ancient system of divinity, and in addition a number of separate stories about the gods and their deeds. The designation of *Edda*, which doubtless means "great-grandmother", probably became attached to the book because its contents were drawn from ancient narratives and songs that had come down from the "days of great-grandmother" herself. *Sæmund's Edda* is a

Introduction

collection of poems celebrating the gods and heroes of
olden times. Just when the collection originated is
uncertain; evidences tend to make it contemporaneous
with Snorri's *Edda;* yet the individual poems are much
older and had lived long in popular tradition before
they came to be written down. *Sæmund's Edda* is also
called the *Elder Edda;* Snorri's, the *Younger Edda.*[1]
Further information about the primitive mythology is
to be gathered from numerous early poems, still extant,
and bits here and there from the saga narratives; but
these sources are as nothing in comparison with the
two *Eddas.* In fine, it is only through Norwegian-
Icelandic sources that satisfactory knowledge of the
ancient mythology is to be obtained.

[1] The *Elder Edda* will be designated in this book as the *Poetic
Edda;* the *Younger Edda* as the *Prose Edda.*—Translator's note.

I

MYTHS OF THE GODS

THE CREATION OF THE WORLD—THE GIANTS—THE ÆSIR—MEN AND WOMEN—DWARFS—VANIR—ELVES

Our forefathers imagined the infinities of space to be a profound abyss, to which they gave the name *Ginnunga-gap;* on one of its confines there were icy frosts and mists; on the other, flame and heat. The frozen reaches were known as the Home of Fogs, or Niflheim; the torrid region as Muspellsheim, which may perhaps be rendered, the Home of Desolation. As the ice of Niflheim gradually melted away before the heat of Muspellsheim, there flowed forth from Niflheim into Ginnunga-gap chill streams of venom (the *Élivágar*), and yet the animating beams from Muspellsheim called the first living beings into life: a prodigious Giant (*jǫtunn*), called Ymir or Aurgelmir, and the cow Audhumla, from whose milk he drew sustenance. From Ymir in turn sprang other Giants, and thus he became the progenitor of all that evil race. The cow Audhumla likewise brought about life anew by licking the icebound boulders of salt. In this manner Buri came into being; his son Borr, with Bestla, daughter of the Giant Bolthorn, had three sons, named Odin, Vili, and Ve. These sons of Borr were good and fair to see; they became the forebears of the race of the Æsir.[1]

When the descendants of Ymir had multiplied beyond number, the sons of Borr put Ymir to death; in

[1] *Áss*, plural *æsir*, genitive *ása.*

[1]

his blood all of the Giants were drowned except Bergelmir, who with his wife saved himself by means of a
boat. The Æsir thus failed in their attempt to exter-
minate the race of Giants, and Bergelmir's kindred
grew to a mighty host. The Giants, or Jotuns, were
also known by the names Thursar (*þursar*), Rime-
Thursar (*hrímþursar*), Ettins (*risar*), Cliff-Ettins
(*bergrisar*), and Trolls (*troll*); they persisted in the
most evil courses. From the body of Ymir the sons of
Borr made earth, sky, and sea. The body itself became the earth, the bones became mountains and
stones, the hair became trees and grass, the skull became the vault of heaven, the brain became clouds,
and the maggots in Ymir's body became small Dwarfs,
who dwelt beneath the earth's surface and in rocks,
and who lived on a better footing with the Giants than
with the Æsir.

Odin, Vili, and Ve, the sons of Borr, were at first
the only Æsir. Not content with shaping inanimate
nature, they brought to life sentient beings as well,
both men and animals. The first human pair, Ask
and Embla, they created from two trees. Odin gave
them breath, Vili[1] gave them soul or understanding,
and Ve (Lodur) gave them bodily warmth and color.
From these two sprang the entire race of men.

The sons of Borr likewise created the celestial bodies.
To this end they employed the sparks that flew into
space out of Muspellsheim. The sun and the moon
were placed each on its wain, and each wain was drawn
by two horses; the horses of the sun were named Arvak

[1] Hœnir, p. 19.

[2]

Myths of the Gods

and Alsvin.[1] Before the sun stands the shield Svalin.[2]
As drivers of the wains were appointed the two beautiful children of Mundilfari, called Sun and Moon.
Mundilfari was so proud of the two that he had
named his daughter after the sun and his son after the
moon; as a punishment the Æsir gave the children the
task of guiding the wains of the sun and the moon.
Moon once carried away from the earth two small
children just as they left the well Byrgir carrying
the cruse Sœg slung from their shoulders on a pole
called Simul. The two children were named Bil and
Hjuki, and their father's name was Vidfinn. Since
that time they have followed the moon in his course.

The Giants or the Rime-Thursar continued without
ceasing to disquiet the Æsir and disturb their labors.
A hideous Giantess, mother of a great brood of Giant
werewolves, bore among the others two called Skoll
and Hati, who took up the pursuit of Sun and Moon,
to devour them. Sun and Moon therefore must needs
make haste in their journey across the heavens; yet in
the end their pursuers will overtake them. Hati was
the more forbidding of the two; he was known also as
Manigarm, or the Moon-Hound. Toward the race of
men the Giants were so ill-disposed that the Æsir
found themselves compelled to build from the eyebrows
of Ymir a great defensive fortress encompassing the
midmost region of the earth. The fortress and all
that it contained bore the name Midgard; beyond its

[1] *Árvakr*, i.e., "the early-waking one"; *Alsviðr*, i.e., "the fleet
one".
[2] "The cooling one".

[3]

confines lay Jotunheim. In the centre of the universe
the Æsir established their own dwelling, Asgard; there
Odin had his own seat, Lidskjalf, from which he might
survey the whole universe, both the heavens and the
earth, and see all that happened there. The race of
the Æsir here grew to a goodly number; Odin particularly had many children.

Aside from the Æsir, the Dwarfs, and the Giants,
our forefathers peopled the universe with other supernatural beings, such as the Vanir and the Elves. To
the Vanir, dwelling in Vanaheim, the direction of the
forces of nature seems particularly to have been attributed. Once upon a time, so the story runs, hostilities
arose between the Æsir and the Vanir; the dispute
ended with a treaty of peace, the terms of which pre-
scribed an exchange of hostages. The Æsir delegated
Hœnir; the Vanir delegated Njord, who in this way
came to be numbered among the Æsir. The other
deities who came from the Vanir were Frey and Freyja.
Of the Elves, beings who associated preferably with
men, some were good and some were evil. The good
Elves, called Bright-Elves (*ljós-alfar*), who were
brighter than the sun, had their abode in Alfheim; the
evil Elves, called Dark-Elves (*svart-alfar, døkk-alfar*),
were blacker than pitch, had their homes beneath the
surface of the earth, and so are often confused with the
Dwarfs.

Myths of the Gods

THE PLAINS OF IDA—VALHALLA—
YGGDRASIL

IN Asgard the Æsir built an immense fortress, in the midst of which lay the Plains of Ida. Here they erected two splendid halls: Gladsheim, which contained high seats for Odin and the twelve peers among the Æsir; and Vingolf, which had high seats for Frigg and the goddesses. Round about Lidskjalf, whence Odin surveys the universe, rose the hall Valaskjalf, roofed with a silver roof.[1] The chief of the halls of Asgard, however, was Valhalla, the banquet hall of the Æsir. Here Odin held high festival not only for the Æsir, but for all the translated heroes (*einherjar*), brave warriors who after death came into his presence. In Valhalla there were 640 portals, through each of which 960 warriors might march in abreast.

Between heaven and earth the Æsir constructed a bridge called Bifrost, or the Rainbow. The ruddy hue of the bridge is the light of a fire that burns without ceasing to prevent the Giants from crossing over it. Bifrost is of all bridges the most splendid and the strongest, and yet at last it will fall asunder, when the end of all things shall have come.

Besides Odin, there were twelve of the Æsir who were held to be chief deities of the universe; among themselves they had apportioned rule over all things, and each day they held counsel about what events should come to pass. Odin was their lord; he was supreme, mightiest of the gods, the preserver of all

[1] See footnote p. 19.

[5]

things, and therefore he was called All-Father. In Gladsheim, where stood the high seats of the gods, they took counsel together. As rulers of the universe the gods bore the titles *regin* or *rǫgn*, governors; *bǫnd* or *hǫpt*, binding or uniting powers; and *véar*, the holy ones. Their high seats were also called judgment seats (*rǫk-stólar*). The gods or Æsir were designated as white, bright, shining, holy, mighty; as war-gods (*sigtívar*) or battle-gods (*valtívar*). They loved the race of men, protected men against Giants, Dwarfs, and Dark-Elves, and upheld righteousness and justice.

When the gods held their solemn assemblies, to which came all the Æsir, they resorted to the ash Ygg-drasil, the tree of the universe. Here was their principal sanctuary. The ash Yggdrasil spread its branches abroad over the whole world. It had three roots: one among the Æsir, another among the Rime-Thursar, a third in the depths of Niflheim. Beside the root in Niflheim there was a fearsome well, Vergelmir; there lay a dreadful serpent, Nidhogg, which, together with a great number of other serpents, gnawed without respite at the root of the tree, threatening to destroy it. Beside the root that rested with the Rime-Thursar there was also a well, which belonged to a Giant, the wise Mimir; in it lay hidden the highest wisdom, and from it Mimir drank each day. Beside the third root, which stretched out to the Æsir, there was also a well, called Urd's Well. It was here that the gods held their assembly. Among the branches of the ash many animals had their resort; there were a sagacious eagle, a hawk, four stags, and the little squirrel Ratatosk, which continually ran up and down bearing evil communications between the eagle and Nidhogg.

ODIN

ODIN, the supreme deity, had, besides the title of All-Father, many other names. He was called Ygg (The Awful), Gagnrad (He Who Determines Victories), Herjan (God of Battles), Har (The High One), Jafnhar (Even as High), Thridi (Third),[1] Nikar, Nikud, Bileyg (One With Evasive Eyes), Baleyg (One With Flaming Eyes), Bolverk (The Worker of Misfortune), Sigfather (The Father of Battle or of Victory), Gaut (The Creator or, the "Geat"), Roptatyr, Valfather (Father of the Slain),[2] etc. Odin was the wisest of all the gods; from him the others always sought counsel when need arose. He drew wisdom from the well of the Giant Mimir. Having placed one of his eyes in pawn with Mimir, Odin invariably appeared as a one-eyed, rather oldish man;[3] otherwise he was represented as strong and well-favored, and as armed with spear and shield. In Valhalla and Vingolf, where Odin gave banquets to gods and heroes, he himself partook of nothing but wine, which to him was both meat and drink; the meat that was placed before him he gave to his two wolves, Geri and Freki.[4] Odin also had two ravens, Hugin

---

[1] These three names, known from *Gylfaginning*, constitute a trinity which at a relatively late period was developed under the influence of the Christian trinity.

[2] Cf. p. 5.

[3] Cf. Harbard, "the graybeard", p. 105.

[4] Both names signify "the greedy one".

and Munin (Thought and Memory), which perched
one on each of his shoulders. To them he owed a
great part of his wisdom; every day they flew forth
through the expanses of the universe, returning at supper to tell him all that they had seen; therefore Odin
was called also the God of Ravens. From his high
seat, Lidskjalf in Valaskjalf, Odin saw all that came to
pass. On his horse, Sleipnir, which was eight-footed
and the fleetest horse in the world, he rode wherever
he wished. His spear Gungnir would strike whatsoever he aimed at. On his arm he wore the precious
ring Draupnir; from it dropped every ninth night
eight other rings as splendid as itself.

The worship of Odin appears to have consisted in
part in a peculiar kind of human sacrifice, and this
circumstance had much to do with our forefathers'
regarding him as a stern and cruel deity. Just as Odin
himself hung upon a gallows, wounded with the thrust
of a spear, and devoted to himself,[1] so, according to
certain legendary narratives[2] it was a custom to dedicate men to Odin by hanging them on a gallows and
piercing them with spears. The skalds thus referred
to Odin as the "God of Hanged Men" or the "Lord
of the Gallows". He bade his raven fly to such as had
been hanged, or he went in person to the gallows tree
and by means of incantations compelled the hanged
man to hold discourse with him. An historian of the
eleventh century, Adam of Bremen, recounts that in
the sacrificial grove near the temple at Uppsala many

---

[1] See note to p. 7.
[2] As, for instance, the story of Starkad and Vikar, p. 221 ff.

Myths of the Gods

human bodies hung from the branches of the sacred trees.[1] This record no doubt has to do with sacrifices to Odin. With these very sacrifices to Odin what Snorri relates in the *Ynglinga Saga* must be closely connected; as the story reads there, Odin immediately before his death caused his body to be marked with the point of a spear, and "dedicated to himself all men who died by force of arms"; "Njord died of disease, but he let himself be marked for dedication to Odin before he died." Thus it was possible for Odin to accept human sacrifice not only by means of hanging but through a ceremonial procedure by which one who wished to avoid dying a natural death made an incision on his body with a spear. And one who advanced to meet an opposing army might, before joining battle, devote the enemy to Odin by hurling a spear over the heads of the hostile force, with the words, "Odin possesses you all." Odin took pleasure in such a sacrifice; to him it was a matter of great moment to surround himself with as many Heroes as possible in preparation for the ultimate warfare against the enemies of gods and men.

Among the Æsir there were several gods of war, but Odin was foremost. From him battle took the name of "Odin's Tempest" and "Ygg's Game"; and the spear, "Odin's Fire". The worship of Odin as the supreme deity was not, however, universally prevalent;

[1] With Adam of Bremen's narrative as a foundation, Hans Dedekam has demonstrated the presence of a sacrificial grove with numerous human figures depending from the trees in the design of a tapestry discovered at Oseberg; see his article, *Odins træ*, in *Kunst og haandverk. Nordiske studier* (Christiania 1918), p. 56 ff.

the cult bound up with his name seems to have come from the South into the North at a comparatively late date. Place names in which the name of Odin forms a compounding element provide valuable aid in determining the limits of Odin worship in various regions.[1]

Jord and Frigg were the wives of Odin; his concubines, the Giantess Grid, and Rind; his sons were Thor (with Jord), Balder (with Frigg), Vidar (with Grid), Vali (with Rind), and besides, Heimdal, Hod, and Bragi; all these were numbered among the chief deities. Other sons are Tyr, Meili, and Hermod, the messenger sent by the gods to Hell upon the death of Balder. Ancient kings and princes were proud to count their descent from Odin; for this reason other sons were later attributed to him, such as Skjold, ancestor of the kings of Denmark, Sæming, ancestor of the Haloigja family (the earls of Lade), Sigi, ancestor of the Volsungs, and still others.

THOR

NEXT after Odin, the principal deity was Thor. He it was who guarded men and their labors from the wild forces of nature, personified as Giants. Thus he held sway—in certain Northern regions—over air and climate, over rain and harvest.[2] As the god of fertility, however, he had to divide his rule with the gods of the Vanir; but thunder and lightning always were

[1] On this point, see § 86 of the original Norwegian text.—Translator's note.

[2] See note to p. 65; cf. p. 118.

Myths of the Gods

the special province of Thor, who according to the Norse myths was constantly engaged in battle against the Giants. He rode in a chariot which, as it rolled along, produced thunder.[1] The chariot was drawn by two goats, Tanngnjost[2] and Tanngrisni;[3] these goats Thor could kill and eat and bring to life once more provided all the bones are gathered up in the hides. Because Thor usually drove these goats, he was called Riding-Thor;[4] he had other names as well, such as Ving-Thor, Lorridi, Einridi.

Thor's realm was known as Thrudvang; there stood his imposing hall, Bilskirnir, the largest in the world, comprising 540 rooms. To Thor belonged three objects of price: the most valuable of these was the hammer Mjollnir, which he carried whenever he gave battle to the Giants; he could make it as great or as small as he pleased, he could hurl it through the air, and it always found its mark and returned of itself to his hand. Again, he had remarkable iron gauntlets with which to grasp the hammer; and he had a belt of strength which, when he girdled it about him, added to his Æsir power. Without Thor the Æsir would have found no help against the Giants; but no sooner did they mention him by name than he gave proof of his prowess. He was wedded to beautiful Sif, of the golden hair;[5] their children were Modi and a daughter

[1] Norw. *torden,* i. e., *Tor-dønn.*
[2] "One who grinds his teeth".
[3] "One who is 'pig-toothed', having distinct interstices between the teeth".
[4] *Øku-Þórr,* from *aka,* "to ride", "to drive".
[5] See p. 30.

named Thrud. With the Giantess Jarnsaxa he had besides a son called Magni.

Thor was hot and hasty of temper; when he rode out to meet the Giants, the mountains trembled and the earth burst into flame. When the gods repaired to Yggdrasil to hold assembly there, Thor did not trouble himself to cross by way of Bifrost but took a shorter road on which he waded the deepest streams. Now and then he might chance to leap before he looked; and so once or twice he came out of some enterprise or other with harm and confusion.[1]

The worship of Thor was very widespread throughout the North. Numerous place names bear witness to his cult,[2] and the sagas contain not infrequent accounts of sanctuaries dedicated to Thor or of invocations directed to him.[3] To our ancestors Thor was tall and strong, handsome and dignified; he had a red beard, and gripped Mjollnir in his hand.

BALDER

THE son of Odin and Frigg is Balder, the god of innocence and piety. He is so bright and fair that light shines from his features; he is also wise, eloquent, gentle, and lenient, and righteous to such a degree that his judgments stand always unshaken. His home and stronghold is called Breidablik;[4] there nothing impure may find lodgment. His wife is the

[1] See p. 56 ff.   See § 86 of the Norwegian original.
[2] Dale-Gudbrand's image of Thor; Thorolf Mostrarskegg's removal of his own shrine of Thor from Hordaland to Iceland.
[4] "Which gleams far and wide".

Myths of the Gods

faithful Nanna, daughter of Nep. His son is the righteous Forseti. Balder was killed by his brother Hod, but after the destruction of the universe he will return again.[1]

The cult of Balder is mentioned only in the late, unhistorical *Fridthjof's Saga;* from this source we learn that he had a great sanctuary, Baldershagi, somewhere in Sogn.[2]

NJORD

NJORD (*Njǫrðr*, originally *Nerpuz*) guides the course of the winds and governs sea and fire; he grants to those who call upon him good fortune at sea and in the chase, and he dispenses wealth, whether of lands or of chattels. Of old he came from Vanaheim.[3] It so befell that when the Æsir and the Vanir were engaged in concluding a treaty of peace, each race gave hostages to the other, the Æsir designating Hœnir and the Vanir, Njord; they all spat in a crock, and from the spittle they made a man, the sapient Kvasir. From that time forth Njord was reckoned among the Æsir and took rank with the foremost of them. His dwelling, called Noatun, is near the sea; outside the walls swim swans and water fowl of all sorts. Njord's children are the god Frey and the goddess Freyja; his wife, their stepmother, is Skadi, a Giantess. The Æsir having brought about the death of her father Thjazi,[4] Skadi went in arms to Asgard to demand recompense. In order to pacify her, the Æsir per-

[1] The detailed narrative of these events will follow, p. 80 ff.
[2] See p. 258.　　　　　　[3] See p. 4.
[4] See p. 53.

mitted her to choose a husband from their number, but she was to see only their feet and to make her choice in this way. She fixed her eyes on a pair of shapely feet and, supposing them to be Balder's, chose accordingly. But her choice fell on Njord, with whom she did not live on the very best of terms; Skadi wished to make her abode in Thrymheim, her old home, but Njord wished to remain in Noatun. So they agreed to live by turns nine nights in Thrymheim and three nights in Noatun. When they had stayed the first nine nights in Thrymheim, Njord said that he was utterly weary of the mountains; the howling of the wolves seemed to him most lugubrious as compared with the singing of the swans. Skadi found herself disappointed likewise; when she had remained three nights in Noatun, she was no less weary of the screaming of the birds and the roaring of the sea, which broke her repose. Thus perforce they went their own ways; Skadi returned to Thrymheim, where she disported herself in skiing and hunting and so earned the sobriquet of the Ski-Deity or the Ski-Goddess (*ǫndurdís*).

Njord was called the Scion of the Vanir, the Vanir-God, the God Without Blemish. According to the testimony of place names,[1] his cult was widespread throughout the North. At the ancient sacrificial feasts, men drank to Njord and Frey next after Odin;[2] and from an early formulary for taking oaths it is manifest that oaths were sworn by Njord and Frey and by the "almighty god" (presumably Thor).

[1] See § 86 of the Norwegian original.
[2] Snorri, *Saga of Hakon the Good*, chapter 14.

Myths of the Gods

FREY

NJORD's son is Frey, who is fair to look upon, mightier
and more valorous than even his own father. He
governs weather and tillage; in his hand lie prosperity,
joy, and peace. Like Njord, Frey is called Scion of the
Vanir, the Vanir-God; also, God of the Seasons and
Giver of Riches. He holds sway over Alfheim and the
Bright-Elves.

Frey has certain priceless talismans that cunning
Dwarfs have made for him. First of these is the ship
Skidbladnir, which sails over land and sea alike; when
its sails are hoisted the winds always favor its course,
and it is so devised that it can be folded together and
kept in a pocket till the time for its use has come.
He has also a marvelous boar, named Gullinbusti or
Slidrugtanni, that races through the air and over the
sea, throwing beams of light from his golden bristles;
Frey often hitches the boar to his chariot when he
wishes to drive abroad. Frey is wedded to Gerd, fair
daughter of the Giant Gymir. Her he caught sight of
one day as he had taken his seat in Lidskjalf to gaze
out upon all the worlds; far to the north he saw her
walking across her father's farmyard; air and sea
shone with brightness as she raised her white arm to
close the door. Frey fell in love with her, and for
sorrow could neither sleep nor drink. His father
Njord sent Skirnir, Frey's servant, to learn what was
amiss with him; then Frey confessed his longing and
commanded Skirnir to run his errand and pay court on
his behalf. Skirnir promised to go if Frey would only

[15]

lend him his magic sword, whose blade, if need be, could strike of its own power. Thus armed he went forth on his quest; and through sorcery he constrained Gerd to promise a meeting with Frey; the appointed tryst was to take place after the lapse of nine nights, and in the interval Frey was beside himself with longing. Frey afterward missed his trusty sword; in a duel with the Giant Beli he was compelled to use the antlers of a stag to kill his opponent. When the end of the world comes, he will feel still more keenly the want of his sword. Snorri relates that his violent love for Gerd was a penalty laid upon him by Odin because Frey had ventured to sit in Odin's seat.

The worship of Frey was general throughout the North, and place names demonstrate that many sanctuaries were dedicated to him.[1] The Swedes showed particular zeal in the cult of Frey; and from Yngvi-Frey (*Yngvi, Yngvifreyr*, also *Ing* or *Ingunar-freyr*) in Uppsala, the family of the Ynglings, Norway's royal house, is said to have descended. There are accounts of horses dedicated to Frey, the so-called Manes of Frey. In Sweden a priestess of his cult was given to Frey for a wife, with whom he is supposed to have lived in actual marriage.

TYR

TYR, Odin's son with the daughter (?)[2] of the Giant Hymir, is bold and courageous; men call upon him in

[1] See § 86 of the Norwegian original.
[2] Cf. p. 66.

Myths of the Gods

battle, and he gives them courage and heroism. Therefore Tyr is the true god of war; he takes pleasure in bringing about strife, and he does nothing whatever for the promotion of concord. Captains and princes are designated after him, Kinsmen of Tyr. No small number of places in the North (mostly in Denmark) commemorate his name; and yet, few traditions connected with him have survived. He has but one hand; the other was bitten off by the Fenris Wolf.[1]

HEIMDAL

HEIMDAL is another of the chief gods; according to report he was considered great and holy, and bore the appellation of the White God. He was born in a miraculous manner of nine Giant maidens, on the confines of the earth, in the morning of time; and he drew his sustenance from the earth. By some he was called Odin's son. His teeth are of gold; by night or day his vision spans a hundred miles of space; he is able to hear the growing of grass upon the ground and of wool on the backs of sheep; therefore he is a fit watchman for the gods. He dwells near Bifrost, which he guards against the Giants. He has an immense horn, the Gjallar-Horn; when he blows it, the sound is heard in all the worlds. His dwelling at the brink of heaven is known as the Mount of Heaven (*Himinbjǫrg*). For the rest, report has little to say of Heimdal. He is also called Gullintanni, by reason of his golden teeth; another of his names is Hallinskidi.

[1] On this myth see p. 23.

The skalds make frequent mention of him; gold they refer to as "Heimdal's Teeth", and to his sword they give the designation "*hǫfuð (manns)*", i. e., "(man's) head", in allusion to an obscure myth. His horse bears the name of Goldtop.

BRAGI

BRAGI, son of Odin, is the god of eloquence and the art of poetry. Our forefathers thought of him as a venerable man with a long beard. After him, according to Snorri, all manner of minstrelsy is given the title *bragr*. Idun is his wife; to her belong the marvelous apples which restore youth to the gods when old age comes upon them.

FORSETI

FORSETI, the son of Balder and Nanna, is the god of justice and conciliation. Those who refer their disputes to him never go away unreconciled. The hall where he sits in judgment is known as Glitnir; its pillars are of gold and its roof is of silver. Forseti must have had no small number of worshippers; a reminiscence of the cult is to be found in a Norwegian place name, Forsetelund in Onsøy, Østfold.

HOD—VALI—VIDAR—ULL

CONCERNING the four major gods Hod, Vali, Vidar, and Ull, few references are found in Norse sources. Hod, the son of Odin, is blind but vigorous; he it is who

Myths of the Gods

unwittingly brings about the death of Balder; he is subsequently killed by Vali and he will not return until after the universe has come to destruction. Vali (also called by Snorri, less correctly, Ali) is the son of Odin and Rind. He has his own house in Valaskjalf,[1] and is a bold warrior and a good archer. He will neither wash himself nor clip his hair until he has taken vengeance upon Hod for the death of Balder, and he will survive the destruction of the universe. Vidar too shall return after Ragnarok. He is the son of Odin and the Giantess Grid, and next to Thor he is the strongest of the gods. He is called The God of Few Words. When Ragnarok, the Twilight of the Gods, is come, he will avenge Odin by cleaving with his thick boot the throat of the Fenris Wolf. His dwelling is in Vidi. Ull is fair to look upon, a mighty bowman and ski-runner; men do well to summon him to their aid in single combat. He is the son of Sif and the stepson of Thor. His dwelling bears the name of Ydalir.

HŒNIR—LODUR

HŒNIR and Lodur are also reckoned, though very infrequently, among the gods. Hœnir's name is found in the *Prose Edda* among the major divinities, and he appears besides as the companion of Odin. According to the *Vǫluspá*, Lodur takes part with Odin and Hœnir

---

[1] This seems to be the meaning of *Grimnismál*, strophe 6. It is not clear whether the name is to be read *Válaskjalf* or *Valaskjálf;* if it is to indicate the dwelling of Vali, it must be *Válaskjalf*. In Snorri's *Edda* it is Odin who possesses *Valaskjálf* (cf. Valhalla`· see above, p. 5.

in the creation of man. These three "mighty and benevolent Æsir" once came down to the seashore, where they found Ask and Embla lying lifeless, without breath, without soul, and without blood; Odin gave them breath, Hœnir gave them soul, and Lodur gave them blood and bodily color. According to the *Prose Edda*, however, it was the sons of Borr, namely Odin, Vili, and Ve, who created Ask and Embla. Odin, Hœnir, and Lodur, or Odin, Vili, and Ve thus function as a sort of trinity of the Æsir. In the *Gylfaginning* something of the kind is to be found in Snorri's formulation of the ancient mythology, namely, the trinity *Hár* (The High), *Jafnhár* (The Equally High), and *Þriði* (The Third). At the end of the war between the Æsir and the Vanir, Hœnir was delivered over to the Vanir as a hostage.[1] As the more complete account runs in Snorri's *Ynglinga Saga:* Hœnir was a tall and handsome man, whom the Æsir declared to be well fitted to be made a chieftain; but for fuller security they sent the wise Mimir with him. Hœnir was at once given leadership in Vanaheim, and all went well so long as Mimir remained at his side; but when Hœnir, in the absence of Mimir, had to make difficult decisions, he invariably declared that "others must determine that". Whereupon the Vanir at length lost patience, killed Mimir, and sent his head back to the Æsir. On the evidence of Snorri's *Edda*, Hœnir was also called The Fleet God or The Long-Footed God or The King of Eld (*aurkonungr*, Snorri's *Edda* I, 168). In the "Saga Fragment" mentioned below,[2] Rœrek

[1] See p. 4.   [2] See note to p. 18, line 5.

Myths of the Gods

Slœngvandbaugi—brother of king Helgi and son-in-law of Ivar Vidfadmir—is compared with Hœnir, who here is called the most timorous of the Æsir. Possibly other myths having to do with him have failed to survive.

LOKI AND HIS CHILDREN

THE twelve major deities in the mythology of the *Eddas* were, as already enumerated,—in addition to Odin—Thor, Njord, Frey, Balder, Tyr, Heimdal, Bragi, Forseti, Hod, Vidar, Vali, and Ull. Next after these is mentioned, among the foremost Æsir, Loki or Lopt, although he is more properly to be counted their enemy. By race he was a Giant, his father being the Giant Farbauti and his mother the Giantess Laufey or Nal; yet he became the foster brother of Odin and was numbered among the Æsir. His brothers were Byleist (also called Byleipt) and Helblindi. Loki was well-favored, but crafty and malicious. To be sure, he was sometimes compelled to make good the evil he had done, and occasionally he even placed his cunning at the service of the Æsir in seasons of great need; yet in all that really mattered he remained their enemy and the secret friend of the Giants. Loki was the actual instigator of the death of Balder. At the last day he will reappear as one of the captains of the Giants, and his terrible progeny will cause much more harm than even he himself. With the Giantess Angerboda in Jotunheim he had three children: Fenrir, Jormungand, and Hel. Fenrir

[21]

was a ravening wolf, known also as the Fenris Wolf; Jormungand was a hideous, venom-spewing serpent; and Hel was a horrible hag. These three were fostered as children in Jotunheim, and the gods foreknew that Loki's offspring would work them great evil. Therefore the All-Father, Odin, commanded them to be brought before him. The gods forebore to put them to death, for the course of fate was not to be broken, neither was the sacred refuge of Valhalla to be contaminated; so the gods sought other means of being rid of the three. Hel they thrust into the depths of Niflheim to hold sway there and to receive in her abode all who should die of illness or old age, whether men or other beings of earth. Jormungand they hurled into the deep sea of the universe, where he grew and waxed so great as to be able to encompass the earth and to bite his own tail. Therefore he is commonly called the Midgard Serpent, since he holds all of Midgard encircled. The Wolf, on the other hand, was nurtured in Asgard and was so ferocious that none but Tyr dared to bring him food. When the gods saw that he was growing altogether too rapidly, they became much alarmed and undertook to bind him fast. They declared that they desired, just in sport, to try his strength by testing his ability to break a chain which they had provided for the purpose. The Wolf, falling in with their wishes, consented to be bound but at once burst his fetters. He did likewise with a second chain, twice as strong as the first. Then the All-Father sent Skirnir on an errand to certain Dwarfs living in the home of the Dark-

Myths of the Gods

Elves, to have them forge a chain that the Wolf should not be able to break asunder. The Dwarfs accordingly made a chain from the sound of a cat's footfall, the beard of a woman, the roots of a mountain, the sinews of a bear, the breath of fishes, and the spittle of birds; this is the reason why the footfall of the cat no longer has any sound, why women have no beards, why mountains have no roots, and so on. The chain, called Gleipnir, was fine and soft as silk. The Æsir led the Wolf out upon the island of Lyngvi in the lake named Amsvartnir and there asked him if he would submit to being bound with Gleipnir. The Wolf, suspecting some trick, gave his consent only on the condition that one of them would place a hand in his mouth as an earnest of his release if the chain should remain unbroken. The Æsir, unwilling to take such a risk, looked doubtfully at one another; finally Tyr stepped forward and laid his hand in the Wolf's muzzle. The Wolf was then bound. The more he struggled to free himself, the tighter held the chain; by no means was he able to break it and, since the Æsir had no thought of letting him go, he bit off Tyr's hand. The Æsir drew the end of the chain through a great slab of rock, thrust it deep into the ground, and laid a huge boulder over it. The Wolf, mad with rage, snapped and bit at everything round about; but they thrust a sword into his mouth so that his jaws gaped wide. He howls dismally, and slaver runs from him like a river. Thus he shall lie bound till the world comes to an end; but then he will gain his freedom, will prove to be the worst enemy of the gods, and will even swallow up Odin himself. But the Wolf will be killed by Vidar.

In regard to all the malicious tricks Loki played on the Æsir and the punishments he suffered in consequence, further accounts will follow. His wife was Sigyn, with whom he had several sons. Besides, he became in a peculiar manner the father, or rather the mother, of Odin's horse Sleipnir. It happened in this way. When Midgard had been created and the gods were meditating the building of a massive stronghold as a bulwark against the Giants, a Giant smith came forward and offered to build the stronghold in a year's time if he might have Freyja, the sun, and the moon by way of payment; but if on the first day of summer any part of the work remained undone, he was to receive no wages. The Æsir felt secure in making such a promise, and crafty Loki urged them on. But the building proceeded more rapidly than they had thought possible; for the Giant's powerful horse, Svadilfari, during the night pulled into place stones as huge as mountains. When only three days remained before summertide, the Giant was already busied with the castle gate, and the Æsir were growing uneasy; at no price whatever were they prepared to surrender Freyja, the sun, and the moon. They commanded into their presence Loki, whose bad counsel was the cause of their trouble, threatened him with death, and thus frightened him into promising to find a way out of their difficulties. Transforming himself into a mare, he ran whinnying out from the forest at evening just as Svadilfari was at his task of hauling stone. Svadilfari

Myths of the Gods

broke loose and followed the mare into the woods, pursued in turn by the builder; that whole night not a stone was hauled, and thus the work was interrupted. The mason was enraged; but Thor crushed his head with Mjollnir. The mare—or Loki—later foaled Sleipnir, the world's fleetest horse, a gray with eight feet.

HERMOD—SKIRNIR

AMONG various subordinate Æsir, who in their own right are powerful enough, but who virtually serve as retainers to the others, appear Hermod and Skirnir. Skirnir, Frey's servant, has already been discussed.[1] Hermod is the son of Odin, and bears the sobriquet, "the resolute"; he is employed in all sorts of errands and embassies. Odin himself presented his son with helmet and byrnie. Hermod is celebrated for his mission to Hel for the purpose of bringing Balder back again. It is Hermod and Bragi who go forth to meet Hakon the Good and to bid him welcome to Valhalla on Odin's behalf.

THE GODDESSES—FRIGG—JORD—FREYJA

AMONG the goddesses there are likewise, besides Odin's wife Frigg, twelve or thirteen of the highest rank, namely: Freyja, Saga, Eir, Gefjon, Sjofn, Lofn, Var, Vor, Syn, Lin, Snotra, Fulla, and Gna; all of these are enumerated together in Snorri's *Edda*. Fulla and Gna,

[1] P. 15.

and to a certain degree Lin as well, are merely handmaidens of Frigg; in their stead may therefore be
placed Idun, Nanna, and Sif, all of whom are far
more important. Next in order come Sigyn, Gerd,
and Skadi, who however are of Giant race; and thereafter some of the daughters of the gods and the goddesses. Jord and Rind are also counted among the
goddesses.

Frigg is the daughter of Fjorgynn;[1] she is the wife of
Odin, the mother of Balder, and chief among the
goddesses. Her house is the splendid Fensalir. The
goddesses Lin, Fulla, and Gna are closely associated
with her. Lin is set to guard those of mankind whom
Frigg desires to preserve from harm. Fulla, a maiden
with long flowing hair and a golden chaplet about her
brow, carries Frigg's hand casket, keeps watch and
ward over her shoes, and shares her secrets. Gna runs
errands for Frigg through the various worlds, especially in matters requiring despatch, in which instances
she rides the horse Hofvarpnir, who races through the
air and over the waters. Something is to be learned of
the cult of Frigg by means of Norwegian and Swedish
place names,[2] and her name occurs also among German
and English tribes.[3] The Frigg of the *Eddas* was no
doubt derived from an ancient goddess of earth or of
fertility, according to the testimony of both her own
name and her father's.[4] Further evidence is to be discovered in the manifest connection between Frigg,

[1] See note.
[2] See § 86 of the original Norwegian text.
[3] See note.
[4] More on this point in the note.

daughter of Fjorgynn, and Jord, Thor's mother, who bears the additional name Fjorgyn.

Freyja, of the race of the Vanir, is a daughter of Njord and a sister of Frey. As the story reads she was, at the treaty of peace with the Vanir, delivered over by them and accepted by the Æsir among the goddesses. She was wedded to Od, but he left her and went out into foreign lands; she often wept over him, wept golden tears. Her daughters, Noss and Gersemi, were so beautiful that from them all precious gems have taken their names; and from Freyja the designation *freyja* or *frúva*[1] is likewise said to have been formed. Freyja was in the habit of driving a cart drawn by two cats; and she had in her possession the magnificent necklace called Brisingamen.[2] She dwelt in Folkvang, in the great hall named Sessrymnir. Of all the heroes who fell in battle, half became her portion; it was her right to choose them, and to her they came in Folkvang. She had special authority in the relations of love, yet she was not the only goddess of love to whom men had recourse; Sjofn had the power to kindle love between men and women, and Lofn to help those who loved each other but who met with difficulties in winning the beloved.

Freyja had several names. She was called Vanadis because she came of the race of the Vanir. At one time she set out in search of Od, on which occasion she adopted various names, as follows: Mardol, Horn (or Hœrn?), Gefn, and Syr.

[1] Meaning "lady".
[2] See p. 79.

Norse Mythology

SAGA—EIR—GEFJON—VAR—VOR—SYN— SNOTRA

In the array of goddesses in the *Prose Edda*, Saga is found next after Frigg; possibly Saga is only another name for Frigg. Her house is known as Sœkkvabek;[1] cool waves wash over her dwelling, and here Odin and she drink each day from crocks of gold. Some generations since, it was a common opinion that she was the goddess of history, "saga"; but it is certain that her name was *Sága* and not *Saga* (with a short vowel). No more reasonable explanation has been proposed than that the name may have been formed from a root found in *at sjá* (Gothic *saihwan*) and thus has the meaning: she who sees—and knows—all things, in common with Odin.[2] Eir is the goddess of healing, her name having originally been the common noun *eir*, "mercy". Gefjon, according to Snorri's *Edda*, was a maiden, to whom came after death all who died maids. Odin says of her in *Lokasenna* that she knows the fates as well as himself. It thus seems as if Gefjon, like Saga, corresponds to Odin's wife Frigg. There is another myth having to do with a Gefjon who was one of Odin's following. She asked king Gylfi of Sweden for as much land as she could plow around in one day, and he promised her the gift. She accordingly transformed her sons into oxen, put them before the plow, and with them she plowed loose all the land that once

---

[1] From *søkkr* or *søkkvi*, " a state of depression", as in the idiom *liggja í søkk* or *í søkkva;* possibly another designation for Fensalir (p. 26).

[2] Concerning Frigg, cf. p. 26.

Myths of the Gods

lay where now lies Lake Mälaren. This parcel of
earth she drew out into the Baltic, and the land is now
called Zealand; there she made her home, and there she
was wedded to Odin's son Scyld. Var [1] hears the
oaths of fidelity that men and women make to each
other. Hence, if report be true, these promises are
known as *várar*, and Var punishes those who break
them. Vor [2] is endowed with prudence; she searches
into all things so that nothing remains hidden from her.
Syn "guards the door of the hall" and prevents the
unworthy from entering; she also hinders men from
bearing false witness in courts of law; thence, says
Snorri, we get *syn*, "the act of denying" (*at synja*).
Snotra is wise and decorous of manner.[3]

IDUN—NANNA—SIF

LITTLE is known of Idun, Nanna, and Sif. Idun,
the wife of Bragi, had in her possession the most priceless treasures of the Æsir, certain apples that restored
youth to those who ate of them. Without them the
Æsir would have become old and feeble. For this
reason they were fearful of losing Idun, so that on one
occasion when she had been carried off by the Giant
Thjazi [4] they were in the most dire straits. Idun was
designated as the "Goddess of Brunnaker's Bench",
presumably the name of the dwelling where she and

---

[1] *Vár*, "a promise", "an oath"; related to German *wahr*,
"true".
[2] Originally a form of the adjective *varr*, "wary", "attentive".
[3] From *snotr*, "wise", "having knowledge of fitting behavior",
"winsome".
[4] See p. 53.

Bragi were housed. Nanna, daughter of Nep, was the wife of Balder, whom she so loved that her heart broke at his death. Sif was the wife of Thor. She had been wedded before, to whom we do not know; and she was the mother of Ull, who is called the stepson of Thor. Sif was fair and had gold hair fashioned for her by cunning Dwarfs. Her name, meaning "kindred", "relationship", indicates that she was thought of as the protector of homes, just as Thor was the protector of Midgard.[1] Sigyn, Skadi, and Gerd have already been discussed.

THE NORNS

NEXT in order to the major gods and goddesses were other powerful divinities, and besides, certain supernatural beings of a lower degree. Most highly regarded were probably the Norns, the goddesses of Destiny. Though their number was rather large, three of them were more prominent than the rest, namely, Urd, Verdandi, and Skuld, who dwelt beneath Yggdrasil, beside the well which after Urd is called Urd's Well, where two swans resort, where the branches of Yggdrasil drip honey dew, and where the gods meet in solemn assembly. The Norns control the destiny of all men and even of the Æsir themselves; and they direct the immutable laws of the universe. At the birth of every child the Norns are present to determine its fate, and no man lives one day longer than the Norns grant him leave. There are both good

[1] See p. 11.

Myths of the Gods

and evil Norns; but the decrees of all alike must be obeyed.

FAMILIAR SPIRITS—ATTENDANT SPIRITS

RELATED to the Norns were the Familiar Spirits (*hamingjur*) and the Attendant Spirits (*fylgjur*). The Familiar Spirits were supernatural, usually invisible feminine beings who accompanied men and directed their course. Each person had his Familiar Spirit, who strove to bring him good luck;[1] it was possible to lend one's Familiar Spirit to another in case one desired to run a risk in his behalf. The Attendant Spirits (*fylgjur*), on the other hand, ordinarily had the shape of animals who walked before men or beside them. Each person had, according to the belief of our fathers, one or more Attendant Spirits; and certain people pretended that they could see the Attendant Spirits and thus ascertain in advance who was drawing near. The Attendant Spirit usually corresponded to the character of the individual in question; powerful chieftains had bears, bulls, and the like as Attendant Spirits, crafty folk had foxes, and so forth. Supernatural beings of this type were not made the object of worship or prayer. Tales have come down to us of sundry men to whom these beings by preference revealed themselves and who by such means gained an uncommon insight into the destinies of other men. Faith in Familiar Spirits and Attendant Spirits per-

---

[1] Hence the word *hamingja* used as a synonym for "good fortune".

Norse Mythology

sisted after the introduction of Christianity; even zealous Christians like Olaf Tryggvason and Saint Olaf were not wholly free from such beliefs. Occasionally both of these classes of tutelary powers were designated outright as Norns; the popular mind appears not to have drawn a sharp distinction in this respect.

THE VALKYRIES

OTHER feminine beings who exercised control over the fates of men and were closely related to the Norns, were the Valkyries. Victory lay in their government, and mortality in battle; Odin sent them forth to "choose the slain" or the heroes who were doomed to fall.[1] They were therefore also called the Maidens of Odin. They were beautiful young girls; armed and fully panoplied, they rode through the air and over the waters, to the ends of the world. At home in Valhalla they served as cupbearers to the Æsir and Heroes in the halls of Odin. There were two classes of Valkyries: an original order, the celestial Valkyries; and another order, half mortal and half divine, who lived for a time among men as mortals but who later came to Odin in Valhalla, evidently a sort of feminine counterpart to the Heroes. The number of the celestial Valkyries is variously computed, as nine or as nine times nine; they were frequently imagined as riding about in three groups. Those most commonly mentioned were Gondul, Skogul (also called Geir-

[1] Thence their name, from *valr*, "the fallen", and *kjósa*, participle *kørinn, korinn*, "to choose".

Myths of the Gods

Skogul, or Spear-Skogul), Lokk, Rist, Mist, Hild, and others. Skuld [1] was also counted among the Valkyries. Besides these, there were other Valkyries who created dissension among the Heroes and who were employed only in the most menial tasks.

Valkyries, Norns, Familiar Spirits, Attendant Spirits, and occasionally even certain of the goddesses, notably Freyja,[2] were known by the general designation of Disir. *Dís* (plural *dísir*) was no doubt originally a term used to denote a distinct group of gods.[3] Worship of them consisted of a special kind of sacrifice (*dísablót*), doubtless a more intimate cult, participated in only by women; the Disir were supposed to have particular concern for the good of the home and the family, and in so far were not noticeably different from the Attendant Spirits of a family (*kynfylgjur, spádísir*), which have been discussed above.[4] From their number, however, proceeded a goddess who was to become the centre of a more general cult; and it must have been this goddess—perhaps *Vanadís*, Freyja—who was worshipped in Disarsal near Uppsala.[5] In connection with the annual sacrifice to the Disir at Uppsala were held also a court assembly (*dísaping*) and a market; until very recent times the market-fair of Uppsala at Candlemass, early in February, was commonly called "Distingen", that is, the Disir court.

---

[1] See p. 30.   [2] *Vanadís*, p. 27.
[3] According to some scholars, death goddesses; according to others, earth goddesses.   [4] Cf. p. 31 and note to p. 32.
[5] *Dísarsalr*, mentioned in the *Ynglinga Saga*, chapter 29, in the narrative of the death of king Adils.

THORGERD HŒLGABRUD AND IRPA

WITHIN one of the greater families, the ancestral Disir might attain the rank of goddesses and become the objects of something more than private worship. Of this there is an example in the goddesses of the Haloigja family, namely Thorgerd Hœlgabrud and her sister Irpa. Thorgerd was the daughter of an ancient mythical king Hœlgi, after whom Halogaland is said to have its name; that is, Hœlgi is the eponymous hero of the district, the personal name having been formed by the operation of myth to explain the place name. Thorgerd Hœlgabrud is also called, but less correctly, Horgabrud [1] and Horgatroll. In more recent saga tradition this designation of "troll" no doubt had some connection with the aid she was supposed to have given to Hakon, Earl of Lade, in the battle of Hjorungavag. According to Snorri's *Edda* (I, 400), her father also was worshipped; the mound in which he was buried was constructed from alternate layers of earth and stone, and of silver and gold— "these were the treasures offered up before him".

THE FORCES OF NATURE—ÆGIR

WHILE the Æsir as major deities governed all the forces of Nature and strove to direct them in the interest of mankind, almost every natural force or element had its own indwelling divinity; this divinity, a kind of personification of the natural force or element itself,

[1] From *hǫrgr*, a certain type of sanctuary.

was able to set those forces in motion but unable to determine their activities wholly. Thus Njord governed the winds and guided their course, but he was not their prime mover; that function was fulfilled by the Giant Ræsvelg (*Hræsvelgr*, that is, Consumer of Corpses) who, sitting in the guise of an eagle at the northern confines of the heavens, produced the winds by the beating of his wings. So long as the rude powers of Nature are left to themselves, their activities are rather harmful than beneficent, for which reason it is no wonder that our fathers commonly regarded these elementary divinities as Giants; for it was distinctly characteristic of the Giants that they were seldom on good terms with the Æsir and that they constantly had to be kept in subjection. The most powerful of these lesser divinities were Fornjot and his kin. Fornjot, according to story, had three sons: Ler, Logi, and Kari. Ler ruled the sea, Logi ruled the fire, and Kari ruled the wind. Kari's son was named Jokul or Frosti; Frosti's son was named Snjo; and Snjo in turn had four children: Thorri, Fonn, Drifa, and Mjoll. Fornjot was no doubt originally a name for Giant;[1] he was probably to be identified with the primordial Giant Ymir. Kari means literally "wind",[2] and Logi means "flame". Jokul means "icicle"; Frosti, "frost"; Snjo, "snow"; Thorri, "black frost"; Fonn, "perennial snowbank"; Drifa, "snowdrift"; Mjoll, "fine driving snow". The names themselves thus indicate what these divinities represented. Most

---

[1] See note.
[2] Old Norse *kári*, in Norwegian dialects *kåre*, "gust of wind".

remarkable of them all was Ler, god of the sea. He was also, indeed usually, called Ægir; and by reason of the similarity in names, Snorri fixes his abode on the island of Læsø in the Kattegat. At first he was no friend of the Æsir. Thor, however, intimidating him with piercing eyes, constrained him to give a banquet for the gods each winter in his own hall; later he in turn paid visits to the Æsir, who received him in a friendly manner. His banquets were in very truth merrymakings, at which ale flowed of its own accord; his hall was lighted by gleaming gold instead of candles; his brisk serving men, Eldir and Fimafeng, ministered to the guests. Yet now and again Ægir's evil nature got the upper hand. He kept meditating vengeance against Thor, who had presumed to lay commands upon him; at length he hit upon the plan of having Thor find for him a kettle large enough to brew ale for all the Æsir together. Such a kettle he knew was to be had from the Giant Hymir alone, and it was only after running many a risk that Thor succeeded in obtaining the kettle and carrying it away with him.[1] Ægir's wife, Ran, endeavored by all possible means to bring mischance upon mankind; she had in her possession a net, with which she made it her constant pursuit to draw seafaring men down to herself in the deeps of the ocean. Ægir and Ran had nine daughters; their names form various designations for the waves, which explains why the skalds sometimes describe the waves as Daughters of Ægir or of Ran. In the kenning for gold, "Ægir's Fire", the

[1] See p. 65 ff.

name of the god of the sea also occurs; gold, it will be remembered, was employed in the lighting of his banquet hall.

NIGHT—DAY

THE divinities of day and of night were also of Giant race. The Giant Norvi had a daughter by the name of Nott (Night), who was dark and swarthy like the rest of her kindred. She was first wedded to Naglfari, with whom she had a son named Aud; later, to Anar, with whom she had a daughter named Jord, who became the wife of Odin; [1] and finally, to Delling, of the race of the Æsir, with whom she had a son named Dag (Day), who was bright and fair like his father's family. The All-Father took Night and her son Day, gave them two horses and two wains, and stationed them aloft in the heavens, where they were to ride around the earth in alternating courses of twelve hours each. Night drives the horse known as Rimfaxi (*Hrímfaxi*, that is, "having a mane of rime"), and each morning the fields are bedewed with froth that drips from his bit. This horse is also called Fjorsvartnir (from *fjǫr*, "life", and *svartr*, "black"). Day drives Skinfaxi ("with the shining mane"); earth and sky sparkle with the light from his mane.

HEL

FAR down beneath the root of Yggdrasil, in darkest and coldest Niflheim, lies the fearful domain of Hel,[2]

[1] Cf. note to p. 27.
[2] Hel is here used to designate the goddess; hell, her realm. —Translator's note.

daughter of Loki and Angerboda. One half of her body has a livid tinge, and the other half the hue of human flesh; she is harsh and cruel, greedy for prey, and tenacious of those who have once fallen under her rule. The dark, deep vales surrounding her kingdom are called Hell-Ways; to go thither men must cross the river Gjoll ("roaring", "resounding"), spanned by the Bridge of Gjoll, which is paved with gold. Lofty walls enclose her dwelling place, and the gate that opens upon it is called Hell-Gate. Her hall is known as Eljudnir; her dish or porringer, as Hunger; her knife, as Famine; her bondman and bondmaid, as Ganglati and Ganglot (both words meaning "tardy"); her threshold, as Sinking to Destruction; her couch, as Sickbed; the curtains of her bed, as Glimmering Mischance. Her huge bandog, Garm, is bloody of chest and muzzle. Her "sooty-red" cock crows to herald the fall of the universe. In the midst of Niflheim stands the well Vergelmir,[1] beside which lies the serpent Niddhogg. The brinks of Vergelmir are called Nastrand (the Strand of Corpses); here is the most forbidding spot in Niflheim. All who did not fall in battle were said to go to Hell; but the general belief seems nevertheless to have been that only the wicked found their way thither.

In the terminology of the skalds, Hel is not infrequently designated as the Daughter of Loki, the Wolf's (the Fenris Wolf's) Sister, and the like. The names Hell (and Niflhel) are often used of the realm of the dead; thence the expression in Norwegian, å slå

[1] *Hvergelmir*, p. 6.

ihjel (*ihel*),—"to strike into Hell", "to kill". When ghosts walked abroad, the saying might commonly be heard, "Hell-Gate is open" (*hnigin er helgrind*); for then it was possible for spirits to slip out.

THE GIANTS

THE Giants, sworn enemies of men and of Æsir, were savage and violent but not always malicious. On occasion they might even manifest downright simplicity and good nature. They were of monstrous size, they often had several heads and hands, and they had dark skin and hair. Many of their women were well-favored, as for example Gerd; others again were most hideous: one might have a tail, another two heads, and so forth. The Giants owned great herds of cattle, bulls with gold horns, sheep, horses, and dogs. They loved darkness and the deeds of darkness; their women, avoiding the light of day, were in the habit of riding forth by night, and so they were sometimes called Dark-Riders or Night-Riders. If the sun's rays chanced to strike a Giant, he turned at once to stone. Now and then it happened that the Giants fought among themselves, throwing huge boulders at one another; but for the most part they were occupied in battle against mankind and the Æsir. The sanctuaries dedicated to the gods were most obnoxious to them, and when the Æsir gave ground before God and his saints, the hatred of the Giants spent itself on the newer deities. Long after the introduction of Christianity, the Giants survived in popular beliefs, and a

multitude of legends bear witness to the hostility of
the Giants against churches and church bells. To this
day in many localities legends are current connected
with great boulders or even mountains which are said
to have been hurled at churches by the Giants. In
earlier times they had as opponents Thor and Odin;
later they did battle with mighty saints, with the
archangel Michael, and above all with Saint Olaf.
To the present day, tradition has preserved legends
about fat and well-fed cattle—always black—owned
by Mountain-Trolls or Jutuls, about Giant women
with long tails which they find it impossible to conceal,
and about the malice and stratagems of these beings
toward mankind, whom they frequently entice to
themselves into the mountains.

The Giants were skilful builders, wise and experi-
enced in all the occult arts. When they became angry,
a so-called Giant valor seized them which made their
strength double what it was before. As already explained, the Giants lived in Jotunheim or in mountains
lying nearer the haunts of men. More than ordinary
fame attaches to Utgard, the Giant counterpart to the
Midgard of mankind. The river Iving, which never
froze over, marked the boundaries between Giants and
gods. When the expeditions into the Arctic seas of the
North began, Jotunheim or Giant-land gave its name
to a real country: the great Russian steppes about the
White Sea or Gandvik (the Bay of Trolls), or more
particularly the regions bordering on the river Dwina.
Here ruled the Giant kings, Geirrœd and his brother
Godmund of Glæsisvoll; and many a daring voyager

who visited them had surpassing dangers to encounter. The actual ruler of Utgard, however, was the crafty Utgard-Loki.

THE DWARFS

THE Dwarfs and the Dark-Elves, between whom a sharp distinction was not always drawn, lived far beneath the surface of the earth or else made their habitat within great rocks or mounds. They were small of stature and ill-favored; the Dark-Elves were commonly reputed to be blacker than pitch. A large number of Dwarfs are mentioned by name in ancient literature; an interpolated passage in the *Voluspá* lists a long array of them, among others their chief Modsognir (or Motsognir?), and next in order after him, Durin. Other Dwarfs were Brokk,[1] Dvalin, and the four whom Odin appointed to hold up the vault of the heavens, namely North, East, South, and West. The chief occupation of the Dwarfs was that of smith, in which they had no rivals. All the most notable weapons and all the precious gems mentioned in the oldest myths were the work of cunning Dwarfs. The Dwarfs hated both gods and men and were unwilling to do them service; if nevertheless they were compelled to do so, they strove to give their handiwork some magic quality of evil omen so that it brought little joy to any one who came into possession of it.

[1] See p. 51.

Norse Mythology

THE VETTIR

ALL supernatural beings, good and evil alike, had one name in common, Vettir (*vættir*, *véttir*, "spirits", "sprites"), which is still to a certain extent in use. The good ones were called Kind Sprites (*hollar vættir*), and the evil ones were called Bad Sprites (*meinvættir*, *úvættir*). To the Kind Sprites belonged the so-called Land-Sprites, guardian divinities of a given country. In Iceland the Land-Sprites were held in high esteem; according to the earliest legal code ("Ulfljot's Law"), it was forbidden to sail a ship of war into any Icelandic harbor bearing at the prow a "gaping head or snout", which might terrify the Land-Sprites. The worst misfortune one could bring to a man was to invoke upon him the hostility of the Land-Sprites. This was exactly what Egil Skallagrimsson did when to gain revenge he raised a "libel-pole" against Erik Bloody-Axe. Before sailing away from Norway, Egil went ashore on an island lying far out to sea. As the story runs: "Egil walked up on the island. Carrying a hazel pole in his hand, he made his way to a rocky headland looking out upon the mainland. Taking a horse's head, he fixed it on top of the pole. Then, making use of a certain formula (a curse), he spoke thus, 'Here I erect this libel-pole, and I turn the libel against king Erik and queen Gunnhild,'—and with these words he turned the horse's head toward the mainland—; 'I aim this libel against the Land-Sprites of this country, to the end that they shall go astray and that no one of them shall reach or find his dwelling until they have driven Erik and Gunnhild forth from the land.' Thereupon he drove the pole into a crevice and left it there. He also turned the head landwards, and on the pole he wrote runes containing all the words of this curse. Then he went on board his ship."

Among the Kind Sprites may be reckoned all Æsir, Vanir, and Bright-Elves; among the Bad Sprites, Giants, Dwarfs, and Dark-Elves. After the coming of Christianity, however, no distinction was made between the Sprites; either they were all regarded as evil, or at any rate they were supposed beyond doubt to imperil the salvation of any man who should remain their friend. The Catholic clergy made it a point to arouse hatred against all the race of Sprites rather than to break down men's reliance on them. Numerous myths eventually sprang up having to do with Sprites that had suffered expulsion by means of the chants, the prayers, or the holy water of the priests, and so perforce had abandoned their dwelling places in stones or mounds. Each spring during Ascension Week in the North, as everywhere else throughout Catholic Christendom, the priests walked in procession around meadows and fields, holy water and crucifix in hand, intoning prayers and benedictions, and thus compelling the Sprites to flee the cultivated acres. During this particular week[1] there were several processional days;[2] besides these, there were two fixed processional days: the "greater", on April 25th; and the "less", on May

---

[1] *Gangdaga-vika:* "procession week".
[2] *Gangdagar.*

Norse Mythology

1st. Ceremonies of just this sort lent themselves directly to the maintenance of belief in the Sprites; even in our own times traditions persist relating to "Sprite mounds" and "Sprite trees", sacred trees that no hand must touch,—where the Sprites not long since were accustomed to receive offerings of food.

Among more recent superstitions concerned with the lesser supernatural beings, those relating to Elves and Giants (Jutuls, Trolls, Mountain-Trolls) are by far the most prevalent. Among the Elves must be counted the Huldre Folk,[1] who occupy a conspicuous place in the superstitions of Iceland. These Elves have quite the appearance of human beings. They make their homes under ground or in the mountains, and are not always hostile toward men but at times rather amiable and friendly; for this reason they are occasionally given the designation Darlings.[2] Among the Norwegians, too, there are numerous stories about the Hidden Folk or the underground people (mound folk, mountain folk), and above all about the Huldre herself, the Hill-Lady. She is often malicious; but at other times she shows a friendly demeanor toward men, as when she appears before the herdsman and speaks and dances with him. The Hill-Lady is often very beautiful as seen from the front, an impression enhanced by her blue smock and white linen hood. From behind she is hideous: her back is hollowed out like a trough and she has a tail that she is never able to conceal.

---

[1] *Huldufólk:* "the hidden folk".

[2] *Ljúflingar, lýflingar,* from *ljúfr,* "dear", "friendly"; a formation like that of German *Liebling,* from *lieb.*

Myths of the Gods

She owns a large herd of fat cattle and dogs to shepherd them ("huldre dogs"). She sings and plays well, but always in a melancholy strain; her tunes are called the "Hill-Lady's harping".

The underground folk are unable to beget children with each other. For this reason they desire to decoy young men or women in order to wed with them. They also have a bad habit of stealing human children; instead they lay one of their own brats in the cradle, the so-called changelings.[1]

Other Sprites are the Nix and the Water-Sprite. They live in rivers and lakes, and in certain localities are considered evil beings; in Telemark, for example, traditional report has it that the Nix demands each year a human sacrifice and that he is impelled to draw down to himself persons who approach the water after nightfall. As a rule, however, these Water-Sprites are guileless and friendly; they are adept at playing the fiddle, and it is possible to induce them to teach the art. Having no hope of eternal salvation, they are melancholy of mood; but they are made happy when any one promises to bring about their redemption, and they often demand the prospect of heavenly bliss as a reward for instruction in playing the fiddle. When the Nix is heard moaning and groaning, it is an omen that some one is about to be drowned. The Nix is able to reveal himself under various guises: as a handsome young man with long hair, as a dwarf, or as an old graybeard.

Out in the ocean dwell Merman and Mermaid.

[1] Old Norse *skiptingr, vixlingr*.

Norse Mythology

They too sing and play beautifully and entice human beings to their haunts. They have the power to foretell future events. The upper part of their bodies has a human shape and the lower part has the likeness of a fish; the Mermaid appears beautiful as long as she does not let her finny tail be seen.

Among the Sprites the Brownie (Modern Norwegian *Nisse*) occupies a position of his own. He is a small boy or a small man dressed in gray clothes and a red cap; the crown of his head remains always moist, and his hands lack thumbs. Lingering about the farmsteads, he makes himself most useful so long as he is well treated; but if he takes umbrage at his hosts, he is capable of causing a great deal of trouble. If the Brownie is pleased with his surroundings, he will help the stableboy feed the horses, will assist the milkmaid in the care of the cows, and will even steal from the neighbors both hay and food to supply the farm on which he lives; but if he grows dissatisfied, he will bewitch the cattle, spoil the food, and bring misfortunes of other kinds upon the house. It may happen that two Brownies from two different farms encounter each other in foraging for hay, and then they will perhaps start a spirited fight armed with wisps of the hay. On Christmas Eve prudent folk are accustomed to set out for the Brownie a dish of Christmas pudding.

Whenever a person in sleep felt a weight upon his chest or when he dreamed disquieting dreams, he had no doubt that the Nightmare or Incubus was abroad, that he was being "ridden" by the Nightmare.[1]

[1] Old Norse, *mara traδ hann:* "the Nightmare was treading him."

Myths of the Gods

According to one account the Nightmare has no head, and is in fact hardly anything more than a mere brown smock; according to another description she is an actual woman who has the faculty of moving about by night and pressing her weight upon the sleeper. Thus the Nightmare does not differ widely from the so-called Werewolves,[1] who by day are actual human beings, but who during the night assume the shape of wolves; in this guise they course about bent on sinister mischief, attacking people in sleep, exhuming and devouring corpses in the churchyards. An ancient legend connected with one of the first Yngling kings in Sweden, Vanlandi by name, relates that a witch named Huld came over him in the form of a Nightmare and choked him to death. So firmly rooted was the belief of our forefathers in such things that the old ecclesiastical law of Eidsifa contained the following provision: "If evidence shows that a woman rides (as a Nightmare) any man or his servants, she shall pay a fine of three marks; if she cannot pay, she shall be outlawed." Nightmare and Werewolf are obviously related to the Dark-Riders or Night-Riders already mentioned,[2] and during later times no great distinction was drawn between them. One who had the ability to disguise his outward semblance was, in the ancient phrase, "multiform" (*eigi einhamr*), and was sometimes also called "shape-shifter" (*hamhleypa*).

---

[1] German *Werwolf*, literally "man-wolf"; this word even as far back as the period of Old Norse had been changed into *vargulfr*.

[2] See p. 39.

Norse Mythology

THE HEROES AND LIFE IN VALHALLA

CONCERNING the mighty deeds and the destinies of the gods much has here been recounted; much less concerning their daily life in Asgard with those of mankind who came into their fellowship. Both Freyja and Odin made the Heroes welcome: Freyja in Folkvang, and Odin in Vingolf and Valhalla. We learn nothing, however, as to which of these domains was to be preferred; we have evidence only as to the manner in which Odin and the Heroes fleeted the time in Valhalla. It would seem that men generally thought of Valhalla as the resort of the fallen Heroes; there they passed their days in mirth and gladness. Odin himself chose them through the Valkyries; and the foremost among them were welcomed by certain Æsir or by doughty elder Heroes who went forth to meet them. In Valhalla the Heroes amuse themselves day by day with battles and banquets. In the morning, donning their armor they sally upon the field to fight and kill one another; yet they rise again unharmed, sit down to eat and drink, and remain the best of comrades. The Heroes are a great company, constantly increasing; but their number is never so great that they do not have enough to eat from the flesh of the boar Sæhrimnir. The cook, named Andhrimnir, each day boils the boar in a kettle called Eldhrimnir; but at evening the beast is just as much alive and unhurt as before. The Heroes drink ale and mead poured out for them by the Valkyries; Odin alone and those whom he desires to honor drink wine. All the mead they drink runs from the udder of Heidrun, a goat that stands on the roof of Valhalla cropping the branches of a tree called Lærad. The mead fills a great drinking-crock in the hall, enough of it to make all the Heroes drunken. Lærad possesses not only the inherent virtue of producing all the mead; on the roof of Valhalla there stands also a hart named Eikthyrnir, who gnaws at the tree and from whose antlers drops fall down into Vergelmir; thence flow forth twelve rivers that water the domain of the Æsir, and in addition thirteen other rivers.

CORRUPTION

IN the morning of time, when Asgard and Valhalla were newly built, the gods lived in innocence, happiness and peace. "Glad in their courtyard they played at chess, nor of gold lacked aught"; so runs the description in the *Vǫluspá* of this golden age of the Æsir. Then came three mighty Thursar maidens out of Jotunheim, and enmity arose between Æsir and Vanir. One link in the chain of strife was the burning in Valhalla of a woman named Gullveig; "three times they burned the thrice born, again and again—yet still she lives." The Æsir take counsel together to learn whether peace may still be preserved. Nothing can be done. Odin hurls his spear over the ranks of the enemy, and the first battle of the hosts begins. The walls of the Æsir stronghold are penetrated and the Vanir pour through the breach into Asgard. Yet eventually peace is declared between Æsir and Vanir,

the story of which has already been told above.[1]
Now the golden age of innocence is at an end; the gods
are compelled to defend themselves against their foes,
sometimes by the use of guile, as on the occasion when
they tricked the Giant mason.[2]   Other Giant women—
Skadi and Gerd, for example—gain entrance to the
dwellings of the Æsir, and Asgard's sanctity is no
more.   The season of tranquillity gives way to a
season of turbulent warfare, in which the gods more
than ever before have need of magical weapons, of the
aid of Heroes.   The gods no longer rule the world as
princes of peace; the most eminent of them become
gods of war.   To this period are to be referred the
numerous myths having to do with valorous deeds and
guileful practices; and the gods fall far short of always
winning victory and glory.   Corruption extends from
gods to men; the divinities of battle, the Valkyries, ride
forth into the world of mortals and here too peace is as
a tale that is told.

THE TREASURES OF THE GODS

Loki's malice was in reality the occasion of the acquir-
ing by the Æsir of all the precious weapons and treasures that served them in such good stead during their
warfare with the Giants.   Once upon a time Loki cut
off all of Sif's hair.   When Thor found out what had
happened, he seized upon Loki and threatened to
crush every bone in his body; he relented only on

[1] P. 4.
[2] P. 24.

Myths of the Gods

Loki's swearing that he would get the Dark-Elves to fashion for Sif hair from gold that would grow like other hair. Loki went with his task to certain Dwarfs known as the Sons of Ivaldi; and they made not only the hair but also the ship Skidbladnir and the spear Gungnir. Loki promptly laid a wager of his own head with another Dwarf, named Brokk, that the Dwarf's brother Sindri was not craftsman enough to make three other talismans as precious as these. Brokk and Sindri repaired to the smithy, where Sindri, laying a pig's hide in the forge, asked Brokk to blow the bellows without pause until he himself returned to take the hide out again. No sooner had Sindri gone than a fly alighted on Brokk's arm and stung him; he kept the bellows going nevertheless, and when Sindri lifted his workmanship from the forge, it turned out to be a boar with golden bristles. Next he laid some gold in the forge, asked Brokk to blow as before, and went away; at once the fly came back, settled on Brokk's neck, and stung him twice as hard as the first time. Brokk notwithstanding held out until Sindri returned and lifted from the forge the gold ring Draupnir. Then he laid some iron in the fire and asked Brokk to blow, insisting that the work would be spoiled if the blowing stopped; but the fly came once more, settled between Brokk's eyes, and stung him on the eyelids so that the blood ran down and blinded him. He could not refrain from loosing his hold on the bellows with one hand to drive the fly away. Just at that moment the smith returned and declared that his handiwork had been on the very point of coming to naught; he lifted it from the forge, and it proved to be a hammer. Giving all three pieces to Brokk, he told him to make his way to Asgard and demand payment of the wager. The Æsir took their places on the judgment seats and came to the decision that Odin, Thor, and Frey were to judge between Loki and Brokk. Loki gave to Odin the spear Gungnir, which never failed of its mark; to Thor he gave the golden hair, which took root as soon as it was fixed on Sif's head; and to Frey he gave the ship Skidbladnir, which always found favoring winds and which could be folded up and placed in a pocket as occasion might befall. Brokk gave to Odin the ring Draupnir, from which each ninth night there dropped eight other rings as heavy as itself. To Frey he gave the boar Gullin-busti, who was able to run through the air and over the sea more swiftly than any horse; no night was so black, no murky region so dark as not to be illumined by his passage, so powerful was the light that shone from his bristles. To Thor he gave the hammer Mjollnir; with it he could strike as hard a blow as he pleased at anything that came in his way, and yet the hammer suffered not the least dent; he could throw it so as always to hit what he aimed at, and the hammer would return to his hand of its own power; when he so desired, he could make it small and put it in his pocket; he had but one fault to find: the shaft was rather short. The Æsir promptly judged that Brokk had won the wager; in Mjollnir they had acquired the very best defence against the Rime-Thursar. Loki wanted to redeem his head, but the Dwarf would not consent. "Catch me if you can," said Loki; and no

Myths of the Gods

sooner had he spoken than he was far away, for he wore shoes that could carry him through the air and over the seas. The Dwarf asked Thor to seize him, and Thor did so. Brokk was about to cut off Loki's head, but Loki declared that the wager called for his head only, and not for his neck. Brokk then began sewing Loki's lips together. He was unable to make an incision with his own knife, but with his brother's awl he managed to make openings through which he could sew the mouth up tight; that done, he tore out through the lips the thong he had used in sewing them together.[1]

THE RAPE OF IDUN

THE story has already been told [2] of how the Giantess Skadi was received into the society of the Æsir and of how Njord was given to her as a husband by way of recompense for the murder of her father Thjazi. Loki's wiles provided the direct occasion for these events. Once upon a time Odin, accompanied by Loki and Hœnir, set forth on a journey that took them across mountains and over wastes where it was no easy matter to find food. At length, on descending into a valley, they caught sight of a drove of oxen; seizing one of the herd they kindled a fire, and began to boil the flesh. When they supposed the meat to be cooked, they took it off the fire; but it was far from done, and they had to let it boil a while longer. The same thing happened a second time; so they fell to debating the

[1] Snorri's *Edda* I, 340–46.
[2] Pp. 13, 50.

strange occurrence and wondering what might be the cause. As chance would have it, they were sitting under a tree, and so they heard a voice above their heads saying that he who sat perched in the tree was to blame for the tardiness of their cooking. Looking more closely, they saw an immense eagle. The eagle said that if they would allow it to still its hunger from the flesh of the ox, the meat would be cooked soon enough. They gave their consent, and the eagle forthwith swooped down and made off with both of the two hind quarters and both fore quarters. Loki became so angry that he picked up a staff and struck at the eagle. The eagle flew away, and one end of the staff stuck fast to the body of the bird and the other end remained fixed to Loki's arms, so that he was dragged over stock and stone till he thought his arms would be pulled from their sockets. He begged the eagle for mercy, but was not freed until he had given his promise to steal Idun out of Asgard, and her apples to boot. Not before he had sealed his promise with an oath was he permitted to return to his companions. When they had come back to Asgard and the appointed hour was at hand, he told Idun that he had discovered certain apples in a wood lying beyond the bounds of Asgard; she would no doubt find them worth having, and accordingly she would do well to visit the spot, taking her own apples along as a means of comparison. Idun permitted herself to be hoodwinked, and the eagle promptly came and carried her off. The eagle, none other than the Giant Thjazi in disguise, bore her away to his own estate of Thrymheim, where he kept her a long while in durance. The Æsir soon noticed that Idun's apples were gone, for they grew old and gray and could find no means of renewing their youth. They met in solemn conclave to inquire into the disappearance of Idun; then some one told that he had seen her walk forth from Asgard attended by Loki. The gods summoned Loki before the assembly and threatened him with death or dire tortures. He became so frightened that he promised to bring Idun back again if Freyja would only lend him her falcon disguise. His request being granted, he flew off to Jotunheim and arrived at Thrymheim at a time when Thjazi happened to be out at sea engaged in fishing, and Idun was alone at home. Loki transformed Idun into a nut and made off with her as fast as he could fly; but just afterward Thjazi returned, and not finding Idun, assumed the shape of an eagle and set out in pursuit of Loki. Little by little the eagle gained on the falcon. When the Æsir saw the two birds drawing near in their flight, they made haste to gather a heap of shavings outside the walls of Asgard, and at the very moment the falcon came inside they kindled the fire. The eagle was unable to come to a stop before it was directly above the bonfire; its wings bursting into flame, it was incapable of continuing the flight. Thus the Æsir got Thjazi into their power and put him to death just within the gates of Asgard.

Thjazi was one of the most formidable of the Giants. His father Olvaldi's wealth was so great that when Thjazi and his two brothers, Idi and Gang, were to divide their patrimony, they were compelled to measure out the gold by mouthfuls. When Thjazi's daughter Skadi came to demand payment of a penalty for the death of her father, she was not satisfied with being permitted to choose a husband[1]; she required in addition that the Æsir should make her laugh, something she deemed to be impossible. Loki again was called upon to deal with the emergency; so he played some vulgar tricks with a goat, and she was compelled to laugh in spite of herself. Odin took Thjazi's two eyes and tossed them up into the heavens, where they became two stars.[2]

THOR'S UNLUCKY JOURNEY TO JOTUNHEIM

THOR, god of thunder, was the most ardent enemy of the Giants; yet he did not always come out the victor in his encounters with them. Once upon a time he drove off with his goats, attended by Loki; as night fell, they found lodging with a countryman. Here Thor slaughtered his goats, flayed them, and caused them to be cooked; then he invited the countryman, with his wife, his son, and his daughter, to share the meat with him, but asked them to throw all the bones down on the goats' hides. They did as he bade them, all but Thjalfi, the farmer's son, who broke a thigh bone to get at the marrow. At dawn Thor rose, donned his garments, raised Mjollnir aloft, and with the hammer consecrated the goats' hides; at once the goats sprang to their feet, as much alive as ever, except

[1] P. 13 f.
[2] Snorri's *Edda* I, 208–14.

that one of them halted on one hind leg. Then Thor understood that the countryman or some one in his house had been careless enough to break the thigh bone; in anger he knitted his eyebrows and gripped the hammer so tightly that his knuckles grew white. The countryman, and his whole family with him, begged for mercy and offered in recompense all that they possessed. When Thor saw how frightened they were, his wrath cooled and he allowed himself to be appeased. By way of ransom he agreed to take the countryman's two children, the son Thjalfi and the daughter Roskva; and these two have followed him ever since.

Leaving his goats with the countryman, Thor continued on his journey to Jotunheim. He reached the seashore, crossed the deeps of the ocean, and stepped on land once more with his followers. Soon they came to a great forest, which they traversed all day until darkness fell. Thjalfi, swift of foot, carried Thor's wallet filled with food, for there was little to be picked up on the way. When night came, they looked about for a lodging and discovered an immense cabin, with a door on one side just as wide as the cabin itself. They went inside and lay down to sleep. At midnight they felt an earthquake so violent that the whole building shook; Thor roused his companions and bade them go into a smaller room through a door in the middle of the wall; as for himself, he sat down at the threshold with Mjollnir in his hand. A dreadful din and rumbling filled his ears. In the morning he went out and saw a gigantic man lying snoring near by in the wood; then he understood what had caused all the noise he had heard. He buckled on his belt of strength but just at that moment the man awoke, and for once, so it is said, Thor found himself little disposed to strike a blow. Instead, he asked the man his name. The man answered: "My name is Skrymir, and small need have I to ask for your name; I know you are Asa-Thor. But what have you done with my glove?" With these words Skrymir bent down to pick up his glove, and Thor saw that what he had taken by night to be a cabin was nothing else than Skrymir's glove, and that the penthouse was the thumb. "Shall we not travel together?" asked Skrymir. "Yes," said Thor. Before starting they ate their breakfasts, each party by itself, Skrymir from his own wallet, Thor and his companions from theirs; then Skrymir proposed that they put their food together in one sack. Thor gave his consent, and so Skrymir tied both their victuals and his own in a bag, which he slung on his back. He walked before them with tremendous paces during the day and at evening chose a night's lodging for them beneath a huge oak tree. "Here I am going to lie down to sleep," he said; "you may take the wallet and eat your supper." Skrymir fell asleep at once and was soon snoring heavily. Thor set about untying the wallet, but with very little success; when he had struggled a long while with his task, he grew angry, seized Mjollnir in both hands, and struck Skrymir on the head. Skrymir awoke and asked if a leaf had not fallen on his head. "Have you had your supper?" he asked. "Yes," replied Thor; "we are just going to bed." In the middle of the night Thor again heard

Skrymir snoring so that the whole forest rang with the sound; he stepped up to him, lifted the hammer high in the air, and struck the man such a blow on the crown that the beak of the hammer sank far into the skull. Skrymir woke and asked: "What is up now? Was that an acorn that dropped on my head? How are you faring, Thor?" Thor hurried away, saying that he had just waked up and that the hour was hardly past midnight. "If I might only strike him a third time," thought Thor to himself, "he should never see the light of day again." He kept watch until Skrymir once more fell asleep a little before morning, then ran up to him, and with all his might struck him in the temple so that the hammer sank into his skull up to the very handle. Skrymir sat up, stroked his cheek with his hand, and said: "There must be birds sitting in the tree above me; something dropped from the branches upon my head. Are you awake, Thor? It is time to get up now, and you have only a little distance to go to reach the stronghold of Utgard. I have heard you whispering among yourselves that I am not exactly small of stature, but you will see bigger men when you arrive at Utgard. And by the way, let me give you a piece of good advice: Do not be too arrogant; Utgard-Loki's men do not put up with much bragging from small boys. Else you had better turn back again, and that might be the wiser thing to do after all. But if you must and will go farther, walk toward the east; my way lies north, toward the mountains you see yonder." With these words Skrymir picked up the bag of food, slung it on his back, and strode off into the forest; and the Æsir were very glad to be rid of him.

Thor and his followers walked on until midday. Then they caught sight of a castle standing in the plain; but they had to bend their necks till their heads touched their backs before they were able to look over the top of it. The portals were barred with a gate that they could not unlock; but they crept in between the wickets and, seeing a huge hall, bent their steps toward it. The door stood open. They walked inside and there saw many men, all of immense size, sitting on benches. Among them sat the king, Utgard-Loki. They saluted him, but he only laughed scornfully, and asked if the little boy was not Riding-Thor. "You are no doubt bigger than you seem to be," he said; "but what kind of manly exercises do you and your traveling companions know? No one is allowed to sojourn here with us who is not able to do something or other better than any one else." Loki, who was standing behind the rest, spoke up: "There is one sport in which I am ready to try conclusions at once; nobody here is able to eat faster than I." Utgard-Loki answered, "We shall soon find out." Then he commanded a man named Logi to step forward from the end of the bench to the middle of the floor to match his skill in eating against Loki's. A trencher full of meat was carried in and placed on the floor; Loki and Logi sat down, one at each end of the trencher, and ate with all their might. They met in the middle of the trencher; but while Loki had eaten only the meat, Logi had consumed the meat, the bones, and the

trencher to boot. So Loki was beaten at this game.
"What is that young fellow there able to do?" asked
Utgard-Loki. "I will try running a race with some
one," answered Thjalfi. "You will need to be swift of
foot," said Utgard-Loki; then he went out into the field
and asked a little fellow named Hugi to run against
Thjalfi. In the first race Hugi was so far ahead that
he turned back at the goal to meet Thjalfi. "You had
better stretch your legs a bit more if you want to win,"
said Utgard-Loki; "for that matter, no swifter runner
than you has ever visited us." In the second race
Hugi reached the goal and turned while Thjalfi still
had a long bowshot to run. "A very pretty heat,"
said Utgard-Loki; "yet I can hardly believe that
Thjalfi would win if you two ran a third time." They
ran once more; but when Hugi had reached the goal
and turned around, Thjalfi had not covered half the
course. All agreed that this contest might very well
be regarded as finished. "What kind of manly sport
are you going to favor us with, Thor?" asked Utgard-
Loki; "we have heard great things about your prowess." "I will drink with any one that cares to
drink," answered Thor. "Very good," said Utgard-
Loki; then he went into the hall and asked his cupbearer to take down the great horn that the king's men
were sentenced to drink from when they had done
amiss. "We consider it well done," said Utgard-Loki,
"if a man is able to empty this horn at one draught;
some require two; but no one is such a weakling that he
cannot drain it in three draughts." Looking at the
horn, Thor did not think it very large but rather long;

thirsty as he was, he placed it to his lips, drank deep, and thought to himself that he should probably not have to bend his head to the horn again. But when he stopped and looked to see how much he had drunk, it seemed to him that there was left not much less than there was before. "You have drunk pretty well," said Utgard-Loki, "but no great amount; to be sure, if any one had told me that Asa-Thor was no better drinker, I should not have believed it; but I am sure you will empty the horn at the second draught." Thor answered not a word, but took as long a pull as he possibly could; still the other end of the horn had not risen as high as he might have wished. When he paused it seemed to him that the level had sunk even less than before, yet now it was possible at least to carry the horn without spilling any of the liquor. "If you care to drink a third time, you have left the greater part till the last," said Utgard-Loki; "but if you are not more skilled in other games than in this, you cannot hope to earn as great a name among us as you have among the Æsir." Thor grew angry and placed the horn to his lips once more. He drank with all his might and kept drinking as long as ever he was able; when he paused to look, he could see that the level had sunk a little, but he did not want to drink any more. "It is easy to see," said Utgard-Loki, "that you are not so great a man as we supposed. Perhaps you would like to try your luck at other exercises, since you have had such bad luck with this one?" Thor answered, "I am willing to risk it; but unless I am much mistaken. my drinking would have earned praise at home among the Æsir." Utgard-Loki replied: "Our young boys sometimes find amusement in lifting my cat off the ground; it is only a small matter, and I should not have thought of proposing such a thing to Thor if I had not seen with my own eyes that you are far from being as mighty as I had supposed." A large gray cat ran out upon the floor of the hall. Thor stepped forward, took hold with one hand under her belly, and lifted; but the more he pulled, the more the cat bent herself into a bow; and when Thor had stretched his hand up as far as he could stretch, the cat raised only one foot off the floor. So Thor was worsted at this game too. Utgard-Loki declared that he might have known as much beforehand, since Thor was small of stature as compared with the big men around him. "Let one of them come out and wrestle with me if you think I am so small," answered Thor, "for now I am really in bad humor." "Not a man in the hall would demean himself so far as to take a turn with you," said Utgard-Loki, "but I will call in my old foster mother, Elli." She accordingly came in and grappled with Thor; but the more Thor tightened his hold, the firmer she stood; at last she began to use tricks of her own, and in the end Thor perforce sank down on one knee. "Perhaps that will do," said Utgard-Loki; "Thor will hardly challenge any one else here to a wrestling match." With these words he showed Thor and his companions to their seats. They remained there the rest of the night, and were entertained with the utmost hospitality.

In the morning they rose and prepared to continue

their journey. Utgard-Loki himself came in and caused a table to be spread for them, laden with all kinds of food and drink. Then they set forth on their way. Utgard-Loki accompanied them out of the castle and, as they were about to depart, asked Thor what he thought of the outcome of his expedition. Thor answered that he knew he had added nothing to his fame and that he felt the keenest disappointment to think that he was leaving behind him the reputation of a mere weakling. "Now I will tell you the truth," said Utgard-Loki, "since you are well outside of the castle. Never with my consent, so long as I live and rule, shall you be allowed to enter it again. And you would never have gained entrance if I had known how strong you were; for you came very near bringing the greatest misfortune upon us. The fact is, you have all been hoodwinked. It was I that you met in the forest; I tied the wallet with troll-iron so that you might not guess how to open it. Each single blow that you struck would have killed me outright if, unknown to you, I had not interposed for my protection the huge mountain you beheld outside the stronghold; there you may see even now three valleys, the one deeper than the other, all of them marks of your blows. The like happened with the games you played: Loki was hungry and ate very well, but Logi (*logi* = flame) was none other than fire itself turned loose, which consumed at one time both meat and trencher. Hugi, the fellow with whom Thjalfi ran his races, was my own thought (*hugr*), which of course was the fleeter of the two. When you drank from the horn, the wonder grew till I could not trust my own eyes; for the other end lay out in the ocean itself. If you look closely you can see how the level has sunk; that is what we call ebb tide. When you lifted the cat, we were all alarmed; she is the Midgard Serpent that encompasses all lands, but you raised her so high that head and tail barely touched the floor together. The wrestling match with Elli was no less a marvel, for never a man lived, nor ever shall live, but must fall before her (*elli* = old age). Now we are to part, and it were best for both of us that you never came back; for the future I will not fail to be on my guard against arts of that kind." Thor lifted his hammer, meaning to smite Utgard-Loki, but in a twinkling he had disappeared. Nor was Thor able again to catch sight of the castle; and so he had to return to Thrudvang. Yet before long he was bound on another expedition, this time against the Midgard Serpent itself.

THOR'S VISIT TO HYMIR

THE story of Thor's visit to the Giant Hymir is told in verse in a poem of the *Poetic Edda* (*Hymiskviða*) and in prose in Snorri's *Edda*. In the Eddic poem the myth begins by recounting how the gods, gathered at a banquet given by Ægir, discovered through magic arts that he had in his possession a huge number of kettles. Thor hinted to Ægir that he was inferior to the Æsir, and in revenge Ægir asked Thor to go out and find a kettle large enough to brew ale for all the Æsir at one time. No one had heard of a kettle of this size, until finally Tyr let it be known that his father (his mother's father?), the Giant Hymir, who lived to the eastward of the Elivagar, had one that was a mile deep; but it was impossible for any one to get hold of it without trickery. Thor and Tyr accordingly drove away from Asgard and in due course arrived at the house of man named Egil; there they stabled the goats and continued on foot to Hymir's farm, only to discover that he had gone out hunting. On walking into the hall they found Hymir's wife (?), a hideous Giantess with nine hundred heads. Hymir's daughter (?), Tyr's mother, nevertheless received them kindly and hid them behind eight immense kettles that were hanging in the room, since, as she said, Hymir was not well disposed toward visitors. After a long time Hymir came home. As he stepped in at the door, the icicles that hung from his frosty beard sent forth a tinkling sound. His daughter greeted him with smooth words and told him that Thor and Tyr had come to see him: "There they are, hiding behind a pillar under the staircase." At the piercing looks that shot from the eyes of the Giant, the pillar burst asunder and the crossbeam broke in two; all the kettles fell down and were shattered into bits except one only, which had come more finely tempered from the forge. Thor and Tyr now had to step out from their hiding; Hymir himself was ill at ease when he saw the deadly enemy of the Giants under his own roof. Three oxen were slaughtered for the evening meal, and of these Thor alone ate two. The next day Hymir proposed that they should go out hunting, to see if they could not bag something really worth eating; Thor, on the

Myths of the Gods

other hand, offered to row a boat out to sea if Hymir
would provide bait for fishing. Hymir pointed to his
own herd of cattle, and Thor was not slow in tearing
the head off an enormous black bull. Thor and Hymir
now rowed so far out to sea that the Giant became
alarmed, and then they began to fish. Hymir pulled in
two whales at once; while Thor, who had taken his
seat aft, baited his hook with the bull's head and
started angling for the Midgard Serpent. And sure
enough, the Serpent took the bait and the hook with it.
Thor hauled his catch up to the gunwale and gave it a
blow on the head with his hammer so that the mountains echoed to the sound and the whole earth quaked;
but the line parted and the Serpent sank back into the
sea. As they rowed homeward Hymir sat in a fit of
temper and spoke never a word. When they touched
land, he asked Thor either to make the boat fast or to
carry in the catch, thinking in either case to put his
strength to the test. Thor laid hold of the boat by the
prow and drew it ashore without bailing out the bilge
water; then he picked up the oars and the bailing dipper
and carried them up to the house, and the whales to
boot, as if they were nothing at all. Still Hymir was
not content; Thor was strong enough both at rowing
and at carrying burdens, but the question remained
whether he had the power to break the Giant's beaker
into bits. Thor hurled it against a stone pillar, but
the pillar broke and the beaker was left whole. Then
Tyr's mother advised Thor to throw it against Hymir's
own hard forehead; Thor did so, and this time the
beaker burst, while the Giant's forehead remained un-

scathed. Hymir felt his loss keenly, yet he said they might have the kettle if they were able to carry it out of the house. First Tyr tried to lift it, but it would not budge an inch. Thor was compelled to bend to the task himself; he took so strong a grip that his feet went through the floor. Finally he succeeded in slinging the kettle over his head, but it was so large that the handles clattered at his heels. Hurrying away, he traveled a great distance before looking back; on doing so at length, he saw Hymir and a whole army of many-headed Giants setting out in pursuit from their rocky fastnesses in the east. He threw the kettle off his shoulders, swung his hammer, and killed every one of the band. He had not gone far on his journey, however, before one of the goats stumbled to earth half dead; it was halt on one foot, and for that mishap malicious Loki was to blame.[1] Thor finally brought the kettle into the presence of the assembled gods; and in it Ægir was thereafter compelled to brew the ale for the yearly banquet which he had to provide for the Æsir.

According to Snorri's *Edda*, Thor set out all alone, in the likeness of a "young lad", without his wagon or his goats, and so arrived one evening at Hymir's dwelling. He remained there during the night, and in the morning got permission to go out fishing with Hymir, although the Giant did not look for much help from a fellow so young and small. Thor asked Hymir

[1] It may be that Loki had misled Thjalfi, Egil's son, to split the goat's thigh bone. As to the supposed time of all these happenings, the Eddic poem reveals nothing; it tells only that the "mountain-dweller" had to pay for the damage with his own children.

for bait, and on being told to provide for himself he tore the head off Hymir's biggest bull, Heaven-Bellower (*Himinhrjótr*). Thor plied the oars; but when Hymir thought they were going rather too fast, he asked Thor to lay by, since they had reached his accustomed fishing banks; Thor for his part, wanted to row farther out. When they had gone on some distance, Hymir declared it would be unsafe to venture beyond a certain point for fear of the Midgard Serpent. Thor nevertheless rowed on and on, until Hymir became very ill at ease. At last Thor pulled in his oars, prepared a stout line and a hook to match, and baited it with the bull's head. Then he dropped the line, and the Midgard Serpent took the bait so that the hook pierced the roof of his mouth. The Serpent gave the line such a violent jerk that Thor's knuckles were dashed against the gunwale; furiously angry, he rallied his Æsir strength and pulled so hard that his feet went through the boat and struck the bottom of the sea. He succeeded in drawing the Serpent up to the gunwale; and a terrible sight it was to see Thor fix his piercing eyes on the Serpent and to see the Serpent glare in turn at Thor, spewing venom meanwhile. Hymir grew pale with terror as he caught sight of the Serpent and saw the waves washing into the boat and out again; fumbling for his bait knife, he cut the line off against the gunwale, and the Serpent sank back into the sea. Thor threw his hammer after it, but did not succeed in killing it. Yet he struck Hymir such a blow with his fist that the Giant tumbled overboard head first. Thor himself waded ashore.

THOR'S VISIT TO GEIRRŒD

ONCE upon a time, as Loki was flying about for sport in Frigg's falcon disguise, he was taken with a desire to see how matters stood on the estates of Geirrœd. Settling on a window ledge, he looked into the hall. Geirrœd bade one of his men take the bird captive; but this was more easily said than done, and Loki was vastly amused at the proposal. He therefore remained sitting on his perch for a while, thinking there would be time enough to escape when the man had clambered up; but when Loki wanted to fly away, his feet clung to the wall and so he was taken in the toils. Geirrœd, on examining his eyes, knew that it was no real bird, but a shape-shifter; he spoke to Loki but received no answer. Geirrœd then locked him up in a chest, where he left him for three months without food. Finally he took him out again, and Loki was compelled to reveal who he was. To save his life he promised to induce Thor to pay a visit to the farmstead of Geirrœd without his hammer, his belt of strength, or his gauntlets. It is not known how Loki managed this affair, but certain it is that Thor set forth on the journey. Loki and Thjalfi went with him. On the way Thor sojourned for a time with the Giantess Grid, who was the mother of the god Vidar and as such a friend of the Æsir. From her Thor learned that Geirrœd was a crafty Giant, with whom it was no simple matter to deal. Accordingly she made Thor a loan of a belt of strength, a pair of iron gauntlets, and her own staff, the "Grid-Staff" (*Gríðarvǫlr; vǫlr* = staff). Thor presently arrived at the banks of a great river called Vimur, across which he was compelled to wade. Girdling on his belt, he braced himself against the current by means of the staff, while Loki held fast to the belt. By the time he had reached midstream, the water flowed over his shoulders. Then quoth Thor:

> Wax no more, Vimur;
> My purpose holds to wade
> To the very home of the Giants.
> Know this, that as thy waxing
> Will wax my Æsir power,
> Even as high as the heavens.

Soon he became aware that Geirrœd's daughter Gjalp was standing astride the river where it narrowed between rocky walls, and that the swelling of the waters was her work. He picked up a boulder from the bed of the stream and threw it at her, saying, "A river must be dammed at the mouth." The boulder found its mark, and now the current bore him so close to the bank that he was able to catch hold of a mountain ash, by the aid of which he pulled himself ashore. From this incident comes the saying, "The mountain ash is the salvation of Thor." Thjalfi—according to a skaldic poem—[1] had seized the thong of Thor's shield and effected his passage in this way. When Thor arrived at Geirrœd's house, he and his companions were lodged in a goat-house[2] where there was but a single chair. Thor sat down in it, but soon noticed that it was being raised with him toward the roof. He thrust

[1] See note.
[2] Some manuscripts of Snorri's *Edda* have "guest-house".

the Grid-Staff up against a beam and let all his weight
sink heavily into the chair, whereupon there at once
arose from below a great crashing and wailing; the din
came from Gjalp and Greip, the two daughters of
Geirrœd, who had lain beneath the chair and whose
backs he had thus broken.   Then quoth Thor:

> Once I made use
> Of my Æsir might,
> Yonder in the home of the Giants;
> That was when Gjalp and Greip,
> Daughters of Geirrœd,
> Would fain lift me up to the heavens.

Now Geirrœd called Thor into the hall to make
trial of his prowess in games of skill.   Great fires were
burning lengthwise of the room, and just as Thor
passed in front of Geirrœd, the Giant picked up with
his tongs a glowing bolt of iron and threw it at him.
Thor caught it in his iron gauntlet and raised it aloft,
but Geirrœd leaped for refuge behind a pillar.   Thor
hurled the bolt with such force that it went through
the pillar, through Geirrœd and the wall, and then
buried itself in the earth.

THOR'S COMBAT WITH RUNGNIR

ONCE upon a time, when Thor had gone off to the east
to kill Trolls, Odin rode on Sleipnir's back into
Jotunheim and pressed forward to the dwelling of the
Giant Rungnir.   Rungnir inquired who the gold-
helmeted man might be, who was thus able to ride
both air and sea—he must be the master of a good

Myths of the Gods

horse! Odin undertook to wager his head that the horse's like was not to be found in all Jotunheim. Rungnir retorted that his own horse, Goldmane, was the swifter of the two; with these words he sprang on his horse in a rage and rode in pursuit of Odin to pay him for his boasting. Odin struck spurs into Sleipnir and maintained his lead; but Rungnir had lashed himself into such a Giant fury that before he knew it he had passed within the gates of Asgard. The Æsir immediately invited him to sit down with them at their drinking, to which he assented and walked into the hall. The beakers were brought forward from which Thor was in the habit of drinking; Rungnir emptied them all without a murmur, and becoming drunk, began to vaunt himself. He would pick Valhalla up bodily and carry it off to Jotunheim; he would level Asgard with the earth and put all the gods to death but Freyja and Sif, and these two he would bear away to his own house. He insisted that Freyja alone had the courage to fill his beaker, and that he would make short work of drinking up all of the Æsir's ale. The Æsir, eventually growing weary of his bragging, summoned Thor; without a moment's delay Thor was on the spot, brandishing his hammer and fuming with anger. Thor demanded to know who had permitted foul Giants to drink there, who had allowed Rungnir to remain in Valhalla, and why Freyja was filling his cup as if it was a banquet for the gods. Rungnir turned unfriendly eyes on Thor and answered that Odin in person had invited him to enter and had given him safe conduct. Thor declared that before the

Giant made his escape he would have reason to rue that invitation. "Thor would gain little glory by killing an unarmed man," said Rungnir; "but have you courage enough to fight with me at the boundary stones of Grjottunagard? I was a fool to forget my shield and whetstone at home, for if I had my weapons at hand we could fight it out at once; but if you kill me while I am unarmed, you will be every man's byword for cowardice." That was the first time any one had offered to stand against Thor in single combat, and so he immediately accepted the challenge. Rungnir rode off at top speed; when he arrived at home in Jotunheim, the Giants paid him the highest compliments on his courage. They realized, none the less, how much was at stake: if Rungnir, their most powerful champion, should be worsted, they might look for all manner of mischances. Accordingly they set about the task of making a man of clay, nine miles tall and three miles broad beneath the arms. They were unable to find a heart large enough for him until it occurred to them to make use of the heart of a mare. Rungnir for his part had a three-cornered heart of stone; his head also was of stone, and his shield as well. Taking his position behind his shield he awaited at Grjottunagard the coming of Thor; resting his whetstone on his shoulder, he presented a most formidable figure. The clay Giant, on the contrary, who bore the name Mokkurkalfi, was so terrified that "he made water as soon as he caught sight of Thor." Thor came on the field seconded by Thjalfi. As they advanced Thjalfi called out, "You have made a reckless choice of position, Giant; Thor is closing in on you from below through the earth." Rungnir then placed his shield beneath his feet and stood on it; no sooner had he done so than Thor, heralded by a burst of thunder and lightning, came upon the scene in all his Æsir might and from a great distance hurled his hammer at the Giant. Rungnir gripped his whetstone with both hands and threw it at Thor, but it struck the hammer in mid air and was shattered to pieces. One part fell to the ground, and from these fragments have come all the mountains of whetstone; the other part, piercing Thor's head, brought him to earth. The hammer struck Rungnir on the crown and smashed his skull to bits; he fell across the body of Thor so that his foot rested on Thor's neck. By this time Thjalfi had won an easy victory over Mokkurkalfi. Neither Thjalfi nor any of the Æsir was able to lift Rungnir's foot off Thor's neck; but presently Magni came upon the field —the son of Thor and Jarnsaxa, a youngster of three years—and raised the Giant's foot as if in play; it was unfortunate, so he said, that he had not come sooner, in which case he would have struck the Giant dead with his bare fist. Thor rose to his feet and praised his son handsomely; he avowed that the boy in time would amount to something, and by way of reward made him a present of Rungnir's horse Goldmane. Odin, however, declared that Thor had not done right in giving so fine a horse to the son of a Giantess instead of to his own father.

Thor now returned to his home in Thrudvang, but the whetstone remained fixed in his head. To be rid of it he sought the aid of Groa, the wife of Aurvandil the Brave. The woman read magic spells over Thor's head until the whetstone loosened its hold. When Thor noticed what was happening, he wanted to please the woman in his turn; so he told her that, on a journey to the north, he had once waded across the Elivagar carrying Aurvandil in a pannier out from Jotunheim. In proof of his story he related that one of Aurvandil's toes, protruding out of the pannier, became so badly frostbitten that he was compelled to break it off; he then tossed it into the heavens, where it turned into a star that had since been called Aurvandil's Toe. No long time would pass, he added, before Aurvandil returned home again. Groa was so happy at hearing his tale that she forgot all about her magic spells; the whetstone consequently was not fully loosened, and so still protrudes from Thor's head. Therefore no whetstones must be thrown crosswise over the floor, for in that event the whetstone in Thor's head will be set in motion.

THRYM STEALS MJOLLNIR

At length it so happened that Thor found an opportunity to steal into Jotunheim and glut his hatred of the Giants. He had lain down to sleep, and when he awoke he missed his hammer. Enraged beyond bounds, he at once sought the advice of Loki, who promised to go out in search of the hammer provided Freyja would lend him her bird plumage. Freyja being willing, Loki flew off to Jotunheim and came into

Myths of the Gods

the presence of Thrym, king of the Thursar, who was sitting on a mound braiding gold cords for his dogs and clipping the manes of his horses. "What news among the Æsir? What news among the Elves? And what brings you to Jotunheim alone?" asked Thrym. "There is something wrong somewhere," Loki answered; "you do not happen to have hidden Thor's hammer, do you?" "Yes," retorted Thrym, "I have hidden it eight miles deep in the earth, and no man will get it before he brings me Freyja to wife." Loki brought the bad news back to Asgard. He then went with Thor to ask Freyja if she would consent to become the wife of Thrym; highly incensed, she gave them a curt "No" for answer. The Æsir accordingly met in conclave to determine what steps were to be taken; no one was able to suggest anything to the purpose until Heimdal proposed that they should dress Thor to take the place of Freyja, decking him out to that end with the Necklace of the Brisings and other appropriate ornaments. Thor pronounced the plan far beneath his dignity but at last gave in; so they dressed him in bridal linen, adorned him with the Necklace of the Brisings, hung jingling keys at his belt, put a kerchief on his head, and wrapped him in the long garments of a woman. Loki, in the habit of a handmaiden, followed in his train. Hitching Thor's goats to the cart, the two drove off at a pace that split mountains asunder and struck the earth into flames. As they drew near the domain of the Thursar king, Thrym bade the Giants rise to their feet and deck the benches for the coming of the bride. "In my possession are cows with gold horns, black bulls, heaps of treasure, and mounds of jewels," said Thrym; "Freyja is now my sole desire." When evening had come, food was borne in before the two guests. Thor by himself ate a whole ox, eight salmon, and all of the delicacies prepared for the women, and washed it all down with three crocks of mead. "Did any one ever see a bride take bigger and harder bites or drink more mead?" asked Thrym. "For eight days on end," answered Loki, "Freyja has not tasted a morsel, so great has been her longing after Jotunheim." Thrym now bowed his head beneath the kerchief to kiss the bride; but she shot such piercing glances upon him that he started back. "Why does Freyja look so grim? Her eyes dart fire." "Eight nights on end," answered Loki, "Freyja has not slept a wink, so great has been her longing after Jotunheim." Just at that moment the hideous old grandmother came in and asked for a bridal gift. Thrym gave commands that Mjollnir should be borne in and laid on the bride's lap so that the wedding might go forward. When Thor once more beheld his hammer, his heart laughed within him. First he slew Thrym, then the old beldame, and thereafter he crushed into atoms all the kindred of the Giants. Thus Thor got his hammer back again after all.

Myths of the Gods

THE NECKLACE OF THE BRISINGS

On most of Thor's expeditions, Loki acted the part of a friend, outwardly at least. Between Heimdal and Loki, on the contrary, there was deadly enmity without ceasing. This enmity showed itself, for example, on the occasion when Loki had stolen the Necklace of the Brisings from Freyja. Loki hid the ornament in the sea at Singastein, and kept guard over it himself in the shape of a seal. Heimdal likewise assumed the likeness of a seal, and so compelled Loki to restore what he had stolen. This is the probable interpretation of the casual references in Snorri's *Edda*,[1] in which case we have here to do with the old and authentic form of the myth.

A variant of the myth, quite different and far less primitive, is to be found in the legendary *Sǫrla þáttr*,[2] dating from the thirteenth century. According to this account, Freyja had received the necklace from four Dwarfs; Odin, however, coveting it, asked Loki to steal it for him. It would prove to be a difficult task, Loki said, for Freyja's house was so well built and so securely bolted that no one would be able to enter without her consent. Odin commanded him to make the attempt nevertheless, and Loki had to obey. When he arrived at the door he could not find even the smallest opening; taking the shape of a fly he crept about the lock a long time, until finally he discovered high up on the door a tiny crevice, through which he succeeded in making an entrance. Freyja lay asleep

---

[1] See note to p. 18, line 5.
[2] *Fornaldar Sǫgur* I, 391 ff.

with the necklace about her neck, the lock facing downward; he accordingly transformed himself into a flea
and bit her so hard on the cheek that she awoke and
turned on the other side. The lock having in this way
been made to face upward, he assumed his natural
shape once more and made off with the ornament.
Escaping through the door, which it was possible to
open from the inside, he brought the treasure to Odin.
Freyja, as soon as she awoke, noticed the theft and
complained to Odin. He answered that she might
have the necklace again on one condition: she was to
stir up strife between two major kings so that they
would wage unceasing war against each other, the
fallen warriors constantly rising to fight again. This
compact came to be the occasion of the Battle of the
Hjadnings.[1]

THE DEATH OF BALDER

AMID confusion and struggle of various kinds life thus
ran its course among the Æsir. Yet Balder still remained to them, the god of innocence and purity;
while he survived, evil and violence could not gain
supremacy in the universe. There came a time, however, when he began to be visited by disquieting
dreams, which filled all the gods with foreboding.
The Æsir and the goddesses held a general assembly
to inquire into the meaning of these portents. Odin
himself rode forth on Sleipnir into the very depths of
Niflheim to take counsel with a departed sibyl or

[1] See note to p. 130.

prophetess. He arrived at the high hall of Hell; and to the east of the door, where lay the grave of the sibyl, he took his station and chanted his incantations to waken the dead. The sibyl, compelled to rise from her grave, asked who had come to disturb her rest. "The snow covered me," she said, "the rain beat upon me, and the moist dews fell over me; I had long been dead." Odin answered, "I am named Vegtam, the son of Valtam; tell me now for whom Hel has adorned her hall." "For Balder the mead is brewed, and the Æsir are sore afflicted." "Who then shall bring death upon Balder?" "Hod shall bring death to Balder," was her response. "Who shall avenge his death upon Hod?" asked Odin. "Rind shall bear a son (Vali) in the West-Halls," she replied; "he shall neither wash his hands nor comb his hair until he has brought Balder's slayer to the funeral pyre; one night old, he shall kill him." "Speak, be not yet silent," said Odin; "still more would I fain learn: who are the maidens that are weeping sorely and throwing their neckerchiefs into the air?" "Now I know that you are not Vegtam, as you have said, but Odin," answered the prophetess. "And you are neither sibyl nor wise woman; you are the mother of three Thursar." "Ride home again, Odin," said the prophetess, "and return to me when Loki has regained his freedom and the Twilight of the Gods is near at hand."

Frigg now bound all things by an oath that they would do Balder no harm—fire and water, iron and all manner of metals, rocks, earth, trees, maladies, beasts and birds, poisons and serpents. Now the Æsir, deeming themselves secure, even found amusement at their assemblies in having Balder stand forward while the others shot missiles at him, aimed blows at him, or threw stones at him; whatever they might do, he suffered no wound. Loki, meanwhile, was not pleased. Assuming the shape of a woman, he paid a visit to Frigg at Fensalir. Frigg asked the woman what the Æsir were occupied with at their assembly. "They are all shooting at Balder without working him the least injury," she said. "Neither weapons nor trees will do him any harm, for I have bound all things by an oath." "Is it really true that all things have sworn to spare Balder?" the woman asked. "All things, except only a tiny sprig growing west of Valhalla, called Mistletoe (*mistilteinn*); I deemed it too young a thing to be bound by an oath." Now Loki went away, tore up the mistletoe, and carried it off to the assembly. Hod, because of his blindness, was standing at the outer edge of the circle. Loki asked him why he too was not shooting at Balder. "I cannot see where he is standing; and besides, I have no weapon," answered Hod. "Nevertheless, you ought to follow the example of the others," said Loki, "and thus pay equal honor to Balder. Take this wand and shoot at him; I will show you where he is standing." Hod grasped the mistletoe, took his position according to Loki's bidding, and let fly at Balder; the bolt sped directly through his body, and he sank down dead. Thus came about the greatest mischance that ever befell gods and men. When the Æsir saw Balder fall to the ground, they were speechless with fear, and none

moved a finger to lift him up; they looked at one another, and all alike were filled with wrath at the man
who had brought that deed to pass; yet they were
powerless to avenge the murder, since the spot on
which they stood had been solemnly set aside as a
sanctuary. For a time they were unable to utter a
word for weeping; Odin above all felt the full force of
the blow, for he saw most clearly what a loss had befallen the Æsir through Balder's death. When the
gods had in part regained their composure, Frigg asked
who among the Æsir would undertake to gain her
favor by riding the Hell-Ways to seek speech with
Balder and to learn from Hel what recompense she
would demand for permitting Balder's release and his
return to Asgard. Hermod the Bold, Odin's son,
declared himself willing; having got the loan of Sleipnir
for the journey, he mounted and took the road with the
utmost speed.

The Æsir took Balder's body and bore it down to the
sea. There lay his great ship, Ringhorni, drawn up on
land; with the intention of using it for Balder's funeral
pyre, they strove to launch it but were unable to move
it from the spot. They were therefore compelled to
send a messenger to Jotunheim to summon the Giantess
Hyrrokkin, and she came riding to them mounted on a
wolf, which she guided by vipers in lieu of reins. She
dismounted, and Odin assigned four Berserks to the
task of holding her steed; they could not restrain the
wolf, however, before they had thrown it to the ground.
The Giantess stepped to the prow of the boat, and at
the first effort shoved it off so fast that the rollers burst

into flame and the whole earth trembled. Thor, his wrath getting the better of him, wanted to crush her head, but all the other gods interceded on her behalf. Now the body of Balder was carried out onto the ship, and when his wife Nanna saw what was happening, her heart broke for sorrow; so her body also was laid on the pyre. The fire was then kindled and Thor came forward and consecrated the pyre with Mjollnir; just at that moment a Dwarf named Lit ran in front of him, and Thor spurned the Dwarf into the fire, where he too was burned. Beings of many kinds came to see the burning. First of all was Odin, and with him Frigg, the Valkyries, and Odin's ravens. Frey drove a cart drawn by the boar Gullinbusti, otherwise called Slidrugtanni. Heimdal rode his horse Goldtop, and Freyja drove her cats. Throngs of Rime-Thursar and Cliff-Ettins presented themselves likewise. Odin laid on the pile the ring Draupnir. Balder's horse also was led fully caparisoned onto the blazing ship.

In the meantime Hermod was on his way to Hell. Nine nights he rode through dark and deep valleys and saw nothing until he came to the river Gjoll and rode out onto the Bridge of Gjoll, which is paved with gleaming gold. A maiden named Modgud, who keeps watch over the bridge, asked his name and kindred. Then she told him that not many days before, five companies of dead men had ridden across the bridge; "and yet," she said, "it thunders as loudly beneath your paces alone as beneath the feet of all of them together. Nor have you the visage of a dead man; why are you riding alone on the way to Hell?" "I am riding to Hell," answered Hermod, "in search of Balder. Have you seen him pass along the Way of Hell?" She told him that Balder had already traversed the Bridge of Gjoll: "The Way of Hell lies downward and northward." Hermod rode on until he arrived at Hell-Gate. There he dismounted, tightened his saddle-girths, mounted once more, and struck spurs to his horse; the horse jumped so high above the gate that he did not so much as touch it with his hoof. Hermod rode straight to the hall, dismounted, and stepped inside; there he saw his brother Balder sitting in the high seat. He remained in the hall during the night; in the morning he asked Hel to permit Balder to ride away with him, telling her at the same time how great was the grief of the Æsir. Hel answered that she meant to assure herself beforehand whether Balder was really so much beloved as he was reputed to be. "If all things on earth," she said, "be they quick or dead, will weep for him, then he shall return to the Æsir; but if there is one thing that will not weep, he shall remain with me." Then Hermod arose, and Balder followed him out through the door and bade him give Odin the ring Draupnir in memory of him. Nanna gave into his charge a kerchief for Frigg and other gifts besides, and for Fulla a finger ring. Thereupon Hermod rode forth on his journey until he came back to Asgard, where he imparted to the gods all that he had seen and heard.

The Æsir now sent messengers throughout the whole world to ask all things to weep for Balder's release from Hell; all things did weep, men, beasts, earth, trees, and all manner of metals, and they can still be seen weeping whenever they pass from frost to heat. But when the messengers, their errand done, were returning home again, they discovered among the rocks a Giantess named Thokk; her too they asked to weep Balder out of the bounds of Hell but she replied:

> Thokk shall weep
> Dry tears
> On Balder's pyre.
> Nor in life nor in death
> Did Karl's son bring me joy;
> Hel hold what she hath!

Balder's homecoming thus came to nought. The Giantess was none other than Loki, who by such means finished his evil deed. Retribution, however, soon fell upon him. Upon Hod as well Balder's death was to be avenged; and according to the sibyl's decree to Odin, vengeance was to come at the hands of Vali, the son of Odin and Rind. The particulars of his doom are not recorded in the *Eddas*.

ÆGIR'S BANQUET—THE CHASTISING OF LOKI

WHEN Ægir had got possession of the huge kettle borrowed by Thor from Hymir, he prepared a great banquet for the Æsir.[1] Odin was one of the guests; others were Frigg, Sif, Bragi, Idun, Tyr, Njord, Skadi, Frey, Freyja, Vidar, Frey's serving men,

[1] See p. 65 ff.

Myths of the Gods

Byggvir and Beyla, with a host of other Æsir and Elves besides. Loki also made one of the number, but Thor was absent on an expedition to the east. Radiant gold lit the room instead of tapers, and the ale poured forth of itself without the aid of any cupbearer. Ægir's servants, Eldir and Fimafeng, were praised highly on every hand for the skilful performance of their duty. Hereat Loki grew angry and killed Fimafeng, although the spot was holy ground. The Æsir brandished their shields, raised an outcry against Loki, and drove him out into the forest; then they sat down to their drinking. Loki nevertheless shortly returned and, meeting Eldir outside the hall, asked him what the Æsir were discoursing about over their cups. "They are speaking of their weapons and their valorous deeds," answered Eldir; "and none among them has a good word to say for you." Loki said that he purposed to go inside and look on at the banquet and that he intended to bring evil and dissension with him and to mingle misfortune with the mead they were drinking. Refusing to listen to Eldir's warnings, he forced his way with threats. All ceased speaking when they saw Loki enter. He asked permission to still his thirst and, no one answering a word, he demanded that they should either show him to a seat or drive him out once more. Bragi declared that the Æsir never would give him a place among them again; whereupon Loki reminded Odin that once in the morning of time they two had blended blood with each other and thus had become sworn brothers, on which occasion Odin had given his promise that no drink should cross his lips that was not offered to both of them alike. Odin accordingly asked Vidar to make room for Loki at his side, and Vidar promptly arose and poured drink into Loki's cup. Loki offered obeisance to all the gods and goddesses and drank to them all—Bragi alone excepted. Bragi now proposed to present him with horse and sword and rings in recompense if he would keep the peace. Loki replied with taunts, maintaining that Bragi had none of the possessions of which he spoke: "Of all the Æsir sitting here, you are most afraid of battle and most wary of flying bolts." "If I were outside the hall, as certainly as I now sit within the hall, I should carry away your head in my hand," retorted Bragi. "You are brave enough while you are sitting in your seat, Bragi Grace-the-Benches," answered Loki; "if you are angry, come and fight it out with me." "I beg of you," said Bragi's wife, Idun, "do not taunt Loki here in Ægir's hall." "Hold your tongue, Idun," rejoined Loki; "of all wanton women I call you the most wanton; with your white arms you have embraced the slayer of your own brother." Idun declared that she only wished to pacify Bragi so that the two would not come to blows. Now Gefjon spoke: "Why do you two Æsir continue to bandy words in this presence? Loki appears not to know that he is on the wrong road, that all the gods are angry at him." Loki at once stopped her lips by reminding her of an amorous adventure in which she had played a part. Hereupon Odin warned Loki to beware of Gefjon's wrath: "For she knows the destinies of men as well as I." Loki immediately turned upon Odin

Myths of the Gods

and said: "You have often granted victory to das-
tards." "You, for your part," replied Odin, "lived
eight winters under ground as a woman, milking cows."
No insult much worse could possibly be thrown in a
man's teeth, and so Loki was not slow in making a
rejoinder no less coarse, to the effect, namely, that
Odin had once sojourned on the island of Samsey
engaged in the practice of witchcraft and sorcery after
the manner of witches. Frigg now took a part in the
discussion, declaring that Odin and Loki had better
not reveal what they had been occupied with in the
morning of time, and Loki immediately countered with
the old story that on a certain occasion when Odin was
absent from home, she had had his brothers Vili and
Ve for husbands. "Had I here in Ægir's hall a son
like Balder, you would not easily escape," answered
Frigg. "You plainly wish me to recount still more of
my evil deeds," said Loki; "know then, it is my doing
that you shall no more see Balder come riding into the
hall." "You are beside yourself," said Freyja, "to
dare relate all the evil and heinous acts of your life;
Frigg knows the course of destiny, though she tells no
man thereof." "Silence," answered Loki; "I know
you only too well. There is scarcely any one in this
company, whether of Æsir or Elves, whom you have
not had for a lover; you are a Troll, wicked through
and through; once the gods surprised you with your
own brother." "It is of little consequence," said
Njord, "that women have lovers; it is far worse that
you, womanish god, venture into our presence."
Loki reminded him that he had once been sent east-

ward as a hostage and that the women of Hymir had covered him with insults. "Even if I was once a hostage, nevertheless I have begotten a son (Frey) who is the friend of all and the bulwark of the Æsir." "His mother was your own sister," replied Loki. Tyr now spoke: "Frey is foremost of the brave men of Asgard, he violates neither maid nor wife, and he looses from bonds all those that are bound." "Hold your tongue, Tyr; never have you been able to bring about peace; do not forget how the Fenris Wolf tore off your right hand." "Nevertheless," answered Frey, "the Wolf lies in bondage until the Twilight of the Gods; and just as he lies chained outside the river's mouth, so may you come to lie fettered if you do not keep silence." "For gold you bought the daughter of Gymir and sold your sword besides, so that when the sons of Muspell come riding across the Dark Woods you will find no weapon ready to your hand." Then spoke Byggvir, Frey's serving man: "If I had offspring like that of Ingunar-Frey and if I lived happily as he does, I would crush this crow of evil omen finer than marrow and break all his limbs asunder." "What is that little thing wagging his tail and whimpering there under the mill? You hid yourself in the straw on the floor when men went forth to battle." On Heimdal's declaring Loki to be drunk, Loki replied: "Hold your tongue, Heimdal. In the morning of time a life most base was dealt out to be your portion, to stand forever with a stiff back, waking and watching on behalf of the gods." Skadi now forecast a threatening future for Loki: "Hitherto your lot has been good, Loki, but you shall not much longer play fast and loose; to the sharp stone the gods shall bind you with your own son's entrails." "None the less was I chief among those that put your father Thjazi to death," answered Loki. Skadi retorted, "Therefore cold counsels will always go out to you from my house and home." Now Sif stepped forward and poured mead into a horn for Loki; she drank to him and asked him to molest Skadi no more, but his only response was to boast that he, if none else, had enjoyed the favors of Sif. "The mountains are trembling," said Beyla; "I think Thor must be coming; he will find a way of stopping the mouth of him who heaps blame on the Æsir." As Loki was berating Beyla, Thor appeared and, fuming with rage, threatened Loki with his hammer. Still Loki had the boldness to say to him: "You will not be so brave when you go out against the Wolf, and the Wolf devours Odin." "I will hurl you into the regions of the east so that no man shall lay eyes on you again," answered Thor. "You had better keep quiet about your journeys to the east," said Loki, adding a further reminder of the cowardly way in which Thor had borne himself in Skrymir's glove and how fast he had found the thongs bound about the wallet; "hale and hearty, you nearly perished with hunger." "If you do not hold your tongue at once, Mjollnir shall strike you, without further ado, down to Hell, even lower than the Gate of Corpses." "I have spoken what I had to speak," said Loki; "I will now depart, on your account alone, for I know that you strike when you are moved to strike." To Ægir he declared that this banquet was his last, that flames were to consume all that he owned.

Loki now took his leave and hid himself in the mountains, where he built a house with four doors so placed that from within he was able to spy in all directions. Often he assumed the shape of a salmon and lurked among the waterfalls of Franang. He pondered much upon what devices the Æsir might employ in order to catch him in the falls; and as he sat in the house brooding on these things, he took flax yarn and wove it into meshes in the manner commonly used in making a net. Before long he saw the Æsir drawing near; for Odin, looking out from Lidskjalf, had discovered his hiding. Losing no time, Loki threw the net on the fire burning before him, and sprang into the waterfall. When the Æsir reached the house, the wise Kvasir was the first to enter; as soon as he saw the ashes of the burned net, he understood that it was a means of catching fish, and he told the Æsir as much. They all set about the task of making a net according to the model in the ashes; when it was finished they went down to the stream and threw the net into the water. Thor had hold of one end, and all the other Æsir held fast to the other end. As they drew the net, Loki swam before it and lay quiet between two stones until the net had passed over him; nevertheless they noticed that the net had touched some living thing. They went up stream and cast in the net a second time, but now they had weighted it so that nothing could pass beneath it. Loki swam ahead of the net until he came within a short distance of the sea; then he leaped over the rope and swam up to the waterfall again. Now the Æsir had caught sight of him; they went up stream a third time and separated into two parties so that each group held one end of the net while Thor waded down the middle of the river. In such a manner they drew the net down toward the sea. In this predicament Loki was compelled either to run out to sea, which would put him in grave danger of his life, or to leap over the net once more. He ventured the leap anew, but Thor seized him and held him fast by the tail, although the salmon slipped a short way through his hands; this is the reason why the salmon tapers toward the tail. Now Loki was taken captive outside the bounds of any hallowed place, and therefore he could expect no mercy. The Æsir carried him off to a cavern in the mountains. There they took three flagstones, placed them on end, and bored a hole in each one. Next they seized hold of Loki's sons, Vali and Nari; Vali, transforming himself into a wolf, at once tore his brother limb from limb. Thereupon the Æsir took Nari's entrails and with them bound Loki in such a position across the three stones that one of the stones stood under his shoulders, the second under his loins, and the third under the tendons of his knees. The bands turned into iron. Skadi caught a venomous serpent and fixed it above him in such a way that the venom would be sure to drip into his face. Sigyn, Loki's wife, stood beside him holding a basin to catch the dripping poison; but when the basin was filled, she had to go away to empty it; and while she was gone the

poison fell on his face and threw him into such violent
contortions that the whole earth trembled. This is
the phenomenon now known as an earthquake. Thus
Loki shall lie bound until the coming of the Twilight of
the Gods.

OTHER NORSE MYTHS CONCERNING THE DEATH OF BALDER (IN SAXO)

The ancient Danish historian Saxo also has an account
—no doubt drawn chiefly from Norse sources [1]—of the
death of Balder. It differs materially from the narrative in the *Eddas*. In Saxo's story the name of
Balder's slayer is Hother, son of Hothbrod. He is
not a blind god, but a bold and well-favored prince who
from his youth has distinguished himself for bodily
strength and adroitness in all manly exercises. He has
no equal as a swimmer and as a bowman, and no one
can match him in playing the harp. He loves Nanna,
the daughter of his foster father Gevar, and she returns
his love. Odin's son, the mighty Balder, sees her and
pays court to her; being disappointed in his suit, he
seeks to kill Hother. From certain Forest-Maidens
Hother learns the entire plot; in consultation with his
foster father Gevar he ascertains that the only means
of wounding Balder is the sword of the Forest-Troll
Miming. With much difficulty he gains possession of
this sword. Balder makes war on Hother and Gevar,
in the course of which he loses a great battle at sea, although all of the gods, even Odin and Thor, fight on his

[1] See Axel Olrik, *Kilderne til Sakses oldhistorie* II (1894), p. 13 ff.

Myths of the Gods

side; Thor crushes down with his cudgel all that oppose him until Hother succeeds in splitting the shaft of it; then even the gods take flight. Now Hother weds Nanna and becomes king of Sweden, which land is his domain by hereditary right. Balder continues the struggle against him, now with a greater measure of good fortune, gains the victory over him in two battles, and thus wins the kingdom of Denmark, which Hother has sought to lay under tribute to himself. But Balder's unhappy love for Nanna consumes his strength. No longer able to walk, he is compelled to ride in a chariot. In order to help him regain his vigor, three Celestial Maidens brew for him a drink made from the poison of serpents. Hother, meanwhile, gains knowledge of the posture of affairs from the same three Forest-Maidens who assisted him before, and makes opportune haste to join battle with Balder; the battle which ensues between them lasts a whole day, and neither side wins a decisive victory. During the night Hother sallies forth to meet the Maidens who are preparing the potent draught; he asks them to give him some of it, but they dare not heed his request, although they are well disposed toward him in all things else. On his return journey by a happy chance he encounters Balder alone. He wounds him with his sword, and Balder dies three days afterward. Hother now becomes king also in Denmark. Odin, meaning to avenge the death of Balder, seeks the advice of soothsayers, and the Finn Rostiophus tells him that Rind, daughter of the king of Ruthenia (Russia) is to bear him a son who will avenge his brother. Assuming a disguise, Odin enters the service of the king as a soldier and performs such incredible deeds of valor that he becomes the king's most highly trusted henchman. Now he pays court to Rind with the consent of the king; but, too haughty to accept him, she sends him away with a box on the ear. The next year he returns in the guise of a smith and fashions for the princess the most lovely ornaments of gold and silver; but instead of the kiss he asks for, he gets only a second box on the ear, the princess being unwilling to favor a man so old. The third time he appears as the gayest of knights, but his courtship meets with no better luck than before. At last he returns in the likeness of a young girl, and so finds a place among Rind's handmaidens. The handmaiden, as he calls himself, pretends to unusual skill in healing. When the princess in the course of time falls ill of a dangerous malady, the handmaiden is summoned and, on being promised her love as a guerdon, restores Rind to health. Thus Odin gains what he has long sought. Rind becomes his consort and bears him a son, whom Saxo calls Bous and who is no doubt to be identified with the Vali of the *Eddas*. Of him Saxo relates only that he makes war on Hother, that Hother falls in battle, but that Bous receives a mortal wound from which he dies on the following day. The *Eddas*, on the other hand, represent Vali as still living, inasmuch as he is one of the small number of gods who are to survive the Twilight of the Gods.

Myths of the Gods

THE DEATH OF KVASIR—SUTTUNG

THE death of Kvasir occasioned the dissemination among men of a knowledge of the poetic arts. It happened in the following manner:

Kvasir [1] was in the habit of journeying hither and thither in the world for the purpose of teaching wisdom to men. Once upon a time he was invited to visit the home of the Dwarfs Fjalar and Galar; they begged permission to speak a word or two with him in private, and promptly killed him. His blood they allowed to drip into two crocks and a kettle; then they mixed honey with the blood and from this pottage they brewed a mead possessing the peculiar virtue that whoever should drink of it would become a skald or a soothsayer. The two crocks are called Son and Bodn, and the kettle Odrœrir. The Dwarfs told the Æsir that Kvasir had been drowned in his own perfect wisdom, no man being wise enough to match wits with him. Some time later the Dwarfs invited into their home a Giant named Gilling and his wife. The Dwarfs asked the Giant to row out to sea to fish with them; as they were rowing along the shore, the boat struck a reef and overturned. Gilling, being unable to swim, was drowned, while the Dwarfs managed to right the boat and reach land. When they told the Giant's wife of the accident, she moaned and wept aloud. Fjalar suggested that it might ease her grief to look out to sea where her husband had perished, and the thought pleased her; whereupon Fjalar directed his brother

[1] See p. 13.

Galar to take a millstone, post himself above the door, and drop the stone on her head as she stepped out, for he was heartily wearied with her lamentations. Galar did as he was told. When Suttung, Gilling's son, learned what had happened, he came upon the Dwarfs, took them captive, and marooned them on a reef over which the sea washed at flood tide. In their distress they begged Suttung to have mercy on them and offered to give him the precious mead in recompense for his father's death. Suttung accepted their proffer, and in this way a reconciliation was effected between them. He hid the mead at a place called Nitbjorg and set his daughter Gunnlod to keep watch over it.

When all these events came to the knowledge of Odin, he set out determined to secure the mead for himself. In his journey he came to a meadow belonging to Suttung's brother Baugi, where he saw nine thralls at work cutting hay. On his asking if they wanted their scythes sharpened they gladly accepted his services. Taking his whetstone from his belt he put such a fine edge on the scythes that the thralls were eager to buy the whetstone from him. He was willing to sell, but finding that each one of them coveted it, he tossed the whetstone into the air; all of them tried to catch it at one time, and thus had the misfortune to cut one another's throats with their scythes. Now Odin found lodging for the night with Baugi. Baugi complained to Odin that his nine thralls had killed one another, and that he was at his wits' end to get laborers in their stead. Odin, who had called himself Bolverk, offered to do nine men's work for Baugi, if Baugi would only procure him a draught of Suttung's mead by way of wages. Baugi answered that, though he had no sort of control over the mead, which Suttung kept in his own charge alone, he was willing to go in the company of Bolverk and try to gain possession of the mead for him. While summer lasted, Bolverk did the work of nine men for Baugi; but when winter came, he demanded his hire. The two accordingly visited Suttung, to whom Baugi explained the agreement between himself and Bolverk; but Suttung refused outright to let them have so much as a single drop. Bolverk then proposed to Baugi that they would have to try to get hold of the mead by some sort of trickery, and Baugi was nothing loath. Bolverk produced an auger called Rati and asked Baugi to bore a hole with it through the mountain, that is, provided the auger would bite rock. Baugi set to work and had not bored a great while before he declared that he had made a hole clear through the stone of the mountain. On Bolverk's blowing into the hole, however, the grit flew back into his face; having thus discovered that Baugi meant to fool him, Bolverk enjoined him to bore again in sober earnest. Baugi plied the auger a second time; and when Bolverk blew once more, the dust flew inward. Bolverk now transformed himself into a snake and crawled through the hole. Baugi tried to pierce his body with the auger but failed. Odin soon made his way to the spot where Gunnlod sat guarding the mead, and remained there with her three nights. She gave him leave to drink thrice of the mead; the first time he drained Odrœrir, the second time Bodn, and the third time Son. Then taking on the form of an eagle, he flew away as fast as ever he could fly. When Suttung became aware of what was going on, he too assumed the shape of an eagle and spread his wings in pursuit of Odin. When the Æsir caught sight of Odin flying toward home, they placed their crocks out in the courtyard. On alighting within the walls of Asgard, Odin spewed the mead into the crocks; but Suttung having by that time nearly overtaken him, he let a part of the mead slip behind him. The gods, however, were not in the least disturbed, and permitted who would to gather up the dregs. Odin made a gift of the mead to the Æsir and to all who understand the art of poetry; the remnants of mead which fell into the mire became the allotted portion of poetasters.

ODIN'S DEBATE WITH VAFTHRUDNIR

JUST as Thor was accustomed to make adventurous sorties in order to discomfit the Giants with material weapons, so Odin from time to time undertook to match wits with them; to this end he would send out challenges inviting them to try their wisdom against his own. Among the Giants was an old wiseacre named Vafthrudnir, famous for his knowledge of the ancient history of the universe and of the gods themselves; with him Odin wished to debate for mastery. Frigg begged him to forgo his purpose on the plea that no one could compete with Vafthrudnir; but since Odin was determined, Frigg could do nothing else than wish

Myths of the Gods

him luck and express the hope that his wisdom would not be found wanting in the hour of trial. Odin accordingly sought out Vafthrudnir; presenting himself under the name of Gagnrad,[1] he let it be known that he had come to discover whether Vafthrudnir was really so wise as rumor had made him out to be. "You shall not escape from my hall," said Vafthrudnir, "if your wisdom does not surpass my own; meanwhile, take a seat and we shall see which of us two knows the more." Gagnrad, declining the proffered seat, declared that a poor man coming to a rich man's house should either speak sound sense or remain silent; if he let his words run wild, he courted certain misfortune. "Tell me, then, Gagnrad, since you choose to plead your cause from the floor," said Vafthrudnir—and he forthwith began to put questions about the horses of Night and Day, about the river Iving that forms the boundary between gods and Giants, and about the plains of Vigrid, where the battle between the gods and the Giants is destined to take place. Gagnrad made ready response to all these questions and then took a seat to propound his own queries. The one who suffered defeat was to lose his head. Gagnrad in his turn questioned Vafthrudnir about the making of the earth from Ymir's body, about the sun and moon, about day and night, about Ymir's or Aurgelmir's origin in the Elivagar, about Ræsvælg, about Njord, about the life of the Heroes in Valhalla, about which of gods and men were to survive the ruin of the universe, and about the passing of Odin. Vaf-

[1] That is, "he who determines good fortune or victory".

thrudnir had an answer for every question. Finally Gagnrad asked what it was that Odin whispered in Balder's ear as Balder was being laid on the funeral pile. This question Vafthrudnir was at a loss to answer, and thus he understood that his opponent was none other than Odin himself. Then he confessed that with the mouth of one doomed to death had he bandied words with his guest; Odin after all remained the wisest of the wise.

ODIN (GRIMNIR) AND GEIRRŒD

On another occasion, too, Odin in person gave a great deal of information about the gods, their manner of life, and their dwellings. King Raudung had two sons, Agnar and Geirrœd. Once upon a time, when Agnar was ten years of age and Geirrœd was eight, they rowed off in a boat to catch fish. The wind drove them out to sea. In the darkness of the night their boat was splintered on the shore, and so they made their way to land. There they came across a peasant, with whom they remained throughout the winter. The wife adopted Agnar as a foster son and the husband adopted Geirrœd. The peasant couple were in fact none other than Odin and Frigg. When spring was come, the husband made the boys a present of a boat; and as he and his wife walked with them down to the shore, the man talked with Geirrœd in private. The boys found favoring winds and finally touched at their own father's boat landing. Geirrœd, who had taken

Myths of the Gods

his station at the prow, leaped on land; as he did so he pushed the boat back into the sea, calling out to his brother: "Go where the Trolls may get you!" The boat drifted out into the ocean, while Geirrœd walked home and received a joyous welcome. Geirrœd's father had died in the meantime. Geirrœd was made king in his stead, and later became a famous man.

Odin and Frigg were sitting one day in Lidskjalf looking out into the universe. "Do you see your foster son Agnar," asked Odin, "living yonder in a cavern with a Giantess and begetting children with her? My own foster son Geirrœd, meanwhile, rules over his lands as a king." "Yet he is so sparing of his food," answered Frigg, "that he stints his guests when he thinks that too many have come to him at one time." Odin declared that there could be no greater falsehood, and so they made a wager to decide the matter. Frigg sent her handmaiden Fulla to king Geirrœd with a message warning him to beware of a certain sorcerer who had found his way into the land, doubtless with the purpose of casting evil spells upon the king; the sorcerer might be easily identified because no dog, however savage, would attack him. It was indeed only idle talk that king Geirrœd was lacking in hospitality; nevertheless he gave commands to seize a man whom, as it proved, no dog would bite. The man, who was wrapped in a blue cloak, gave his name as Grimnir—in reality it was Odin himself disguised.[1] When they laid hands on him, he had little to say for himself, and therefore the king caused him to be

[1] *Grima*, "a covering for the face", "a mask".

tortured in order to loosen his tongue, by placing him between two fires and forcing him to remain there eight nights. King Geirrœd at the time had a son, ten years of age, who bore the name Agnar after his father's brother. Agnar, stepping up before Grimnir, gave him a drink from a well-filled horn, saying that his father did ill in torturing a man charged with no misdeed. Grimnir drained the horn to the lees, by which time the fire had come near enough to singe his cloak. Then he chanted a long lay, in the course of which he sang the praises of Agnar and reckoned up all of the thirteen dwellings of the gods: Thrudheim, Ydalir, Alfheim, Valaskjalf, Sœkkvabek, Gladsheim, Thrymheim, Breidablik, the Mounts of Heaven, Folkvang, Glitnir, Noatun, and Vidi, the home of Vidar. Furthermore he sang of the meat and drink of Valhalla, of the dimensions of Valhalla and Bilskirnir, of Heidrun, of Eikthyrnir, of the rivers in the realms of gods and men, of the horses of the gods, of Yggdrasil, of the Valkyries, of the horses of the sun and of the wolves that pursue them, and of the creation of the world. At last he recounted all of his own names and gave Geirrœd to understand that he had played the fool and that he had forfeited the favor of Odin. When Geirrœd heard that the man was Odin, he sprang up to help him away from the fire. The sword which had lain across his knees slipped from his hand with the point upward, and the king stumbled and fell forward upon the sword in such a way that it pierced him through the body; Odin at once disappeared from sight. Agnar, however, ruled many years as king over the land.

Myths of the Gods

HARBARD AND THOR

ONCE upon a time when Thor had been away in the regions of the east carrying on his warfare with the Giants, he came on his homeward journey to a sound, on the other side of which stood the ferryman by his boat. Thor called to him, and the ferryman called out in turn, asking who it was that was waiting on the other shore. Thor answered: "If you will only ferry me across, you shall have food from the basket on my back; I ate herrings and oatcakes before starting on my journey and even now I am not at all hungry." The ferryman, who later disclosed that his name was Harbard, retorted with taunts, ridiculing Thor as a barefooted vagrant without breeches. "Bring your boat to this side," said Thor; "and tell me who owns it." "The owner is Hildolf the Wise, of Radseysund," answered Harbard; "he has just given me express commands not to ferry vagabonds and horse thieves across the water, but only honest folk that I myself know well; so tell me your name if you want to cross the sound." Thor told with great pride who he was— "Odin's son and Magni's father"—and threatened to make Harbard pay for his obstinacy if he did not bring the boat over at once. "No, I will stay here and wait for you," said Harbard; "and you will meet no man more difficult to deal with than myself, now that Rungnir is dead." "You see fit to remind me of Rungnir and his head of stone," answered Thor; "and yet he sank to earth under my blows. What were you doing while I did that work?" "I was a companion of

Fjolvar five full winters on the island of Algrœn; there we sped the time in battle, cutting down warriors; we endured many hardships, but nevertheless we gained the love of seven sisters. Did you ever do the like, Thor?" "I slew Thjazi and tossed his eyes into the heavens," retorted Thor; "what do you say to that?" Harbard replied: "By artful practices I enticed the Dark-Riders to leave their husbands. Lebard, it seems to me, was a Giant hard to cope with; though he made me a gift of a magic wand, yet I played him false so that his wits forsook him." "An evil return for a good gift," said Thor. "One oak gains what is peeled from another;[1] each man looks to his own interest— but what else have you done, Thor?" "I invaded the east and there put to death Giantesses as they made their way to the mountains; great would be the progeny of the Giants if all of them were suffered to live, and small would be the number of men in Midgard. Is there anything else you have done, Harbard?" "I was in Valland and took my part in battle; I egged the heroes on but never reconciled one to another; to Odin belong the earls that fall in battle, and to Thor the thralls." "You would mete out unequal justice among the Æsir if it lay in your power to do so." "Thor has much strength but little courage; fearful as a coward you squeezed yourself into the glove, most unlike what Thor should be; you dared not make the slightest noise, afraid as you were that the Giant might hear you." "Harbard, dastard that you are!

[1] A proverb, the meaning of which is that one man's loss is the other man's gain.

Myths of the Gods

I would kill you if I could only reach across the sound."
"Why should you do so? You have no reason whatever. Have you done anything else worth mentioning?" "Once in the realms to the east, as I stood guard at the river (Iving?), the sons of Svarang sought my life; they hurled stones at me, but victory did not fall to their lot; they themselves had to sue for peace. What have you done?" "I too was in the east, and there trifled with a fair maiden who was not unwilling to pleasure me." "I took the life of Berserk women on the island of Læsey; they had left undone no evil deed, had bereft men of their senses by means of witchcraft." "Only a weakling, Thor, would take the lives of women." "She-wolves (werewolves) they were, not real women; they smashed my boat as it lay leaned against the shore; they threatened me with iron bands, and kneaded Thjalfi like dough. What were you doing meanwhile?" "I was among the armed men marching hither with flying standards to redden their spears in blood." "Perhaps it was you, then, who came and offered us most evil terms?" asked Thor. "I will offer you a recompense of arm rings, as many as they shall deem right who may choose to reconcile us to each other." "Who has taught you such biting words of scorn, the like of which I never have heard before?" "The ancient men who dwell in the mounds at home." "That is a fine name you give to the barrows of the dead. Yet," continued Thor, "your mocking will prove dearly bought if I wade across the sound; no wolf shall howl more hideously than you if I strike you but once with my hammer."

"Sif has a man visiting her, whom you may want to meet; prove your strength there, where your duty demands it." Thor said it was a shameless lie; but Harbard only crowed over having delayed Thor on his homeward journey, and Thor had to own the justice of his taunts. "I should never have believed," said Harbard, "that a boatman would be able to hinder Asa-Thor in his travels." "I will give you a piece of advice, then: row the boat across, and let us bandy words no more." "Leave the sound if you choose; I will not ferry you over." "Show me the way, at any rate," begged Thor, "since you will not help me cross the water." "That is too small a favor to be denied," answered Harbard, "but it is a long way to go: first some paces to 'Stock' and then to 'Stone'; then take the first turning to the left until you reach Verland; there Fjorgyn will meet her son and show him the road to the land of Odin." "Can I finish the journey today?" "With toil and trouble you may reach your journey's end before the sun sinks, if I am not mistaken." "Our parleying might as well stop, since you do nothing but pick new quarrels; but you will pay for your stubbornness if we ever chance to meet again." "Go where the Trolls may get you!" said Harbard by way of a last word.

RAGNAROK—THE TWILIGHT OF THE GODS

At last the time draws near when the existing universe must perish and the gods must succumb before higher powers. This period is called in the ancient myths the

Myths of the Gods

Dissolution or Destiny (*rǫk*) of the gods or rulers (*ragna*, genitive plural of *regin*); a later form is *ragnarøkkr*, the Darkness of the Gods. The gods themselves have foreknowledge of its coming, which is foreshadowed by many signs. Evil and violence increase. The Æsir's cock with the golden comb (Gullinkambi) crows to waken the Heroes of Odin's retinue; the dun cock in Hel's keeping crows likewise; so also crows the red cock Fjalar in the world of the Giants; and Garm bays vehemently outside the rocky fastness of Gnipa. For the space of three years the earth is filled with strife and wickedness; brother kills brother for gain's sake, and the son spares not his own father. Then come three other years, like one long winter; everywhere the snow drifts into heaps, the sun yields no warmth, and biting winds blow from all quarters. That winter is known as Fimbul Winter (the Great Winter). The wolf Skoll swallows the sun, and Hati or Manigarm swallows the moon so that the heavens and the air are sprayed with blood. The stars are quenched. The earth and all the mountains tremble; trees are uprooted; all bonds are burst asunder. Both Loki and the Fenris Wolf shake off their shackles. The Midgard Serpent, seeking to reach dry land, swims with such turbulent force that the seas wash over their banks. Now the ship Naglfar once more floats on the flood. The ship is made from dead men's nails, and therefore the nails of all that die should be trimmed before their burial, to the end that Naglfar may be the sooner finished. Loki steers the ship, and the crews of Hell follow him. The Giant Rym comes out from the east, and with him all the Rime-Thursar. The Fenris Wolf rushes forth with gaping maw; his upper jaw touches the heavens, his nether jaw the earth; he would gape still more if there were more room. His eyes are lit with flame. The Midgard Serpent, keeping pace with the Wolf, spews venom over sky and sea. Amidst all the din and clamor the heavens are cleft open, and the Sons of Muspell ride forth from the south with Surt in the van, fires burning before him and behind him. His sword shines brighter than the sun. As they ride out over the bridge Bifrost, it breaks asunder beneath their feet. One and all, the Sons of Muspell, the Fenris Wolf, the Midgard Serpent, Loki, Rym, and all the Rime-Thursar direct their course toward the fields of Vigrid, which measure a hundred miles each way. The Sons of Muspell muster their hosts for battle, and the radiance of their levies gleams far and wide.

Meanwhile, on the part of the Æsir, Heimdal rises to his feet and sounds the Gjallar-Horn with all his might in order to rouse the gods. They meet in assembly and take counsel together. Odin rides to Mimir's Well to seek guidance there. The ash Yggdrasil trembles, and all things in heaven and earth are seized with dread. Æsir and Heroes don their panoplies and march upon the fields of Vigrid. Foremost rides Odin, girt with his golden helmet and magnificent byrnie; brandishing his spear Gungnir, he presses on against the Fenris Wolf. At his side walks Thor; but as he soon finds himself in mortal conflict with the Midgard Serpent, he can give no aid

Myths of the Gods

to Odin. Frey joins battle with Surt, and Tyr with
the dog Garm, who also has broken from his fetters.
Heimdal fights against Loki.

Thor in the end kills the Midgard Serpent but is
himself able to walk only nine steps after the struggle
is over; then he sinks to the ground dead, borne down
by the venom spewed over him by the Serpent. The
Wolf swallows Odin, and so the god lives no more; but
Vidar at once steps into the breach, thrusts one of his
feet into the nether jaw of the Wolf, grasps the upper
jaw with his hand, and thus tears open the Wolf's
throat; his foot is shod with a heavy shoe made from
all the slivers of leather that men have cut from their
boots at the toe or the heel; consequently men should
always cast such patches aside in order that they may
serve the uses of the Æsir.[1] Frey falls at the hands of
Surt, no longer having at his need the good blade he
once gave to Skirnir. Tyr and Garm, and likewise
Loki and Heimdal, kill each other.

Thereupon Surt hurls fire broadcast over the whole
earth and all things perish. The wild, warlike order
passes and a new life begins.

Out of the sea there rises a new earth, green and fair,
whose fields bear their increase without the sowing of
seed. The sun has borne a daughter as beautiful as
herself, and the daughter now guides the course of the
sun in her mother's stead. All evil is passed and gone.
On the plains of Ida assemble those Æsir who did not
fall in the last great battle: Vidar, Vali, and the sons of

---

[1] Thus runs the story in Snorri's *Edda;* according to the *Voluspá*,
Vidar kills the Wolf by means of his sword.

Thor—Modi and Magni. Thither resort also Balder and Hod, now returned out of Hell, and thither comes Hœnir out of Vanaheim. Once again the Æsir make their dwelling on the plains of Ida, where Asgard stood before; in the grass they find scattered the ancient gold chessmen of the gods, and thus they recall to memory the old days and speak together of the vanished past. Now that Thor's battles are done, Modi and Magni fall heir to Mjollnir. Nor are all among mankind dead. Lif and Lifthrasir have saved themselves from the fires of Surt at a place called Hoddmimir's Holt, where they find subsistence in the dews of the morning; from these two spring forth a new race of men. At Gimle stands a hall thatched with gold and brighter than the sun. There a righteous generation shall dwell, in joys that never end. "Then shall come from above the Mighty One, he who governs all things."

ON THE MYTHOLOGY OF THE EDDAS

WE may with some justice speak of a system of divinity or a mythology of the *Eddas;* but this does not mean the same as the actual religion of our forefathers, their systems of belief and worship. As to the worship of the gods, we have scattered items of information in ancient written records, of which an account will follow, p. 267 ff. Besides, the appendix will contain a summary of the knowledge supplied by Norwegian place names as to the worship of the gods in pagan times.[1] Of the actual belief in the gods, of the funda-

[1] This appendix on Norwegian place names, pp. 210–44 of the original, is omitted in the present translation.—Translator's note.

Myths of the Gods

mental forces supporting pagan religious feeling, it is much more difficult to give a searching analysis, since the materials for an exposition of this character are most various and of a kind which, in the present state of scholarly investigation, would require a series of critical studies at first hand. So far as this phase of the religion of our fathers is concerned, we must rest content with the indications furnished in the foregoing division of the book, on the "Myths of the Gods, or the Mythology Proper".[1] Express emphasis, however, must be laid on the fact that the particular form assumed by the myths of the gods depends to a great extent on the literary vehicle—be it poem or prose narrative verging on folk tale—by means of which it has been delivered to us.

With reference to both worship and creed it would be necessary, by reason of the nature and the chronological distribution of the sources, to take up the discussion on an historical basis; but a history of Northern religions is still to be written.[2] Such a work cannot be written until some further progress has been made in clearing the ground by separating out the relatively late Christian elements, a task begun by Sophus Bugge in his *Studier over de nordiske Gude- og Helte-*

[1] In general, reference may be made to V. Grønbech, *Vor folkeæt i oldtiden* (Our Race in Antiquity), particularly vol. III (Hellighed og helligdom: Holiness and Sanctuary) and vol. IV (Menneskelivet og guderne: Human Life and the Gods), Copenhagen, 1912; cf. the same author's *Religionsskiftet i Norden* (The Change of Religion in the Northern Countries), Copenhagen, 1913.

[2] Cf., however, Karl Helm, *Altgermanische Religionsgeschichte* I, Heidelberg, 1913, of which up to the present time only the period down to the "Roman era" has been published.

Norse Mythology

Sagns Oprindelse (1881–89), and during the present generation carried forward principally by Axel Olrik [1] and Kaarle Krohn (*Skandinavisk mytologi*, Helsingfors 1922). In the works named, the comparative study of folklore takes a conspicuous place; especially have Finnish borrowings from the Northern peoples proved to have great significance. [2] Much also remains to be done toward a true estimation of the value of Norse literature as source material. The situation in this respect, however, is such that it is possible—and defensible from the standpoint of the history of religion— to attempt an exposition of what may be termed the Norse mythology. The fact is that our principal sources, the poems relating to the gods in the *Poetic Edda*, together with a group of skaldic poems, present a closely correlated unity as to content, period, and surroundings; [3] under such a unified aspect Snorri viewed the religious poetry from the close of the pagan era, principally the tenth century, and on it he built his consecutive presentation in the *Gylfaginning*, the first section of his *Edda*. It is of great importance that we keep clearly in mind the position occupied

[1] Cf. note to p. 112.
[2] Cf. J. Fritzner, *Lappernes Hedenskab og Trolddomskunst sammenholdt med andre Folks, især Nordmændenes Tro og Overtro*, in [*Norsk*] *Historisk Tidsskrift* IV, 1877, p. 135 ff.; Axel Olrik, *Nordisk og lappisk gudsdyrkelse* in *Danske studier* 1905, p. 39 ff.; Wolf von Unwerth, *Untersuchungen über Totenkult und Odinn- verehrung bei Nordgermanen und Lappen* (*Germanistische Ab- handlungen* 37), Breslau, 1911; Kaarle Krohn, *Skandinavisk mytologi*. Cf. the literature cited in the notes to p. 16, p. 25, line 7, p. 86.
[3] Cf. A. Olrik, *Eddamytologien* (*Nordisk tidsskrift* 1917, p. 81 ff.).

Myths of the Gods

by the two *Eddas* in the intellectual life of the Norse race.[1]

Now that we have given an orderly view of the my-thology of our forefathers, some mention should be made of the chief sources from which the account has been drawn. These are, as often pointed out, the two *Eddas*. One of the two, Snorri's *Edda*, dates back no farther than the thirteenth century. It is a learned work intended as a handbook for skalds, wherein they might find easy access to the ancient mythology form-ing a basis for the poetic phraseology of the time; in the course of our discussion occasional examples have been given of skaldic kennings based on the myths of the gods. Snorri thus had the task of collecting and re-telling all of the myths known to his day; and it is clear that his sources were of three kinds: various poems preserved in the *Poetic Edda*, other poetry and skaldic verses, and finally nonmetrical tales that had run current in popular tradition. But since his work was begun several centuries after the pagan faith had died out, there is reason to believe that the myths of the last class especially had not come down in their original form. At any rate, there is no certainty in the matter. And inasmuch as Snorri was not content with re-telling the individual myths, but also in great measure gave them a systematic arrangement of his own, his personal interpretation of the vague myths must have influenced his treatment of the whole.

[1] Cf. Finnur Jónsson, *Den oldnorske og oldislandske litteraturs historie*, 2nd ed., vol. I, 1920 (on the literary history of the Eddic poems).

Norse Mythology

The second principal source of our knowledge of the ancient mythology is the collection of poems known as the *Poetic Edda*. These poems no doubt possess greater authority for the purpose than Snorri's *Edda;* but even they do not come from a period when the ancient faith flourished in its fullest energy. They belong to the Viking Age, to an era during which the Northern peoples maintained the liveliest relations with the outside world; and during those last centuries of paganism—as also in earlier times, when communication with nations of a superior cultivation was by no means slight—the Northern races surely received impulses from without which must have affected various elements in their mythology.[1] Great care must therefore be exercised in seeking ancient native material in the myths of the *Eddas*. The warlike spirit which marked the Viking Age (a spirit which was by no means wanting in the preceding period) doubtless was very influential in making the mythology of the *Eddas* take on the coloring of a religion for warriors. It is only the fallen warrior who is received into the company of the Heroes in Valhalla, and not even death itself puts an end to the life of battle; the war-god Odin is of all gods the king, in comparison with whom the other gods take subordinate rank. Moreover, the evidence of the sagas goes to show that the Viking Age was an era of intellectual ferment during which many men gave up their faith in the deities of old, and put their trust in their own right arms instead; a rational movement of this type must have had a strong influence

[1] See notes to p. 7; to p. 25, line 7; to p. 86; and to p. 112.

Myths of the Gods

on the poetic elaborations of the mythology which sprang up during this period. The gods of paganism are without exception created in the image of man; and the Norse Asa-religion is to so great a degree an expression of the Viking Age that it may well be regarded as bearing in significant particulars the plain impress of the period.

To discover, in the next place, to what extent the religion of our forefathers may be primitive and domestic in origin, recourse must perhaps be had especially to indications lying outside the range of the Eddic mythology itself. Place names and cult reminiscences surviving in later folk custom and folk beliefs provide a great deal of information.[1] To a less degree, literary sources other than those purely Norse, are of value.[2] One of the most important of these sources is the chapter in Tacitus's *Germania* containing the account of the worship of Nerthus (Njord); this passage gives us, when compared with other later materials,[3] glimpses of a distant past when culture divinities had the foremost place in public worship. The worship of these gods maintained itself until paganism was extinct, and even then had force enough to perpetuate itself in newer popular customs; but these gods had only a slight attraction for the poets of the *Edda*.[4] Another important source is Adam of Bremen's account (*The History of the Bishops of*

---

[1] Cf. Gudmund Schütte, *Hjemligt Hedenskab i almenfattelig Fremstilling*, Copenhagen 1919.
[2] Cf. pp. ix–xii.
[3] See note to p. 16.
[4] See, however, p. 17; and *Skírnismál*.

Norse Mythology

Hamburg IV, 26–27) of the gods of the temple at Uppsala in the eleventh century, probably based on the description of an eyewitness, Sven Ulvsson: "In this temple the people bow down before the images of three gods so arranged that the mightiest of them, Thor, occupies a throne in the centre, on one side of him Wodan (Odin), and on the other side Fricco (Frey). Thor governs the air and rules over thunder and lightning, wind and rain, fair weather and harvests. The second, Wodan, that is, the raging one, makes war and gives men courage in the face of the enemy. The third is Fricco, who grants peace and delight to mortals; his image sometimes is represented with a large phallus. Wodan they present armed, as we are accustomed to present Mars. To Thor, on the other hand, wielding a sceptre, they give the appearance of Jupiter. They also worship gods whose origin was human, men who for their mighty deeds have been immortalized. All of the gods have their several priests, who make offerings on behalf of the people. In case of threatening pestilence or famine, sacrifices are offered to Thor; in case of impending war, to Wodan; when weddings are to be celebrated, . . . sacrifice is made to Fricco. The common sacrificial festival of all the Swedes together is held each ninth year in Uppsala."

This passage shows how the worship of the Swedes differed from that which has been delivered to us through the tradition of the *Eddas*. Great interest attaches to the circumstance that Thor here is definitely represented as the god of fruitfulness.[1] For the

[1] Cf. p. 12 and note to p. 65.

Myths of the Gods

rest, literature outside of the Norse domains supplies only the sparsest references to faith and worship. The surviving evidences are for the most part limited to a mere recital of the names of the various divinities; one of the very few exceptions is to be found in the myth about Wodan, Frea, and the origin of the name of the Longobards.[1]

[1] See note to p. 27.

II.
THE HEROIC LEGENDS

INTRODUCTORY REMARKS

ACCORDING to views common during the Romantic period, the heroic legends were at once mythical and historical, and thus closely allied to the myths of the gods. More recent scholarship, which reckons only to a slight degree with domestic legendary traditions dating from a remote antiquity, has formed quite a different opinion. At the present time the heroic legends are studied not only according to their contents, according to their motives; considered as a complete whole, the heroic legend exists merely in and by means of the literary form it has assumed; consequently, for the proper investigation of the heroic legend a peculiar literary-historical method must be adopted, differing from the method used in the study of mythology, in that the literary forms dealing with the gods must be correlated with the fixed, distinctly local ceremonies having to do with the *worship* of the gods.

The heroic literature has for its subject human destinies which by their elevation above the commonplace have made a strong appeal to the poet. In their most compact form, where the chief interest gathers about strong-willed personalities moulded by the great moments of life, we come across the heroic legends in brief epic lays which can be traced back to the period of the national migrations and which in pre-Christian times ran their course among all of the Germanic tribes. Heroic lays of this type, in their more uncontaminated ancient forms or in literary adaptations of Norse origin (dialogue verse without direct narration) provide the bulk of the heroic poetry of the *Poetic Edda*. During historic times in Norway and Iceland, this heroic poetry had a continued existence in the so-called "sagas of antiquity" (*fornaldarsǫgur*), saga-like stories which drew their themes from antiquity, from a prehistoric, pagan era. The legendary materials in these sagas frequently have their roots in prose adaptations of ancient heroic lays;[1] yet newer materials make their appearance during the Viking Age, and popular taste takes another direction.[2] These heroic sagas, which lack the firm outlines of the ancient heroic lays, are subjected to influences from all sorts of vagabond themes, for instance folk-tale themes, and at length we find an entire group of sagas of antiquity which must be regarded as nothing more than independent compositions dealing with arbitrarily invented personages whose lifetime is laid in the era of the petty kings anterior to the unification of Norway.[3]

Of the heroic legends as a whole it is to be said in general that, contrary to the practice of historians of a generation ago, they are not to be treated as historical sources. The poetic elements have gained the ascendancy over the historical elements and created

[1] *Hervarar Saga*, p. 130 ff; *Vǫlsunga Saga*, note to p. 159.
[2] The adventures of the hero in love and war, as in *Ragnar Lodbrok's Saga*, p. 245 ff, a typical saga from the Viking Age.
[3] Thus no doubt *Fridthjofs Saga*, p. 256. Many of the "antique sagas" have given rise to popular ballads. On this subject reference may be made, once for all, to K. Liestøl, *Norske trollvisor og norrǿne sogor*, Christiania 1915.

Heroic Legends

combinations of a kind that bids defiance to history and chronology alike. What may be authentic history in such poetic versions of the legends we can not discover so long as we have to rely solely on the legends themselves; we must seek the aid of veracious historical documents and the testimony of trustworthy foreign historians to get at the residuum of truth, as, for example, in the case of the legends dealing with Ragnar Lodbrok and his sons. As a rule the outcome of such a procedure is that the legends disclose no historical facts not already known through these foreign sources. In a number of the legends even this expedient is denied us, since history fails to confirm the events recited in the legends; this holds true, for instance, with the Helgi legends, for which reason it is difficult if not impossible to ascertain their origins. Other legends have made their way to the Northern nations from neighboring countries, for example, the legends of the Volsungs and the Gjukungs; but these also have suffered many changes in form in the fresh soil to which they were transplanted.

Among the heroic legends there are several that show a closer mutual relationship, and therefore are designated as a legendary cycle; still others are isolated, showing no connection with anything else. It has been further demonstrated that the legendary process tends in the course of time to draw together various originally distinct legends and thus to create new cycles. Among the great cycles, those of the Volsungs, the Niflungs, and the Gjukungs are most prominent. Among the independent legends, those dealing with

Wayland Smith, with Frodi and his handmaidens, and with the Battle of the Hjadnings emerge above the rest.

WAYLAND

THE legend of Wayland runs as follows: Once upon a time there were three brothers, named Slagfinn, Egil, and Wayland; their father was king of the Finns. It so befell that they went out on their skis to hunt and came to a place called Wolf Dales, lying near a body of water called Wolf Lake; there they built themselves a house. One morning they chanced to see three beautiful women sitting on the shore weaving linen; beside them lay their swan cloaks, by which token the brothers knew them to be Valkyries. They carried the three women home and wedded them. Slagfinn took to wife Ladgunn Swanwhite; Wayland took Hervor Allwise; and Egil took Olrun. The first two were the daughters of king Lodvi, and the third a daughter of king Kiar of Valland. When they had lived together seven years, a longing for battle came over the Valkyries, and in the absence of the brothers they flew away. Egil and Slagfinn at once set out in search of their wives; Wayland remained alone at home in the Wolf Dales, busying himself in his smithy with the forging of objects of price. While he awaited the return of his wife, he sped the time in fixing precious stones in settings of gold and in fashioning magnificent rings. The fame of his handiwork reached the hearing of Nidud, the evil and greedy king of the Njarir. One night, in the waning of the moon, he marched forth with an armed band and reached the house in the Wolf Dales while Wayland was away a-hunting. By this time Wayland had finished seven hundred rings, which he had left hanging all together on one rope; Nidud lifted one of them off, and lay in wait for the homecoming of Wayland. Wayland returned, sat down before the fire to roast bear's meat, and in the meantime counted his rings. Missing one of them, he thought that his wife must surely have come home; but while he sat pondering the matter, he fell asleep. Awakened by the weight of heavy fetters on his hands and feet, he asked who had laid shackles upon him. Nidud called out to learn how Wayland had dared to seize his treasures in the Wolf Dales, to which Wayland answered that all of his possessions were his by right. Nidud now carried Wayland off to his own court, took from him even his splendid sword, and gave the ring to his own daughter Bodvild. But Nidud's queen, fearing the vengeance of Wayland, spoke words of warning to her husband. "His eyes glitter like those of a serpent every time he sees the sword and catches sight of Bodvild's ring," she said; "sever his sinews and expose him on the island of Sævarstead." They did her bidding; having severed Wayland's sinews at the knees, they placed him on the island, where he was employed in forging for the king all manner of precious things, and where none but the king was permitted to visit him. Many a time Wayland bemoaned his fate; without sleeping a wink he plied his task at the smithy and never ceased to meditate on means of repaying Nidud for his treachery.

Norse Mythology

At last fortune favored his designs. One day Nidud's two sons came out to the island and asked leave to look at his treasures. Opening a chest, he showed them many magnificent things; on the next day they were to return in secret, and he would give them all that he possessed. They came as they had promised, and no one in the palace knew of their coming. Wayland once more opened the chest; and while they stood looking down into it, he let the heavy lid fall in such a way as to cut off their heads. The bodies he hid beneath the floor, but the skulls he silvered over and sent them to Nidud for drinking vessels; the eyeballs he employed as jewels in ornaments for the queen; and from the teeth he fashioned brooches for Bodvild. Now after a time it so happened that Bodvild was unfortunate enough to crack the ring Nidud had given her. Not daring to let her father find out about her misadventure, she secretly sought out Wayland to have him mend it for her. He promised to do so. Since he treated her with great kindness, she suspected no evil when he offered her something to drink; the liquid being strong, she grew giddy and drowsy and so fell an easy prey to his purposes. Now Wayland donned a feather cloak and in this guise flew into Nidud's courtyard, where he settled to rest on the palings. He found Nidud sitting sleepless, brooding over the fate of his sons; divining that Wayland had caused their death, the king questioned him about them. Wayland then told how it all had come about, how the king's sons had been killed, how gems had been framed from their skulls, their eyes, and their teeth, and how Bodvild had been dishonored. Wayland flew away laughing, and Nidud had to stand in helpless rage watching him escape. He called Bodvild to him and asked if it was true that she and Wayland had sat together on the island. "Yes, it is true," replied Bodvild; "we sat together one whole fearful hour—I had no power to resist him."

THE HJADNINGS

THE legend of the Battle of the Hjadnings is recounted as follows in the *Prose Edda*: King Hogni had a daughter named Hild. Once upon a time, when Hogni had gone to a meeting of kings, she was taken captive by king Hedin Hjarrandason. As soon as Hogni learned that his realm had been sacked and his daughter carried off, he set out at the head of his soldiery in pursuit of Hedin. He got news that Hedin had taken flight toward the north; but when Hogni reached Norway, he was told that Hedin had shaped his course over the western seas. Hogni set sail in the wake of his enemy and at length touched the Orkney Islands, where he encountered Hedin off the island of Haey. Hild went to her father and offered him terms of peace in Hedin's name; or, in case he refused, an alternative struggle for life or death. Hogni would not accept the proffer of conciliation. The two kings thereupon landed on the island and marshalled their warriors for battle. Once again Hedin made overtures of peace; calling out to his kinsman, he offered him by way of recompense a heap of gold. But Hogni answered: "It is too late; I have already drawn the sword Dainsleif, forged in the smithy of the Dwarfs; each time it is bared some man must lose his life; its stroke can never be arrested; and the wounds it makes are never healed." "You boast of your sword," said Hedin; "but that does not mean that you shall boast of the victory; that sword is the best which does not fail its master at his need." Then they began the battle, to be known ever afterward as the Battle of the Hjadnings. During the whole day they fought on, and at night the kings went aboard their ships. In the course of the night Hild went out upon the field of battle and by means of her magic roused into life all of the fallen warriors. The next day the kings marched up on land and began the struggle anew, and with them all those who had been slain the day before. Thus they continued their warfare day after day. All who fell and all weapons and shields that were left on the field turned to stone; but as each new morning broke, the slain rose up armed and ready for the fray. In this way the Battle of the Hjadnings is to go forward until the coming of the Twilight of the Gods.

THE LEGEND OF TYRFING

ANOTHER sword, a match for Dainsleif, bore the name Tyrfing. It was forged under durance by the Dwarfs Dulin and Dvalin for Svafrlami, the brave grandson of Odin. Svafrlami had surprised them outside of their rock and had made haste to cast spells over them to prevent their getting back into the stone. He then threatened to take their lives unless they promised to forge for him a sword with hilt and handle of gold, a sword which would never rust, which would always bring victory, and which would cut iron as if it were so much cloth. The Dwarfs gave unwilling assent and finished the sword within the designated time; but when Dvalin had given it into the king's hand, and while he was still standing at the door opening into the rock, he said: "Your sword will take the life of a man each time it is unsheathed, and with it three dastard's deeds will be done; it will also bring death upon yourself." Svafrlami struck at the Dwarf with the sword, but failed to touch him. After that day he kept the sword in his possession a long time and with it won many a victory in battle and in single combat.

On the island of Bolm dwelt a great Berserk named Arngrim, who fared far and wide as a Viking. It so happened that in harrying the domains of Svafrlami he came face to face with Svafrlami himself. Svafrlami aimed a blow at Arngrim with Tyrfing, but succeeded only in striking his shield, from which he cut off a portion, while Tyrfing buried its point in the earth. In a moment Arngrim severed Svafrlami's hand from his body, laid hold of Tyrfing, and cleft Svafrlami's body in twain from head to foot. Thus a part of the prophecy of the Dwarf came to be fulfilled. Arngrim now took Svafrlami's fair daughter Eyfura captive, carried her off to Bolm, and made her his wife. They had twelve sons, all of them tall men, strong and warlike, who from their earliest years sped the time in Viking forays, to their own increasing renown. The eldest, named Angantyr, was a head taller than his brothers and as strong as any two of them; the others bore the names Hervard, Hjorvard, Sæming, Rani, Brami, Barri, Reifnir, Tind, Bui, and the two named Hadding, who were twins. Angantyr fell heir to Tyrfing, Hervard had the sword Rotti, Sæming had Mistiltein. Now and again the Berserk rage came over them, and during such periods it chanced a time or two that they killed some of their own men; in order to prevent happenings of this sort, when they felt the Berserk rage taking hold of them they went ashore out of their ships and fought with boulders or with the timbers of the forest. No king ever crossed their purposes, to such a degree were they held in awe for their wildness and cruelty.

One evening at Yuletide the champions of Bolm sat making vows over their flowing bowls. Angantyr avowed his intention of possessing the fair Ingeborg, daughter of king Yngvi of Uppsala. The following summer the brothers journeyed to the court of Yngvi and at once marched into the hall; Angantyr recounted his vow and demanded an immediate answer. On hearing what was said, Hjalmar the Haughty promptly came forward. For a long while he had spent his winters in the retinue of Yngvi and had rendered him most important services. Reminding the king of all his services, he asked Yngvi rather to bestow Ingeborg upon himself than upon so evil a Berserk as Angantyr. Yngvi declared that Ingeborg herself must make the decision, and she chose Hjalmar; whereupon Angantyr

challenged him to single combat on the island of
Samsey. Hjalmar promised to appear at the designated place the next summer, and so the brothers
returned home. In the spring the sons of Arngrim
first paid a visit to Earl Bjartmar, where Angantyr
wedded Svava, the earl's daughter. At the time
agreed upon, both Hjalmar and the sons of Arngrim
set sail for Samsey; in Hjalmar's company went his
brother in arms, the mighty and famous Norseman
Orvar-Odd (Arrow-Odd). Hjalmar elected to fight
against Angantyr, and Orvar-Odd against the eleven
other brothers. The combat now began, and Odd
was fortunate enough to slay all of the eleven; but
when he came to see what had befalled Hjalmar, he
saw Angantyr lying dead at his enemy's feet, while
Hjalmar himself was sitting on a hummock, pale as
death. Odd asked how the battle had gone with him,
to which he answered: "I have sixteen wounds, my
byrnie is worn with the fray, and Tyrfing has pierced
me beneath the heart; draw this ring from my finger
and carry it to Ingeborg in token of my love." Thus
his life ended. Odd laid all the Berserks fully armed
in barrows, but Hjalmar's body he bore with him to
Sweden. Ingeborg died of a broken heart and was
buried in the same mound with Hjalmar.

Some time later Svava, wife of Angantyr, gave birth
to a daughter whom they gave the name Hervor
and who became the foster child of Bjartmar. She
grew up to be tall and well-favored, but even at an
early age she showed a vehement and headstrong
character; she inclined more to the use of sword and

shield than to employments befitting a woman. When she was fully grown, she set out to visit her father's barrow in Samsey, meaning to reclaim Tyrfing from burial. Dressing in men's clothing, she took the name Hervard, joined a band of Vikings, and sailed to the coasts of Samsey. Here she went ashore alone, her companions being afraid of the spectres and evil spirits that were said to harbor there. She did in fact meet with many manifestations of devilry; the barrows appeared to be on fire; not a whit deterred, she strode straight through the flames to the barrows of the Berserks. There she called to Angantyr and his brothers with many incantations, thus compelling her father to answer her summons. Angantyr charged her with madness in rousing dead men in such a way from their repose; he refused to deliver Tyrfing up to her and even maintained that the sword was not in his keeping. Then she demanded it still more vehemently, asserting that the Æsir would grant him no further rest if he denied to his only child her rightful inheritance. "Beware of Tyrfing," Angantyr then answered; "it will destroy all your kindred; it is lying beneath my shoulders, swathed in fire; no maiden I know will dare take it in her hand." "I fear not your fire," said Hervor. At length Tyrfing flew hurtling into her hand, and she gave many thanks for the gift. "I had rather possess Tyrfing," she continued, "than hold sway over all of Norway." Angantyr notwithstanding reiterated his foreboding prophecy; to which she answered that she cared not what fate might befall her sons. Then he spoke these words:

Heroic Legends

Long shall you keep
Hjalmar's bane,
Long shall you bear it;
Wield it but warily,
Touch not its edges;
In the twain there is venom,
Worst of all evils
That men may suffer.

Daughter, farewell!
In your hands rest
Twelve men's lives,
If you can believe me;
Power and hardihood,
All good things soever
That Arngrim's sons
Have left behind them.

Now she took her departure; but the Vikings had
already fled in fear from that haunted place. She was
therefore compelled to find other shipping to carry
her thence; later she visited king Gudmund of Glæsisvoll, with whom she remained throughout the winter,
still in the garb of a man. Gudmund being stricken
in years, his son Hofund virtually governed the
realm. Once while she was playing chess with Gudmund, and had laid Tyrfing aside, one of the men of
the retinue drew it from its scabbard to admire its
burnished edge; Hervor at once sprang up and drove
the sword through his body, inasmuch as the blade
demanded the blood of man once it was unsheathed.
Despite this deed Hervor was permitted to depart unmolested; soon falling in with other Vikings, she made
common cause with them for a time; when she had
tired of their forays, she returned home to her mother's
father, where she practised needlework and tapestry
like other maidens. The fame of her beauty meanwhile spread far and wide. Hofund paid court to her
and won her for his wife. They had two sons, Angantyr and Heidrek. Angantyr was gentle and winsome,
and his father loved him most; Heidrek, who was the
foster son of the wise champion Gissur, was malicious

[135]

of spirit and yet his mother loved him the most; both were tall, strong, and handsome men. Once upon a time Hofund gave a great banquet, at which Heidrek and Gissur were not asked to be guests. Heidrek was offended; he nevertheless presented himself at the banquet, where he made such bad blood between two of the guests that one of them killed the other. Hofund, a most upright man, laid the ban of outlawry on Heidrek; whereupon Heidrek, with a mind to causing his father the utmost grief, drew Tyrfing, given him by his mother as a gift, and killed Angantyr. This was the first of the dastard's deeds destined to be done with Tyrfing. As Heidrek was taking his leave, Hofund sped his parting with certain wise counsels, which were to bring him good fortune if he would only follow them. They were as follows: 1) He was never to give aid to any man who had played false to his rightful overlord; 2) he was to leave no moment's peace to any man who had murdered his own sworn brother; 3) he was not to permit his wife to visit her own kin too often, no matter how much she begged for leave; 4) he was not to stay late with his mistress;[1] 5) he was not to ride his best horse if he was in a hurry; 6) he was never to act as foster father for the children of men holding higher rank than himself; 7) he was never to greet a guest with a joke; 8) he was never to lay Tyrfing down at his feet. Heidrek, however, thinking Hofund's counsel to be devised with evil intent, averred that he would give no heed to it. He

[1] Or to tell her weighty secrets, it might be added on the witness of the following events in the saga.

Heroic Legends

soon allied himself with a band of Vikings, but not before he had taken occasion to redeem from death two miscreants, one of whom had played false to his overlord and the other of whom had brought about the death of his own sworn brother.

Heidrek before long became a captain of Vikings. Having offered his services to Harold, king of Reidgotaland, he promptly brought defeat upon two earls who had been harrying the land. By way of reward he won Harold's fair daughter Helga and one half of the kingdom. Heidrek and Helga had a son, whom they named Angantyr; of equal years with him was a son whom Harold had begotten in old age, and whose name was Halfdan. In course of time a severe famine visited the realm; and when wise men invoked the decree of the gods, they received the answer that they were to offer the most highborn youth of the land in sacrificial atonement. Now each man sought to spare his own son. Harold declared that Angantyr was the nobler of birth, and Heidrek imputed the honor to Halfdan; finally they agreed to leave the decision to the upright Hofund. Heidrek visited his father in person, and Hofund told him that Angantyr held the higher rank, but at the same time taught him an artifice by which the execution of the judgment might be evaded. When Heidrek returned to Reidgotaland he signified his willingness to offer up his son as a sacrifice provided only that every second one of Harold's men would first swear absolute obedience and fealty to himself. They did according to his will, but Heidrek made use of the occasion to create dissension between

Harold and Halfdan, further contending that Odin would receive his due if the king, the king's son, and a number of his men were offered up as a sacrifice. No sooner said than done; the battle at once began, and Heidrek slew his own kinsman Halfdan with Tyrfing. That was the second of the dastard's deeds. The blood of Harold and Halfdan was sprinkled on the altar of the gods, and Heidrek dedicated to Odin all who had fallen on the battlefield. But queen Helga, no longer wishing to live, hanged herself in the vale of Disardal.

Heidrek now subjected the whole realm to his own rule and also harried many foreign countries. After gaining a victory over king Humli of the land of the Huns, Heidrek took the king's daughter Sifka captive, kept her by him for a time, and then sent her home to her father's house, where she gave birth to a son, who was called Lod. Not long afterward he took to wife the daughter of the king of Saxland, but soon drove her away because on one of her many visits to her father's court she had played him false. He continued to ponder on ways and means of acting contrary to his father's counsels; accordingly he paid a visit to the mighty king Rollaug of Holmgard in Russia and offered to take the king's son Herlaug under his charge. On Rollaug's giving his consent, Herlaug left the kingdom in Heidrek's company. Some time later, Heidrek paid a visit to Russia and brought with him his mistress Sifka and Herlaug. One day Heidrek went out hunting with Herlaug but returned home alone; under the pledge of secrecy he told Sifka that he had by chance drawn Tyrfing from the scabbard and therefore had come under the necessity of piercing Herlaug's body with the sword. Sifka, unable to keep the secret, revealed it to Herlaug's mother. A great commotion ensued. Heidrek and his men were surprised, he himself was bound with chains, and in this action no one showed more zeal than the two miscreants he had once ransomed. Heidrek was about to be carried out into the forest and hanged, but he was saved by a band of his own men, whom he had had the foresight to place in ambush there. He returned to Reidgotaland, mustered a huge army, and swept with fire and sword through Rollaug's domains; meanwhile the news had come out that Herlaug had not been killed but was safe and sound at Heidrek's court. Rollaug made proffers of peace; Heidrek accepted the terms and later wedded Rollaug's daughter Hergerd, receiving by way of dowry a region called Vindland, contiguous to Reidgotaland. One evening as Heidrek, mounted on his best horse, was bringing Sifka home, who sat with him in the saddle, the horse stumbled just as they reached the banks of a river, and Sifka suffered a broken leg. Heidrek and Hergerd got a daughter, who was given the name of her father's mother Hervor; the child was put under the care of Earl Ormar. Heidrek now forsook his warlike enterprises and devoted himself to establishing law and justice in the land. He forbade all civil conflicts and chose twelve wise men to be judges in all matters of dispute. He offered sacrifice by preference to Frey, in whose honor he reared a boar that grew well-nigh to the size of an ox, and so fair that each hair seemed as if made of gold. Every Yuletide Eve the king and his men swore oaths by the boar, laying one hand on his head and the other on the bristles of his neck. On one occasion the king made the vow that whatsoever a man might do amiss, he should still have the right to lay his cause before the twelve sages for equitable judgment, and he should be privileged to escape his due punishment if he could put riddles that the king would be unable to read.

In Reidgotaland there lived a mighty man named Gestumblindi. He had the misfortune to incur the displeasure of the king and was therefore summoned before the tribunal of the twelve sages. Fearing the worst of evils, he offered sacrifice to Odin for aid. One evening Odin actually appeared before him and promised to help him by going before Heidrek in his stead. Gestumblindi accordingly hid himself, while Odin assumed his likeness and presented himself before the king. Here he was asked if he would like to try his luck at riddling with the king, but Gestumblindi (Odin) showed no eagerness to make the venture. At length he made up his mind to the attempt, and essayed a multitude of riddles, the greater number having to do with nature and some few with divinity; but Heidrek read them all. The following are examples of his riddles:

Gestumblindi: From home I fared,
From home I journeyed,
On my way I saw roadways,
Roadways beneath me,

Heroic Legends

Roadways above me,
Roadways on all sides.
Heidrek, king,
Rede me this riddle.

Heidrek: Good is your riddle,
Gestumblindi,
Yet do I rede it:
Birds flew above you,
Fish swam beneath you,
A bridge was your roadway.

Gestumblindi: What was the drink
I drank yesterday?
Neither water nor wine,
Neither mead nor ale,
Nor was it food,
Yet I thirsted not.
Heidrek, king,
Rede now this riddle.

Heidrek: Good is your riddle,
Gestumblindi,
Yet do I rede it:
You walked in the sun,
You rested in shadow,
Dew fell in the dales;
There did you sup
On the dews of the night,
And so cooled your palate.

Gestumblindi: Who are the men
That ride to the moot,
At one in their counsels?
Troops are sent forth,
Now hither, now thither,
Wardens of home.
Heidrek, king,
Rede now this riddle.

Norse Mythology

Heidrek: Good is your riddle,
       Gestumblindi,
       Yet do I rede it:
       Itrek and Andad [1]
       Year in, year out,
       Play blithe at chess;
       In concord their troops
       Lie couched in the casket;
       On the board the chessmen do battle.

Gestumblindi: Four are walking,
       Four hang downward,
       Two point the way,
       Two defend against dogs;
       One brings up the rear
       Ever and always,
       Most often unclean.
       Heidrek, king,
       Rede now this riddle.

Heidrek: Good is your riddle,
       Gestumblindi,
       Yet do I rede it:
       That beast surely
       To you is well known;
       Four feet she has,
       Fourfold is her udder,
       Horns defend her,
       The tail follows after.

Gestumblindi: Who are the twain
       That ride to the moot?
       They have three eyes together,
       Ten are their feet,
       But one tail only;
       So they traverse all regions.
       Heidrek, king,
       Rede me this riddle.

[1] The white king and the black king.

Heroic Legends

Heidrek: Good is your riddle,
Gestumblindi,
Yet do I rede it:
Odin sits mounted,
Riding on Sleipnir;
One eye has he,
But the horse has twain;
Odin has two legs,
The horse has eight;
The horse alone has a tail.

Finally Gestumblindi—Odin—put the same question with which he once stopped the mouth of Vafthrudnir:

Now tell me this only,
Since you deem yourself
Wiser than other kings:
What words did Odin
Whisper to Balder
Ere on the pyre they laid him?

Then Heidrek spoke in anger:

Evil and malice,
All the world's infamy,
Prattle, buffoonery, nonsense!
No man knows your words
But yourself alone,
Wretched, malevolent spirit.

With these words he drew Tyrfing and was about to cut Odin down; but Odin took the shape of a falcon, and the sword struck only his tail, from which it shore off a part; this is the reason why the falcon has a stubbed tail. Odin said: "Because you broke your promise and drew your sword against me, the most miserable of your thralls shall be your death." And having spoken, he flew away.

A short time afterward the king was murdered by nine thralls who had been freemen in their own land but had been taken prisoners of war by Heidrek. These thralls during the night broke into the king's bedchamber and slew him with Tyrfing. Thus the sword performed the third dastard's deed, and the curse was lifted from it. Angantyr, son of Heidrek, now became king. He set out at once in pursuit of the thralls and came upon them as they sat fishing from a boat in the river Graf. As one of them was cutting off the head of a fish with Tyrfing, Angantyr heard him say jocosely: "The pike in the river of Graf must pay the penalty for the killing of Heidrek at the foot of the mountains of Harfada." That very night Angantyr put them to death and carried away Tyrfing. Having thus avenged the slaying of his father, he gave in honor of his own succession a great banquet in his palace of Danparstad in Arheim.

When his half brother Lod got wind of his father's death, he journeyed to Arheim, where Angantyr still was holding his festival, and sat down among the men who were drinking at the table. Angantyr invited him to a seat with himself, but Lod answered: "We have not come to fill our bellies but to demand our rightful inheritance; I lay claim to one half of all the possessions of Heidrek, one half of all that has a point and all that has an edge, of treasures, of cows and calves, of mills, of serving men, of thralls and their children, of the boundary forest Dark Wood, of the sacred grove in the land of the Goths, of the precious stone in Danparstad, one half of fortresses of

Heroic Legends

war, of lands and people, of gleaming gold rings."
Angantyr replied: "Shields shall clash and spears
cross each other in flight and many a man shall bite
the grass before I divide Tyrfing with you, Humlung,[1]
or give you a half of my inheritance; I will give you
gold and fee, twelve hundred men, twelve hundred
horses, twelve hundred armor-bearers; each man shall
receive rich gifts; to each man will I give a maiden, to
each maiden a necklace; I will surround you with silver
when you sit down and heap gold about you when you
arise, so that rings overflow on all sides; you shall hold
sway over one third of the lands of the Goths."
Heidrek's old foster father, Gissur Grytingalidi, who
was still among the living, heard these words, and
said: "The serving man's son might well be content
with such gifts as these!" When this taunt fell on the
ears of Lod, he was enraged and hastened home to his
mother's father Humli; the two together mustered a
mighty army against Angantyr. When their forces
were ready they marched through the boundary
forest Dark Wood to the uttermost plains of Gotaland,
where Angantyr's sister and her foster father Ormar
were stationed in defence of a frontier stronghold
against the Huns. Early one morning Hervor became aware of a great cloud of dust; soon after, she
saw the glittering of helmets and knew that it marked
the army of the Huns. She chose to fight rather than
to flee; defending herself bravely she fell in the ensuing
battle, and many men with her. Ormar fled the field
and rode day and night until he came to Arheim,

[1] Daughter's son of Humli.

where he told Angantyr of the battle with the Huns and of Hervor's death. Angantyr's lips twitched with grief as he spoke the words: "In most unbrotherly wise were you betrayed, glorious sister." Then, looking about among his retainers, he spoke again: "We were once many as we sat about our flowing bowls; now that we should be many we are few; I see no man in my retinue who has the strength of will to ride forth against the Huns to offer them battle, even though I promise him a guerdon of rings." Then old Gissur lifted up his voice and said, "I will ride, nor ask for gold or fee." Donning his weeds of war he leaped into the saddle, brisk as any youth, pausing only to ask:

> Whither shall I bid
> The Huns come to battle?

Angantyr answered:

> Bid them come to Dylgja,
> To the Heaths of Dun,
> Bid them join battle
> At the foot of Mount Josur;
> There the Goths often
> Gladly made war,
> There gained victories,
> Fair with renown.

Gissur did according to Angantyr's command, and summoned the Huns to battle on the Heaths of Dun. "Marked for death is your war lord," he said; "may Odin turn the flight of the spear after the bent of my words." Lod wished to take him captive; but Humli opposed such a course, and Gissur said, "We do not fear, Huns, your horn bows." Angantyr with his

army came to meet the Huns, who were twice the
number of the Goths. Yet by day and by night warriors streamed to Angantyr's banner from all parts of
his kingdom, and after a day's battle the Goths had
the upper hand. Angantyr strode out from beneath
the shelter of the stronghold of shields and with Tyrfing hewed down both men and horses. He exchanged
buffets with his brother, and both Lod and Humli fell;
so many of the Huns were stricken to earth that
rivers were dammed in their course and whole valleys
were filled with bodies of the slain. Angantyr came
across his own brother lying dead. "I offered you
chattels and riches," he said; "now you have nought,
neither land nor gleaming rings. A curse rests on our
kin; I have brought you down to death. Evil is the
doom of the Norns."

THE LEGENDS OF THE VOLSUNGS—
HELGI HJORVARDSSON

LIKE the legends centering about Tyrfing, the legendary cycle of the Volsungs is made up of a number
of separate legends. The action lies in both northern
and central Europe, and the legends themselves are
found among all the races belonging to the great
Germanic family. The Eddic poems begin the cycle
with the story of Helgi Hjorvardsson.

In Norway there was a king named Hjorvard who
had made the vow that he would possess the most
beautiful woman in the world. He already had three
wives, each of whom had borne him a son; he and his

retinue all held these boys to be the handsomest in all the world. Once upon a time, however, Atli, a son of one of Hjorvard's earls named Idmund, happened to be walking abroad in a grove. A bird sitting in a tree heard Atli's men say that no women on earth were fairer than Hjorvard's wives. The bird began to twitter and asked Atli if he had ever laid eyes on Sigrlin, daughter of king Svafnir, who was the fairest of all maidens. Atli asked the bird to reveal to him what it knew about her; it promised that the king should win Sigrlin if he would build for it a temple and many altars and there offer in sacrifice many gold-horned cattle. On Atli's telling all these things to Hjorvard, the king sent him off to ask Svafnir for the hand of Sigrlin. But her foster father, Earl Franmar, persuaded Svafnir to deny the king's suit, and Atli had to return home with his errand unfulfilled. Hjorvard now determined to go in person, and Atli went with him. In the meantime another powerful king, by name Rodmar, had paid court to Sigrlin; he also had met with a refusal and in his wrath had killed Svafnir and harried his realms. Franmar concealed Sigrlin with his own daughter Alof in a lonely house, transformed himself into an eagle, and so kept watch over the maidens by means of magic arts. When Hjorvard and Atli reached the top of the mountains and caught sight of the reaches of Svavaland, they saw nothing but fire and desolation on all sides; nevertheless they descended and lay down to rest for the night beside a river not far from the house where the maidens were hidden. The eagle perched on the roof had fallen asleep; Atli killed it with his spear, entered the house, found the young women, and led them before Hjorvard. The king took Sigrlin to wife, and Atli took Alof. Hjorvard and Sigrlin got a son, who grew to be tall and handsome; but he was dumb, and no name was given to him.

One day, as the king's son was sitting on a mound, he saw nine Valkyries riding toward him, one of whom far surpassed the others in beauty. She said to him: "Helgi, if you persist in your silence, it will be long before you have gold rings to give and before you win renown." Then Helgi found the power of utterance and said: "What will you give me as a gift, fair maiden, now that you dower me with a name of my own? I will not accept the name unless you give me yourself with it." She answered: "In Sigarsholm lie six and forty swords, one of which is better than the others; it is adorned with gold, a ring is fixed in its hilt, courage is in its middle and terror in its point, and along the edge lies a serpent flecked with blood, winding his tail about the handle." The Valkyrie's name was Svava, daughter of king Eylimi; from that day on, she gave great aid to Helgi in the fighting of his battles.

Helgi now went before his father and asked for armed men in order to march against Rodmar to avenge the death of his mother's father, Svafnir. Hjorvard having put the men under his command, Helgi sought out the sword designated by Svava; then he sallied forth together with Atli and took the life of Rodmar. As time passed they performed many a deed of prowess. Helgi killed the mighty Giant Hati, whom he found sitting on a mountain side. Afterward he and Atli sailed into Hatifjord, where Rimgerd, Hati's daughter, sought to harm them by sorcery; but Atli, who was keeping watch during the night, artfully contrived to keep her listening to his speech so that she forgot to hide from the rising sun, and so was turned into stone. Thereupon Helgi paid a visit to king Eylimi, where he took Svava to wife; they loved each other beyond measure, but she remained a Valkyrie as before.

Meanwhile Helgi's elder half brother Hedin had remained at home with his father in Norway. One evening at the Yuletide, while he was out in the forest alone, he came upon a Troll woman mounted on the back of a wolf which she was guiding by means of serpents instead of reins; she offered to go with him, but he would not consent. Then she said, "You shall pay for that at your drinking." At evening, as the wassail bowl went round and vows were being made by the great boar, Hedin swore that he would possess Svava, his brother Helgi's wife. No sooner had he spoken the oath than he was smitten with remorse and set off on unbeaten paths toward the south to meet his brother Helgi. Helgi received him gladly, asked for tidings from Norway, and wanted to know whether he had been banished, since he was making such a journey alone. Hedin made a clean breast of his trouble, telling how the Troll woman had bewitched him into making the vow concerning Svava. Helgi comforted him and said that the vow might after all

Heroic Legends

be fulfilled. "Rodmar's son Alf," he declared, "has challenged me to meet him in combat when three days have passed, and no one knows whether I shall leave the field alive." Helgi had a premonition that he was marked for death, the Troll woman being none other than his own attendant spirit. Alf and Helgi fought at Sigarsvoll near Frekastein (the Wolf Stone); there was a great battle, in the course of which Helgi received a mortal wound. He dispatched Sigar to summon Svava to hasten to his side before he died. When she came Helgi begged that she would, after his own death, wed Hedin and give him her love; but she answered that when she gave her troth to Helgi she had vowed never to wed another in his stead. Both Helgi and Svava were born anew, as Helgi Hundingsbane and Sigrun.[1]

VOLSUNG—SIGGEIR—SIGMUND—SINFJOTLI

THE legends dealing definitely with the Volsungs begin with the story of Odin's son Sigi, who was driven into exile because he had killed the thrall of another man of high degree, and who later won for himself a kingdom in Hunaland. In the end he was betrayed and put to death by his own brothers-in-law. His son Rerir became king in his stead, avenged the murder of his father, and won great renown for his own prowess in war. Rerir and his wife, deeply grieved at their childless state, prayed devoutly to the gods to grant children to them. Frigg and Odin heard their prayers,

[1] See pp. 164–65.

and Odin sent his Valkyrie Ljod, daughter of the Giant Rimnir, to carry an apple as a gift to the king. The queen ate of it, and their wishes were fulfilled. But for the space of six years she remained unable to give birth to the child; the king meanwhile died and the queen at length, weary of days, caused the child to be cut from her side in order to save its life. It was a large and well-shaped boy. He gave his mother a kiss before she died. He got the name Volsung and became king of Hunaland after his father. With his wife Ljod, who had brought the apple to Rerir, he had a daughter named Signy and ten sons; the eldest and bravest of them all was Sigmund, twin brother to Signy. The Volsungs, as they came to be called, excelled all other men in all manner of prowess and manly sports. King Volsung caused a great and splendid hall to be built, in the midst of which stood a tall tree, stretching its fruitful boughs out over the roof; this tree they called the Stem of the Children.

A mighty king, Siggeir of Gautland, paid court to Signy and secured the promise of her hand from Volsung and his sons, against her own will. The marriage was celebrated with great pomp in king Volsung's hall. While the festival was in progress an old, one-eyed man with a broad hat on his head came into the hall and thrust a sword into the Stem of the Children up to the hilt, with the words that he who proved able to draw it out again should have it as a gift and would find for a certainty that he had never laid eyes on a better sword. Thereupon he went out of the door; it was Odin in disguise, and no one knew whence he

Heroic Legends

came or whither he went away. The guests all tried to draw the sword but to no avail; at last Sigmund came forward and pulled it out at the first trial. Every man praised the sword, all avowing that they had never seen one so good. Siggeir offered Sigmund for it three times its weight in gold, but Sigmund said: "You might have drawn it forth as well as I; I will not sell it for all the gold in the world." At these words Siggeir became incensed and at once began to meditate revenge.

The next day Siggeir made it known that he intended to take his departure while the weather was still fair, at the same time inviting king Volsung and his sons to pay him a visit after an interval of three months, on which occasion, he added, they might make up for what they were now losing of the marriage feast by reason of his early leave-taking. Signy said to her father that she was reluctant to go away with Siggeir and that she could foresee great misfortunes as the aftermath of the wedding; but Volsung brushed aside her misgivings with fair words, consoling her as best he could. Siggeir took his departure, and three months later Volsung and his sons set out on their voyage with three well-manned ships. On their arrival in Gautland late one evening, Signy hastened to meet them with the tidings that Siggeir had mustered against them a great army, meaning to play them false. Volsung nevertheless would entertain no thought of flight but marched up into the land to face Siggeir's hosts, who at once attacked him. Volsung and his sons fought with great courage; eight times they broke Siggeir's lines, but the ninth time they were worsted, Volsung himself was slain, and his ten sons were taken prisoner. Siggeir meant to put them to death, but Signy persuaded him to expose them out in the forest with their feet bound to a stake, so that she might have, at least for a time, the pleasure of beholding their features. Siggeir did as she wished. But during the night Siggeir's old mother, who was skilled in sorcery, transformed herself into a she-wolf, bit one of the brothers to death, and ate his body; she did likewise during each of the following nights until Sigmund alone remained alive. Signy, who had appointed watchmen to bring her news of all that happened, now caused Sigmund's face to be smeared with honey. When the she-wolf came again and smelled the honey, she began to lap it up; when she reached Sigmund's mouth, he seized her tongue in his teeth and thus held her fast. The wolf in attempting to escape thrust her feet against the stake; but the stake sprang asunder, the wolf's tongue was torn from her jaws so that she died forthwith, and Sigmund regained his freedom. Signy, learning what had befallen, herself went out to see him, and conspired with him that he was to build himself an earth house in the forest and that Signy was to carry to him anything that he might need. Siggeir now believed that all of the Volsungs were dead.

Signy and Sigmund kept pondering upon some suitable form of revenge. Signy had borne two sons to Siggeir. When the eldest of these was ten years of age, she sent him out to the forest to give Sigmund any assistance that he might require. One day Sigmund asked the boy to knead dough for bread and for this purpose gave him a sack of meal. On returning Sigmund found that the boy had done nothing; he had been afraid to touch the sack because some living thing stirred within it. Now Sigmund knew that the boy lacked the required courage, and he said as much to his sister. "Kill him then," answered Signy; "he does not deserve to live." Sigmund did so. The next year Signy sent her second son, and he fared likewise. She then got a witch to exchange shapes with her and in this guise she herself went out to her brother, who failed to recognize her. After remaining with him three nights she returned home and assumed her former likeness once more. Some time later she gave birth to a large, strong, and handsome son, who was given the name of Sinfjotli and who in all respects resembled the Volsungs. When he reached the age of ten, she sent him out to Sigmund. Meanwhile she had put him to the same tests she had used in the case of the other sons: she had sewed their kirtles fast to their arms through skin and flesh; the two elder sons had complained, but Sinfjotli when his turn came gave no sign. She tore his kirtle off so that his skin came away with the sleeves, but he paid no heed. "That is a small matter to one of the Volsungs," were his only words. When he arrived at Sigmund's house he was set to kneading the dough, the same task that had been given to his older brothers. When Sigmund returned home, Sinfjotli had already baked the bread. Sigmund asked if he had not found something in the meal. "Yes, it seemed to me at first that there was some living thing in it, but I kneaded the whole into one mass," answered Sinfjotli. "You have kneaded into the meal a most venomous serpent," said Sigmund; "and you will have to eat that very bread this evening." As it happened, there was this difference between father and son, that while Sigmund was able to swallow poison without suffering the least harm, Sinfjotli on the other hand was able to endure poison only on the surface of his body but could not eat or drink it unhurt.

Sigmund deeming Sinfjotli still too young to assist in carrying out his revenge, determined first to accustom him to dangers and difficulties, and to this end took the boy with him on robber forays during several summers. Still having no inkling that the boy was not the son of Siggeir, he was amazed at Sinfjotli's often putting him in mind of his purposed vengeance on Siggeir. On one occasion they came across a house in the forest where two men lay sleeping with great gold rings on their fingers, two princes who had been turned into wolves and who were able to cast off their wolfish likeness once in ten days, and no oftener. This happened to be one of the days, and their wolf pelts hung above them as they slept. Sigmund and Sinfjotli sprang into the pelts and thereafter roved about a long time in the guise of wolves, doing what harm they could do throughout Siggeir's domains. Each tenth day they became men again. Once Sigmund chanced to bite Sinfjotli's throat so hard that he lay a long while seemingly dead; Sigmund fell to

Heroic Legends

cursing the wolf's clothing, but as he did so he caught sight of an ermine biting another to death and waking the dead to life again by means of a leaf. Sigmund did likewise to Sinfjotli, who immediately came to life; they went up to the earth house, waited till the time once more came for the shifting of shapes, and then burned the wolf's pelts, for which they had no further use.

When Sinfjotli had no more than reached man's estate, Sigmund led him to Siggeir's house for the purpose of carrying out his revenge. Having agreed with Signy that the hour of vengeance was to strike during the night, they hid themselves in the anteroom. Meanwhile the two small children of Signy and Siggeir were running about the floor of the hall, playing with gold rings. One of the golden bands rolled out into the anteroom where Sigmund and Sinfjotli were sitting, and the boy who ran to pick up the ring caught sight of two tall, hard-favored men in broad helmets and gleaming byrnies. The boy hurried away to tell his father what he had seen. Siggeir at once had his misgivings; but Signy led the two little children out into the anteroom and asked Sigmund to kill them so that they should tell no more tales. Sigmund would not do her bidding, but Sinfjotli killed them both and threw their bodies out into the hall. The king started up and gave commands to seize the men sitting in the anteroom; after a long and brave struggle, Sigmund and Sinfjotli were taken captive, bound fast, and placed in the midst of a huge pile of stones and turf in such a manner that a large stone slab set on end in the middle of the heap separated them. Just as the last pieces of turf were being laid over the mound, Signy came forward and tossed an armful of straw down to Sinfjotli. In the bundle of straw was hidden a piece of meat, within which lay Sinfjotli's sword, a blade capable of cutting stone as easily as wood. Sinfjotli told Sigmund what had happened, and Sigmund was very glad. Sinfjotli now thrust the point of the sword over the upper edge of the slab so that Sigmund could seize hold of it; in this manner they were able to shear the slab in two from top to bottom, and so they found themselves side by side in the mound. Then they severed their own fetters and cut their way out of the mound itself. They now went straight to the king's hall, heaped up wood round about it, and set it on fire; the hall immediately burst into flames, before any who were within knew what was going on. At length Siggeir woke out of sleep and at once understood it all. Sigmund bade Signy make her escape from the hall, but she answered: "Now I have taken full vengeance against Siggeir for the death of my father Volsung; I caused our children to lose their lives, I went to Sigmund in the shape of a witch, and Sinfjotli is his son and mine. I have done all in my power to end the days of Siggeir; now I will die with him as gladly as I once lived with him unwillingly." She kissed Sigmund and Sinfjotli, and then entered the hall and allowed herself to perish in the flames together with Siggeir and his whole retinue. Sigmund and Sinfjotli mustered a band of men, took ship and set sail to the kingdom which Volsung once ruled over. There Sigmund took the government into his own hands and came to be a mighty and a famous king.

HELGI HUNDINGSBANE

SIGMUND took to wife Borghild of Bralund and with her had two sons, Helgi and Hamund. Of Helgi we read in the Eddic poem:

> In the morning of time,
> While eagles screamed,
> Holy rains fell
> From the Mounts of Heaven:
> Then was Helgi,
> Proud of heart,
> Borghild's son,
> Born in Bralund.
>
> Night covered the court;
> Then came the Norns,
> Who for the atheling
> Numbered his days:
> Bade him become
> Boldest of captains,
> And among heroes
> Hold highest renown.
>
> Mighty they were:
> They laid life's threads,
> While the towers
> Broke in Bralund;
> Forth they stretched
> The golden cords,
> Fixed them midmost
> In the hall of the moon.
>
> In the East, in the West,
> The ends were hidden,
> The lands of the king
> Lay between them:

Norse Mythology

Far to the North
Neri's kinswoman (the Norn)
Fastened the one end,
Bade it hold firmly.

The ravens perched in the trees were already yearning for the time when Helgi should become a man and give them their fill of carrion corpses. Once Sigmund had been away from home fighting the battles of the realm; on his return he went in to his son, gave him a leek, and dubbed him Helgi, at the same time giving him as naming gifts Ringstad, Solfjall, Snjofjall, Sigarsvoll, Ringstead, Hatun, and Himinvang, and a goodly sword besides. Helgi was then given over as a foster child to a man named Hagal. Sigmund presently became involved in warfare with king Hunding. When Helgi reached the age of fifteen, Sigmund sent him out in disguise to spy upon Hunding's retinue. At first all went well with Helgi, but as he was about to leave Hunding's court he could not refrain from revealing his true name. He asked a certain goatherd to say to Heming, Hunding's son, that he whom they had treated as a guest and whom they supposed to be Hamal, Hagal's son, was none other than Helgi himself. Hunding sent men to Hagal's estate to search for Helgi, and he had no other recourse than to don the garb of a bondwoman and to busy himself in turning the mill. One of Hunding's men, to be sure, found that the bondwoman had rather sharp eyes and that she put a good deal of force into her grinding; but Hagal said that this was no wonder, since she was a shield-maiden before Helgi made her a captive. Some

Heroic Legends

time later Helgi set sail in his ships of war; engaging in battle with Hunding, Helgi laid his enemy low, and thereby gained the surname of Hundingsbane. After the victory he lay with his fleet in the bay of Brunavag. Presently the Valkyrie Sigrun, daughter to king Hogni, came riding through the air to his ship and entered into speech with him. She asked him his name, and then told him that she already knew of the mighty deeds he had done. "I saw you beforetime," she said, "on the long ships, as you stood in the blood-red prow and the cold waves played about you." Sigrun then left him; but the four sons of Hunding challenged Helgi to battle in order to avenge the death of their father, and Helgi slew them all at the mountains of Loga. Wearied from the struggle, he sat down to rest at the foot of Arastein (Eagle Rock). There Sigrun came riding toward him a second time, threw her arms about his neck, kissed him, and told him that she was hard bestead. Her father Hogni had promised her in marriage to the hateful Hodbrod, king Granmar's son, of Svarinshaug. Helgi undertook to free her from the compact and for that purpose gathered a great force of ships against Hodbrod; Sinfjotli was one of the company. At sea they encountered a perilous storm. Lightning played about them and shafts of fire shot down on the ships. Then they saw Sigrun come riding through the air with eight other Valkyries, and she stilled the tempest so that they made land in safety. The sons of king Granmar were sitting on a mountain side near Svarinshaug as the ships sailed in toward the shore. One of them, named

Gudmund, leaped on a horse and rode to spy on the strangers from a hill overlooking the haven; he arrived just as the Volsungs were furling their sails. Gudmund asked who they might be, and for answer Sinfjotli raised a red shield aloft at the yardarm. They berated each other until at length Helgi came forward and said that battle would be more becoming to them than bandying words. Gudmund thereupon rode home with a summons to war, and the sons of Granmar mustered a large army. Many kings made common cause with the brothers, among them Hogni, Sigrun's father, with his sons Bragi and Dag; and Alf the Elder besides. The battle was joined at Freka-stein (Wolf Stone). All of the sons of Granmar fell and all of their captains but Dag, who made his peace by swearing fealty to the Volsungs. After the battle Sigrun went out among the slain and there found Hodbrod at the point of death. She gave thanks to Helgi for the deed he had done. Helgi was grieved to think that he had caused the death of her father and her brother, and she herself wept; but he consoled her with the assurance that no man could escape his destiny. Helgi took Sigrun to wife and made Granmar's kingdom subject to his own rule. But he did not reach old age. Dag, the brother of Sigrun, offered sacrifice to Odin to obtain vengeance for his father's death, and Odin lent his own spear to him. With it he thrust Helgi through the body at Fjoturlund and then rode home to tell Sigrun what he had done. Sigrun put him in mind of the sacred vows he had

sworn to Helgi and which he had now broken; then she
spoke these words:

Let not the ship sail on
That glides beneath you,
Though the winds follow
Fair as your wishes!
Let not the horse run fleet
That runs beneath you,
Though he might carry you
Far from your foes!
Let not the sword be edged
That your arm lifts aloft,
Save when it sings
About your own head!
Meet would that vengeance be
For Helgi's death,
If you were a wolf
In the forest wilderness,
Wanting all worldly goods,
Wanting all joys,
Finding no provender,
Filled with no carrion.

Dag declared that his sister was mad thus to curse
her own brother. He laid the blame for all that had
passed upon Odin and offered to give her red gold
rings and one half of his kingdom; but she answered
that nothing could atone for Helgi's death. A cairn
was thrown over the body of Helgi, and when he
entered into Valhalla Odin invited him to sit in counsel
with himself; but on Hunding, Helgi laid commands
to carry out the meanest tasks. One evening Sigrun's
handmaiden, chancing to pass Helgi's mound, saw
him riding toward the cairn followed by many men;
she asked whether she was only seeing visions, whether
the Twilight of the Gods had come inasmuch as the

dead were riding, or whether the Heroes had got leave
to revisit the earth. Helgi answered that the Heroes
had been granted leave for their homecoming, and
these tidings the handmaiden brought back to Sigrun.
Sigrun went out to the cairn, glad of heart to see Helgi
once more. "Yet," she asked him, "why is your hair
covered with rime, why are you flecked with blood,
and why are your hands cold as ice?" "You alone
are the cause," he replied, "since you weep such bitter
tears each night before you go to rest; each tear falls
on my breast, icy cold, burning, freighted with woe.
But though we lack lands and joys, we shall yet drink
with one another costly drinks, and no man shall sing
dirges for the wounds he sees in my breast." Sigrun
now prepared a couch in the mound so that she might
lie down to rest in his arms. Then Helgi said: "Now
nothing is beyond the bounds of belief since you, fair,
living daughter of a king, rest in my arms, the arms of
one who lives no more; but the time has come for me
to ride forth on the reddening roadway; westward I
must journey across the bridge of Heaven before
Salgofnir (the cock of Valhalla) wakens the victorious
men (the Heroes)." Helgi then rode away, but the
next evening Sigrun awaited his return in vain.
Sigrun lived no long time thereafter, so great was her
sorrow and affliction.

Helgi Hundingsbane and Sigrun were none other than
Helgi Hjorvardsson and Svava, Eylimi's daughter,
born again in other bodies. It is said that Helgi
Hundingsbane and Sigrun were likewise born anew.
In this reincarnation he bore the name of Helgi Had-

dingjaskati, and she bore the name of Kara, daughter of Halfdan.

SINFJOTLI

SINFJOTLI, son of Sigmund, passed his time in continual warfare. Once upon a time, happening to see a woman of uncommon beauty, he paid court to her; but his stepmother Borghild's brother had the same design; enmity sprang up between the two, the end of which was that Sinfjotli killed his rival. When he returned home, Borghild wanted to drive him away; but Sigmund offered her wergild for her brother, and so she could do naught else than come to terms. She then made a great banquet for her brother, to which she invited many mighty men as guests. In the course of the banquet she brought to Sinfjotli a large drinking horn, in which she had mingled poison with the intent to take his life. On looking into the horn he said to Sigmund, "The drink is muddied." Sigmund, being immune to all poisons, took up the horn and drained it. Borghild brought Sinfjotli a second horn; once more he suspected evil, and Sigmund again drank in his stead. A third time she brought a horn to him and bade him drink if he had the courage of a Volsung. Sigmund, being by this time well drunken, said, "Drain the drink through your beard." Sinfjotli drank, and at once fell down dead. Sigmund, lifting up his son's body, bore it away with him; when he had carried his burden a long distance he came at length to a narrow fjord, where he found a boat and a man sitting in it. The man offered to ferry Sigmund across the water; but when the body had been taken on board, the boat was incapable of supporting an added weight, and so Sigmund was compelled to walk on foot around to the other side. But no sooner had the man launched his boat out from the shore than he was lost to sight, and the boat with him. Sigmund on returning home drove Borghild away. Hitherto, during the whole time he was wedded to her, he had lived in her own kingdom of Denmark; now he took his departure, directed his course southward to a kingdom of his own in the land of the Franks, and made his home there.

THE DEATH OF SIGMUND

THERE was a great and powerful king named Eylimi; to his fair daughter Hjordis Sigmund paid court after he had put Borghild away. King Lyngvi, son of Hunding, who had escaped from the field at Frekastein, also sought her hand. King Eylimi permitted his daughter to make her own choice, and she chose Sigmund for his fame, in spite of his years. He wedded Hjordis and took her home with him, king Eylimi bearing them company. King Lyngvi and his brothers marshalled their forces and marched against Sigmund to summon him to battle. Sigmund at once accepted the challenge; but before taking the field he transported Hjordis with her serving maid and a great store of goods into a forest to keep her safe from the enemy. Sigmund bore himself bravely in the battle,

and no one was able to stand against him until an old
one-eyed man, dressed in a broad-brimmed hat and a
blue cloak, and carrying a spear in his hand, entered
Lyngvi's ranks. He advanced upon Sigmund, whose
strokes he warded off with his spear, and Sigmund's
splendid sword shortly broke asunder. From that
moment the fortunes of war took a turn, the outcome
of which was that Sigmund and Eylimi fell, and with
them the greater part of their men. Lyngvi hastened
to the king's palace, meaning to take Hjordis captive,
but found neither her nor any of the goods; so, con-
tenting himself perforce with laying the kingdom
under his own sway, he returned home. The night
after the battle Hjordis went out onto the field and
found Sigmund still among the living. She asked him
if he had any hope of being healed of his wounds. But
he would not so much as try, since luck had forsaken
him. "Yet you shall give birth to a son," he said,
"who shall become the greatest of our race. Keep for
him the two pieces of my sword; from them a goodly
sword can be forged, which shall be called Gram.
That sword he shall bear at his side and with it do
many a deed of passing prowess." Hjordis remained
sitting by Sigmund until he died; then she took up the
fragments of the sword, changed her own clothing for
that of her handmaiden, and made her way to the
seashore. There certain Viking ships were lying,
under the command of Alf, the son of king Hjalprek
of Denmark. He received them well. The handmaiden told the story of Sigmund's death and showed
Alf where the treasure lay hidden; accordingly he

sailed with them to Denmark, believing all the while that Hjordis was the handmaiden and that the handmaiden was a princess. But his mother noticed that Hjordis was the more beautiful and had more courtly manners than the other, and so Alf determined to put them to the test. When the occasion came he asked them a question: "By what token can you mark the coming of morning when neither moon nor stars are visible?" The handmaiden answered: "As a child I was accustomed to drinking a great deal toward dawn and therefore I have formed the habit of waking at that time; this is the sign I am governed by." The king laughed and said, "The king's daughter was not brought up as well as might be." Hjordis said: "My father gave me a gold ring that had the property of turning cold on my finger as dawn drew near; that is a sure sign to me." The king replied: "Gold there must have been in plenty since bondwomen were in the habit of wearing it; now I know that you have deceived me, and of that you had no need; nevertheless you shall become my wife as soon as your child is born." She then confessed all that she had done and gladly entered into accord with him.

SIGURD FAFNIRSBANE

Hjordis bore a son who got the name Sigurd. He proved to have inherited the sharp eyes of his father; and as he grew to manhood it soon appeared that he excelled all others in height and in bodily prowess. He received his early nurture in the court of king

Heroic Legends

Hjalprek, his foster father being a cunning smith named Regin, who was skilled in all manner of manly exercises, in magic runes, and in speaking with tongues, in all of which arts Sigurd came under his tutelage.

Regin, the son of a wealthy man named Reidmar, had two brothers, Oter and Fafnir.[1] Oter often took the shape of an otter and passed his time in catching salmon in a waterfall not far from Reidmar's house. The waterfall bore the name of the Cascade of Andvari, because the Dwarf Andvari frequented the waters in the guise of a pike. Once upon a time Odin, Loki, and Hœnir, being on a journey, came to the waterfall and there saw an otter feeding on a salmon; in eating, it closed its eyes, not being able to endure seeing the fish grow smaller and smaller. Loki picked up a stone, threw it at the otter, and killed it. Then he boasted of having bagged an otter and a salmon with one stone. Taking their catch with them they went on to Reidmar's house, where they asked for a night's lodging, at the same time showing him their booty. Reidmar at once recognized the otter's pelt, which they had flayed off; and with the aid of Regin and Fafnir he took the Æsir captive and put them in bonds. The Æsir offered in ransom for their lives anything that he might choose to demand, whereupon he decreed that they were to fill the otter's skin with gold and to cover its surface with gold besides. Having sealed their promise with an oath, they were released from their bondage. Loki hastened to Ran and borrowed her net, with which he then returned to the waterfall

[1] Or *Faðmir*, that is, "the embracing one."

and caught the Dwarf Andvari. Loki threatened to put Andvari to death if he did not at once surrender all the gold in his possession. The Dwarf yielded up his hoard under compulsion; but Loki, noticing that he kept back a small gold ring, forced him to give that as well. All of the Dwarf's entreaties availed him not a whit; Loki took the ring. But as the Dwarf darted back into his rock, he stood at the opening long enough to say these words: "The Dwarf's gold shall be the death of two brothers and a sign of division to eight athelings; no one shall find joy in the holding of my hoard." Thus was a curse fastened upon the gold, above all upon the ring—just as on the sword Tyrfing[1] —and Loki rejoiced that the treasure would bring no good to Reidmar. When Loki returned with the hoard, Reidmar first filled the skin and raised it on end, and then covered it over on the outside; in this way all of the gold was spent with the exception of the ring, which Odin kept for himself. Reidmar, however, discovered that a single hair near the mouth had not been covered up. Odin was compelled to surrender the ring of Andvari; Loki, for his part, reiterated the curse spoken over the Dwarf's hoard.

Regin and Fafnir now asked their father for a share of the gold in wergild for their brother; on his denying their request, Fafnir killed him as he lay asleep. Fafnir then took all of the gold as his own patrimony. Regin, bereft of his inheritance, removed to the court of king Hjalprek and there took service as the king's smith. Fafnir had in his possession also a forbidding

[1] P. 130 ff.

helmet [1] and a costly sword named Rotti. Transforming himself into a venomous serpent, he made a lair for himself on Gnita Heath, and there remained brooding over his hoard.

Regin egged Sigurd on to kill Fafnir and seize the treasure, by which means he would be able to win great renown for himself. From Hjalprek Sigurd got the excellent horse Grani, of the race of Sleipnir, on whose back no man before himself had ever ridden; and Regin wrought a sword for him. But when Sigurd came to try the sword and brought it down on Regin's anvil, it broke in two; the same thing happened with a second sword forged for him by Regin. Then Sigurd's mother gave him the pieces of Sigmund's sword, from which, at his command, Regin forged a marvelous blade to which was given the name Gram. Gram stood the test of the anvil; Sigurd cleft it from top to bottom without so much as turning the edge of the sword. Then, carrying the weapon down to the river Rhine, he let a ball of wool float with the stream against the edge of the sword, and Gram cut it in two.

Regin now bade him set forth without delay against Fafnir; but Sigurd declared his determination of first avenging his father's death. On seeking counsel from a wise man named Gripir, brother of queen Hjordis, he learned the whole course of his destiny. He now besought Hjalprek for men and ships with which to make head against the sons of Hunding. His every wish was fulfilled. It was a gallant sight to see his

[1] Literally, "terror-helmet".—Translator's note.

ship as he set sail. Presently a severe storm came upon them, which compelled them to lay by in the shelter of a headland. At the edge of the cliff stood a man who hailed the ships to ask who the voyagers might be. Regin answered that the fleet was under the command of Sigurd and then in turn asked the man to tell his own name. His name was Nikar, came the reply, but they might call him Old Man of the Mountain, or Feng, or Fjolnir, whatsoever they pleased. They took him aboard, and at once the winds began to blow from the right quarter. On Sigurd's asking him what were the most favorable auguries for one who was going forth to battle, he answered: "It is a good sign to be followed by a black raven. It is a good thing to meet, as you set out on your journey, two heroes whose thoughts are fixed on fame. It is good to hear the wolf howling beneath the ash tree. Luck will attend you against your enemies if you see them before they catch sight of you. No man should fight with the setting sun in his eyes, for they who can see to carry on the battle shall enjoy the victory. It is a great mischance if a man stumble on his way to the field. Every man should take care that he is combed and washed and filled with food in the morning, for no one knows what the evening may bring in its train." They now continued on their course, and before long a battle to the death was fought between Sigurd and the sons of Hunding. Lyngvi was taken captive, and his brothers were killed. As for Lyngvi himself, a blood eagle was carved on his back, which is as much as to say that his ribs were shorn from his back and his lungs were pulled out through the aperture.

When all these things were done, Sigurd and Regin made their way to Gnita Heath bent on the killing of Fafnir. Regin gave the counsel that a trench should be dug straight across the path along which Fafnir was in the habit of creeping in quest of water; Sigurd did so, Regin meanwhile hiding himself away in terror. Just then an old man with a long beard came to Sigurd and persuaded him to dig a number of trenches. In one of these he was to lie in wait himself, while the others were to provide an outlet for the overflow of venom spewed out by the serpent; if he failed to take such a precaution, he might come to grief. Herewith Sigurd got his first inkling that Regin meant to play him false. After digging a number of trenches, Sigurd hid himself in one of them. When Fafnir came, spitting venom and rolling so violently that the earth shook, Sigurd lost no time in thrusting his sword into the serpent's left side up to the very hilt. Sigurd then sprang to his feet, and the serpent, feeling that the wound was mortal, asked him to reveal his name; for if Fafnir could succeed in learning that secret and in cursing the slayer by name, he would have his revenge. Sigurd at first thought to conceal his true name, but on the serpent's taunting him, he told the truth. Fafnir reiterated the curses once fastened upon the gold, which was now to pass into Sigurd's keeping. Sigurd put a number of questions to Fafnir on divers matters pertaining to the gods; after giving answers to these questions, Fafnir died. While

Sigurd stood wiping the blood from the sword, Regin came to him and prayed good fortune to attend the mighty deed he had done, but added the hint that since Fafnir was his own brother, Sigurd owed Regin something by way of wergild for the life he had taken; he would ask no more than the heart of Fafnir, which Sigurd was to roast for him. Regin now cut the serpent's heart out with his sword Ridil, drank of Fafnir's blood, and lay down to sleep. Sigurd kindled a fire and set about roasting the heart on a spit; but as he touched it with his finger to see if it was done, he burned himself. He therefore put the finger in his mouth; when Fafnir's heart's blood touched his tongue, he became aware that he had learned to understand the song of birds. He heard the tomtits twittering in the bushes: "Sigurd would do more wisely in eating the heart himself; he would do well to kill Regin, who is plotting to betray him, and to seize Fafnir's hoard and ride away with it." Sigurd accordingly cut off Regin's head, ate Fafnir's heart, and drank his blood. Then he heard the birds singing once again: "It behooves him to ride to the top of Mount Hindarfjall, to a hall standing swathed in flames, there to force an entrance and to awaken a shield-maiden who lies entranced by magic arts." Sigurd now made his way to Fafnir's lair, which he found to be a house of beams and doors, all wrought out of iron. The gold lay buried in the earth; he took the whole hoard and also Fafnir's other treasures, the forbidding helmet, a gold byrnie, and the sword Rotti. Filling two huge chests he bound them to a packsaddle on Grani's back, one on each side; he meant to drive the horse before him, but Grani would not move a foot before Sigurd himself mounted. From this time forth Sigurd bore the name Fafnirsbane.

THE NIFLUNGS—THE SLAYING OF SIGURD

SIGURD now rode south toward Frankland and up to the top of Mount Hindarfjall. On the mountain he saw a great light, as if a fire were burning there; when he drew nearer he caught sight of a stronghold of shields, above which was reared a standard. On going within the stronghold he found a woman fully panoplied lying asleep. He attempted to remove the armor; but the byrnie clung tight as if it had grown fast to the flesh itself, and so he had to cut it loose with Gram. Sitting up, the woman asked who it was that had roused her from so profound a sleep. Sigurd told his own name and asked what her name might be. She was called Sigrdrifa and was a Valkyrie; on a certain occasion she had laid low a king to whom Odin had given a pledge of victory, and in punishment Odin had stung her with sleep-thorns, had declared that she should never more win victory in battle, and had foretold that in due time she should wed. She had vowed, for her part, that she would never wed a man capable of feeling fear. Thereupon she had sunk into her deep magic trance, from which Sigurd was the first to waken her. Sigurd now asked her to teach him wisdom, what lore she might have learned from all the worlds that be. Taking a horn filled with mead and turning her face toward the sons of Day and the daughters of

Norse Mythology

Night, toward the Æsir and the goddesses, she besought their favor; then she gave the horn into his hand, and said: "I bring you a drink, warrior champion, in which are blended power and glory; it is filled with songs and with tokens of strength, with goodly incantations and with gladdening runes.

"Runes of victory you must carve if you desire to be victorious, some on the blade and some on the haft; and twice you must speak the name of Tyr" (that is, the name of the rune for the letter T).

"Ale-runes you must know if you would not have the wife of another betray your trust; carve them on the horn and on the back of your hand, and mark on your finger nail the word 'need'" (that is, the rune for the letter N). "Bless the beaker, stand on guard against deceit, lay a leek in the liquor; then can mischance never be mingled with your mead.

"Birth-runes you must know if you would lend aid to a woman bearing a child; carve them on the palms of your hands, clasp the woman about her waist, then pray to the Disir to help her.

"Wave-runes you must know if you would save ships at sea; carve them on the prow and rudder and burn them into the oars; then will the waves never be so steep or the seas so black but that you shall safely reach the shore.

"Branch-runes you must know if you would learn healing and the treating of wounds; carve them on the bark and on the trunk of a tree whose branches lean to the east.

"Speech-runes you must know if you would take

vengeance for your harms; twist them, twine them, wind them all together, at the judgment seats where all the counselors are assembled in judgment.

"Thought-runes you must know if you would be wiser than all other men; them Odin devised from the sap that ran from Heiddraupnir's head and Hoddrofnir's horn. On the mountain he stood with Brimir's sword and with a helmet on his head. Then spoke the head of Mimir for the first time and gave utterance of trusty tokens: these were carved on the shield that stands before the shining god, on Arvak's ear, and on Alsvin's hoof, on the wheel under Rognir's (Odin's) wagon, on Sleipnir's teeth, on the runners of the sledge, on the paw of the bear and on Bragi's tongue, on the claws of the wolf and the beak of the eagle, on bloody wings and on the bridge's head, on freeing hand and on healing footprints, on glass, on gold, and on amulets, in wine, in simples, and on seats of joy, on Gungnir's point and on Grani's breast, on the Norn's nail and on the owl's beak. All those that were carved were shaven off again, mingled with holy mead, and sent forth on far ways; some are with the Elves, some with the Æsir, some with the wise Vanir, and some with the race of men. There are book-runes, birth-runes, ale-runes, and excellent magic-runes for every one who is able to use them without mischance, without misadventure. Turn them to your happiness if you have understood them, time without end. Now make your choice further, between speech and silence; for all harms have their destined bounds." "I should not flee even if you knew me to be fated to die," said

Sigurd, "for I was born without fear." Then she continued her discourse: "Be free from fault in your dealings with kinsmen, and seek not revenge if they wrong you. Swear no false oaths. At the assembly dispute not with fools, for the unwise man often speaks words of worse meaning than he is aware; yet there is danger in all things if you keep silence, for so you will appear to be afraid, or what is said will have the color of truth: rather kill him the next day, and thus reward men for their lies. Never take lodging with a witch, even if night has come upon you unawares. Let not fair women deceive you. Contend not with drunken men. Yet with brave men you must fight, rather than let them burn the roof over your head. Entice no maiden and no man's wife. Give seemly burial to the dead. Put no faith in him who has lost a kinsman at your hand: a wolf lurks in a young son, even though he have accepted gold for wergild. Beware of guile in your friends."

From Hindarfjall Sigurd journeyed to the home of Heimir in the Dales of Lym and abode there for a time. Here he chanced to see Brynhild, daughter of king Budli and foster daughter of Heimir, and was taken with an overpowering love for her. She was a shield-maiden, and when Sigurd paid court to her she answered that the fates would not permit them to live together; yet at length she gave her consent, and he placed the ring of Andvari on her finger. Afterward she bore him—according to a late legend[1]—a daughter, who was named Aslaug.

[1] P. 246.

Heroic Legends

Thereafter Sigurd rode farther on his way until he came to the court of king Gjuki, whose kingdom lay south of the Rhine. The children of Gjuki, the Gjukungs, were fairer and stronger than all others; the sons were named Gunnar, Hogni, and Guttorm, and the daughter's name was Gudrun. Gjuki's wife, a woman skilled in magic, was called Grimhild. Here Sigurd was received as a welcome guest; it was Grimhild's greatest wish that he should become her son-in-law, but he loved Brynhild too dearly and all his thoughts were bent upon her. Grimhild accordingly had recourse to magic; she made a drink capable of stealing memory away, and this she gave to Sigurd. No sooner had he drunk of it than he remembered Brynhild no more; soon he came to love Gudrun instead, wedded her, and entered into a compact of sworn brotherhood with her brothers. Sigurd gave Gudrun to eat from Fafnir's heart, which he had carried with him, whereupon she grew even more grim of mood than before.

Grimhild now counseled her son Gunnar to pay court to Brynhild, daughter of Budli. King Budli making no objection, the Gjukungs[1] journeyed together with Sigurd to the Dales of Lym, where Brynhild still had her abode. Heimir, who received them kindly, declared that Brynhild should choose according to her own desire. Round about her hall there burned a ring of fire, and she had made known her intention to marry none but that man who could ride through the flames. When Gunnar rode his horse Goti toward the fire, the

[1] Also called Niflungs.

horse recoiled. Sigurd made him a loan of Grani, but Grani would not stir a pace. Sigurd and Gunnar now each took upon him the likeness of the other, whereupon Sigurd in the guise of Gunnar mounted Grani, with Gram in his hands and golden spurs on his feet. Grani at once ran forward, while the fire crackled, the earth shook, and flames darted up to the very heavens. Sigurd thus made his way into Brynhild's hall and there wedded her, but during the night he laid the sword Gram between her and himself. They exchanged rings, so that Sigurd once more got possession of the ring of Andvari and gave her another ring in its stead. When three nights had passed, he rode out again and restored Gunnar's likeness in return for his own. Brynhild gave into the charge of Heimir her own and Sigurd's daughter as a foster child; later she went with them to the realm of Gjuki, where her wedding with Gunnar took place. Yet Sigurd's deception brought its revenge; he now remembered the oaths he had sworn to Brynhild, but in no wise betrayed his true feelings.

Once upon a time Brynhild and Gudrun went out into the river Rhine to wash their hair. Brynhild waded out the farther of the two, saying that since she had the braver husband she would not wash herself in the rinsings of Gudrun's hair. Gudrun followed her, maintaining that it was her right to stand the farther up stream, inasmuch as no man could compare with Sigurd Fafnirsbane. "A braver deed it was," said Brynhild, "of Gunnar to ride through the fire, a thing which Sigurd dared not do." Gudrun laughed and answered, "Do you think it was Gunnar who rode through the fire? No, it was Sigurd; he slept with you and took the ring of Andvari from your hand—here it is." Brynhild recognized the ring and now understood all that had happened; she grew pale but spoke no word. During that evening and throughout the following day Brynhild was silent and downcast. Gudrun bade her be of good cheer, but Brynhild replied, "You are passing cruel toward me." "What is it that troubles you?" Gudrun asked. "You shall pay dearly for the winning of Sigurd in my stead, for I do not yield him to you with good grace." Gudrun answered, "You have made a better marriage than you deserve." "I might have rested content," said Brynhild, "if your husband had not surpassed my own; Sigurd has no peer, he won the victory over Fafnir, and that deed is worth more than the whole of Gunnar's realm. Sigurd killed the serpent, and that stroke will be known as long as the world shall stand; but Gunnar dared not ride through the flames." "It was Grani who would not stir with Gunnar on his back," answered Gudrun; "Gunnar himself had courage enough." Brynhild said: "Grimhild alone is to blame; may you find joy in Sigurd just so much as I shall find joy in a life marred by treachery."

Brynhild took to her bed sick at heart; Gunnar went to her side to comfort her and prayed her to confide in him, but she would not. He then asked Sigurd to try what he might do. Sigurd spoke with her, confessed his love for her, and even promised to put Gudrun away and marry her instead. But she

was too proud to listen to his entreaties, whereat
Sigurd was so stricken with grief that the rings of his
byrnie burst at both sides. Rather than wed with
him on such terms she would prefer to see him lying
dead, so that neither she nor Gudrun should rejoice
in him again. She egged Gunnar on to kill Sigurd;
he had, as she said, betrayed them both. Gunnar,
being readily swayed to her purpose, sought counsel
with his brother Hogni, but Hogni was unwilling that
they should lay violent hands themselves upon Sigurd,
since they were bound to him by oaths of brotherhood.
He proposed instead that they should persuade the
thoughtless Guttorm to undertake the deed, a youth
who had no part in their oaths. To heighten his
courage, they gave him to eat the flesh of serpents and
wolves. Having eaten, he became so fell of mood that
he was at once ready to do his dastard's work. Coming upon Sigurd asleep at Gudrun's side, he pierced
his body with a sword. Sigurd always kept his own
sword Gram by his side; when he felt the wound, he
threw the sword after Guttorm with such force that
it cleft him through the middle. The young son of
Sigurd and Gudrun lost his life at the same time.

Gudrun sat by the body of Sigurd, unable to weep,
though her heart was ready to burst. Men and women
coming to comfort her could do nothing. Not until
Gullrond, daughter of Gjuki, drew aside the cloth that
had been spread over Sigurd, so that Gudrun once
more beheld his glazed eyes and his bloody head, did
she sink back weeping; as the tears ran down her
cheeks, she found words to utter her grief. Brynhild

on her part laughed when men told her of Sigurd's
death, till the whole house rang with her mirth:

> Long may you revel
> In lands and men,
> You who laid low
> The boldest of princes.

Then she said furthermore: "Once I lived honored and
glad with Atli, my brother. No man did I desire until
the Gjukungs rode into the courtyard. Then gave
I my troth to the hero who sat on the back of Grani;
he was a man, Gunnar, unlike you. This you shall
know, that Sigurd was never false to you; the sword
Gram, its edge tempered in venom, he laid down between me and himself; but you have broken your oath.
Now I will live no longer, for Sigurd alone did I love,
and desperation drove me on all my ways. My
brother Atli will know what vengeance to take for me
and my sorrows; and he shall remain a mightier man
than you." Gunnar earnestly prayed her not to seek
death; but Hogni said that nothing could hold back
one born, like her, to misfortune. Brynhild then took
a sword, turned the point against her side, and sank
down among the pillows. Before she died she besought Gunnar to lay her and Sigurd on one and the
same funeral pyre, and to deck it with draperies and
shields, to cover it over with splendid garments and
with thralls. "Burn," she said, "at Sigurd's other
side my retainers, adorned with amulets, two at the
head and two at the feet, and my two falcons with
them; once more lay Gram between us, even as on the
wedding night. In such wise shall Sigurd go forth

proudly; since there follow him so many, five bond-women and eight henchmen, the portals of the hall shall never clang shut at his heels." The pyre was made ready as she had given command, and on it she and Sigurd were burned. As Brynhild passed along the Hell-Ways in a magnificent chariot, a certain Giantess meeting her on the road made as if to deny her passage, and derided her for the life she had lived. But Brynhild charged Gudrun with all the blame; Gudrun had egged her to evil, speaking falsehoods of her and of Sigurd.

All too long	Yet shall we live
Life endures	Our lives together,
For man, for woman,	Sigurd and I.
Burdened with sorrows;	Sink, witch, from sight.

ATLI

GUNNAR and Hogni fell heir to all Sigurd's treasures after his death. Atli, Brynhild's brother, maintaining that the two men had caused the death of Brynhild, threatened them with war. Peace was nevertheless established between them on such terms that Atli was to have Gudrun as his wife. Shortly after the death of Sigurd, Gudrun had given birth to a daughter, whom she had named Svanhild and with whom she had fled to Denmark, where for seven half years she took refuge with Thora, daughter of Hakon. Gudrun's mother Grimhild and her brothers now journeyed to Denmark for the purpose of persuading her to marry Atli, but she curtly refused; Grimhild then gave her a drink of forgetfulness and so gained her consent.

Heroic Legends

With Atli, Gudrun had two sons, named Erp and Eitil. Atli, moved by a desire to secure the rich possessions of his brothers-in-law, sent his crafty servant Vingi, also called Knefrœd, to invite them to a festival. Gudrun, however, knowing that some treachery lay at the bottom, charged the messenger to carry with him warning runes which she had cut for her brothers and at the same time to deliver to them a ring to which she had bound a wolf's hair. On the way Vingi read the runes and altered them so that they bore a contrary message and gave them over thus changed to Gunnar and Hogni. The two brothers made a great banquet and promised to proceed without delay to take part in Atli's festival. But during the night, when all men had gone to bed, Kostbera, the cunning wife of Hogni, looked at the runes and saw that at first something else had been written there than was now to be read. She told Hogni what she had found, but he put no faith in her words. Glaumvor, Gunnar's wife, the same night, dreamed foreboding dreams, and she likewise warned her husband against undertaking the journey; notwithstanding he held to his purpose as stoutly as his brother, and so they set forth on their visit to Atli's court. Yet before leaving home they hid Fafnir's gold in the river Rhine. As they neared Atli's court, he came out to meet them in hostile array; a stubborn battle took place, in which the Niflungs defended themselves bravely, but at last they were overpowered and both brothers were taken prisoner. Atli came to Gunnar, who was sitting apart from his brother, and tried to get him to say where the hoard was hidden. Gunnar answered: "Not until Hogni's heart shall lie in my hand, bleeding, cut from the hero's breast." Atli went away and caused a thrall's heart to be cut from his body; but when Gunnar saw it he said: "This is the heart of Hjalli, the weakling, quite unlike the heart of the hero Hogni; as much as it trembles lying there on the platter, it trembled twice as much in the breast of the thrall." Atli now caused Hogni's heart to be cut out in earnest, but he only laughed as the knife drew near his heart. When they brought this heart to Gunnar, he knew it to be his brother's; "but," he said, "I alone now know where the gold lies hidden, and the river Rhine shall rule over the hoard." No one ever afterward uncovered Fafnir's gold, and so Atli's treachery was bootless. In his wrath he threw Gunnar, whose hands were bound, into a den of serpents. Gudrun sent her brother a harp, on which he played so wondrous well with his toes that no man had ever before heard the like. All of the serpents fell into a doze but one; this one gnawed its way into his breast and struck its fangs into his heart.

When Gudrun heard of the death of her brothers, she gave no sign; she let it appear as if she accepted Atli's offer of renewed amity and the wergild he paid for the lives of the slain. She held a funeral feast for her brothers, but in her heart she meditated grim revenge. First of all she killed the two small sons she had by Atli, made drinking vessels from their skulls, and gave the king wine to drink from them, in which was blended the blood of the children; she gave him

also their hearts to eat. Afterward she told him all
that she had done, and he was filled with sorrow for the
death of his sons and with fear for her surpassing cruelty. But she went still farther in exacting vengeance.
Together with a young son and heir of Hogni she went
by night to Atli's bedside and thrust a sword into the
king's breast, her brother's son helping her. Atli
waked from his sleep at the stroke; and before he died,
man and wife held discourse together. Gudrun declared that she had never been able to love him, that
she had lived happier days with Sigurd, the greater
hero, and yet that she would give him befitting funeral
obsequies. And she kept her promise. But she set
fire to Atli's hall; and so his men too went to their
death.

JORMUNREK

WHEN Gudrun had thus compassed her revenge, she
had no desire to live longer and so threw herself into
the sea. Yet she was not drowned; the waves bore her
across the water to the land of king Jonaker, where she
became the wife of the king. They had three sons,
Sorli, Hamdir, and Erp. Jonaker also caused Svanhild, Gudrun's daughter, to be brought before him,
and her he adopted as his foster daughter. She was
like her father in beauty and had the same sharp eyes,
the gaze of which no man could meet.

The fame of her loveliness, spreading abroad, reached
the ears of a mighty king named Jormunrek. He accordingly sent his son Randver and his counselor Bikki

to pay court to her on his behalf. Gudrun, to be sure, gave utterance to the fear that the marriage would not prove happy; but Jonaker held that a man like Jormunrek was not to be lightly dismissed, and so Svanhild was sent away in the care of Randver. In the course of the journey the malicious Bikki broached the suggestion that a man so old as Jormunrek was no fitting match for a woman so young and fair as Svanhild, that in short it was more meet that Randver, being young like herself, should have her to wife. Randver found some reason in Bikki's words. But as soon as they arrived at home, Bikki told all that had happened to Jormunrek, who became so wroth that he bade Bikki cause Randver to be hanged. As Randver was being led away to the gallows, he plucked the feathers from his falcon and sent them to his father. Jormunrek understood the token: old as he was, and soon to be without an heir, he would be like a plucked bird, lacking in all that might aid and sustain him. He at once commanded that Randver's life should be spared, but it was too late: Bikki had made all possible haste in carrying out the king's behest. Jormunrek's wrath now turned in full measure against Svanhild, whom he held to be the cause of his misfortunes. As he came riding home from the hunt and found Svanhild sitting at the gate drying her hair in the sun, he trampled her to death under the hoofs of his horses. At first they dared not move upon her, but started back before her piercing glances; then Bikki caused a sack to be drawn down over her eyes, and so she lost her life.

When Gudrun learned of all these things, she egged

her sons into wreaking vengeance on Jormunrek for his cruelty. They made ready for the journey, and she gave them byrnies and helmets that no iron could pierce. Then she gave them this counsel, that when they came into the presence of Jormunrek, Sorli and Hamdir were to sever his hands and feet and Erp was to cut off his head. As they rode on their way, the two brothers asked Erp what aid he meant to give them. "Such help," he replied, "as the hand may give to the hand or the foot to the foot." Thinking such a promise a thing of naught, they put him to death. A moment later, Hamdir stumbled and thrust out his hand to support himself; the like happened to Sorli, who succeeded in checking his fall with his foot; in this manner they learned that one hand may well help another, and the one foot the other, and that therefore they had done evil toward Erp. Coming to the hall of Jormunrek by night as he lay asleep, they cut off both his hands and both his feet. Jormunrek started out of sleep and called to his men; then Hamdir said: "His head would now have fallen had Erp been here." The men of the king's bodyguard sprang up and rushed upon the intruders, but found their weapons useless in their hands; an old one-eyed man now came and told them to stone the brothers to death, and they did as he bade them. The two brothers lost their lives, and with them the whole race of the Gjukungs came to an end.

Norse Mythology

ASLAUG

WITH the death of Jonaker and Jormunrek this legendary cycle in the *Poetic Edda* comes to an end. The *Prose Edda* makes a brief reference to Sigurd's and Brynhild's daughter Aslaug; in the *Vǫlsunga Saga* and in the related saga of Ragnar Lodbrok there is a circumstantial account of her fate.[1]

After the death of Sigurd and Brynhild, Heimir suspected that men would be sent out to search for Aslaug for the purpose of putting her to death. He therefore caused a harp to be made, large enough to hide both the little girl and her treasures; carrying the harp and Aslaug within it, he then traveled about in the guise of a poor minstrel. When he came to the banks of lonely streams, he took her from her hiding place and bathed her, but he kept her concealed while he passed through populated places. For food he gave her a kind of leek, so nourishing that she required nothing else to eat; and when she wept, he played for her on the harp. At length he arrived at Spangereid in Norway, where he halted from his journey at a little farm kept by two old people named Aki and Grima. The man happened just at the time to be out in the forest, but Grima was at home. Heimir prayed her for a night's lodging. She did not deny his request but kindled a fire so that he might warm himself; as she did so, she caught sight of some bits of fine raiment protruding from a crack in the harp and also discovered a costly gold ring beneath the tatters that swathed his arm. She now

[1] Cf. p. 245 ff. and p. 178.

understood that he was not what he seemed to be, and so she determined to kill him and rob him of his treasures. She gave him lodging in a rye granary outside the house; for, as she said, she and her husband were accustomed to talk together late into the night after he came home. There Heimir lay down to sleep, keeping his harp by his side. When Aki returned, his wife had not nearly done her work, and he upbraided her for her sloth. She answered: "Do not be angry; at one stroke we can secure more than is needed to keep us the rest of our lives." Then she told him of Heimir and of the plans she had hatched. Aki was unwilling to betray his guest; but since it was the woman who ruled in that house, he was compelled to yield, and so it fell to him to give Heimir the killing blow as he slept. Heimir was so big and strong that the whole house clattered down and the earth shook at his death struggle. The woman now tried to pick up the harp; but she could not lift it, and so they had to break it to pieces. When their eyes fell on Aslaug, they were rather abashed; but they found riches enough besides. Aslaug would not tell her name or even speak a word; for a long time therefore they thought that she lacked the power of speech. They determined to pretend that she was their own daughter, and they laid all the hard work on her. Being loth to have any one see how beautiful she was and thus suspect that the kinship was not all that they pretended it to be, they cut off her hair, smeared her head with tar, and gave her a broad hat and wretched garments to wear. They named her Kraka, after the mother of Grima. The story of her marriage with Ragnar Lodbrok will be told below.[1]

GERMAN LEGENDS DEALING WITH SIEGFRIED AND THE NIBELUNGS

THE Germans also knew the legends of the Volsungs and recorded them in various forms. The chief source is the well-known heroic poem, the *Nibelungenlied*. This poem is built upon earlier popular ballads, no longer extant. It dates from about the year 1200, and the presentation has lost much of its antique character for the reason that the legends have been adapted to the requirements of medieval chivalry. Thus mention is made of feudal castles and of tournaments; the heroes have become Christian knights and are no longer pagan champions. Many of the individual events are likewise presented in a form totally different from the form that is characteristic of Northern poesy. Several legends only lightly touched in the Northern sources are fully detailed in the German; such, for example, are the legends of king Thjodrek, the celebrated Theodoric of Verona, who in German legend bears the name Dietrich of Bern. The names have other forms and are in some cases wholly different. The following are the contents of the *Nibelungenlied* in brief:

Siegfried was the son of Sigmund, king of Xanten in the Netherlands, and of his queen Sigelind. From his earliest youth he distinguished himself in many a

[1] See p. 245 ff.

dangerous enterprise. On one such occasion he killed a dragon and, having bathed himself in its blood, was by this means made immune to wounds, except in one spot where the leaf of a linden had clung to his body. He conquered king Nibelung and thus won for himself the immense treasure of the Nibelungs and the sword Balmung, and he took from the Dwarf Alberich his cap of invisibility ("Tarnkappe"). In the city of Worms, Gunther, king of the Burgundians, at that time held his court; his mother was Uote, and he had two brothers, Gernot and Giselher. The king's sister, Kriemhild, was famed far and wide for her beauty. Siegfried, learning of her renown, went to Worms to sue for her hand. Though he was received with the greatest kindness by the kings, he remained in the city an entire year without being permitted to see Kriemhild. A war now broke out, in which the Burgundians were victorious, thanks to the help of Siegfried; on his return the hero saw Kriemhild for the first time at a festival celebrating the success of their arms. He dared not hope to win her, and yet he let himself be persuaded to remain a while longer.

News presently reached Gunther of queen Brunhild of Iceland and her marvelous beauty; rumor related that it was her custom to put her suitors to proof in trials of strength and to have them put to death as soon as she had worsted them. Gunther determined to pay court to her; but, not being confident of his own prowess, he sought the aid of Siegfried. Siegfried promised to help him in return for the hand of Kriemhild. From her fastness of Isenstein Brunhild witnessed the approach of the kings and their retinue; supposing that it was Siegfried, whose fame had reached her ears, that was coming to claim her hand, she was much disappointed on Gunther's making his own desires known. Siegfried acted as Gunther's vassal, stood at his side during the trial of strength, and helped him to win the victory. The two wedding festivals, that of Gunther and that of Siegfried, now took place in Worms; but Siegfried was called upon once more, this time invisible, to assist Gunther in the final proof of puissance, and on this occasion he carried Brunhild's ring away with him. Siegfried now returned with his wife to his own kingdom. Brunhild still held him to be a vassal of her husband and so was surprised to learn that he fulfilled no feudal obligations; suspecting some secret and being determined to learn what it was, she persuaded Gunther to invite Siegfried and Kriemhild to pay them a visit in Worms. As queen of the Burgundians she insisted that they should recognize her greatness. Once while the company was on the way to church, a dispute arose between the two queens as to the right of precedence. Kriemhild taunted Brunhild, disclosed the deceit that had been practised,—that it was really Siegfried who had prevailed over her, and showed the ring in proof of what she said. Shamed and angered at the trickery that had been used against her, Brunhild at once began to nurse thoughts of vengeance. With this purpose she persuaded Hagen, a kinsman of the royal house and one of Gunther's chief vassals, to help her in bringing about the death of Siegfried. Gunther, believing that his honor had been betrayed by Siegfried, unwillingly lent himself to the plot. Hagen, for his part, tricked Kriemhild into revealing what part of Siegfried's body was vulnerable, on the pretext that through this knowledge he would be better able to protect Seigfried in the course of an impending war. While a hunt was in progress in the forest of Odenwald, Siegfried was pierced by Hagen's spear as he bent down, unarmed, to drink from a fountain; and Gunther was a witness of the murder. Hagen caused the body to be laid during the night at Kriemhild's door, and the queen at once suspected the truth. Defiantly she accused her brother and Hagen of the crime, and from that day she lived at Worms in the deepest sorrow, never speaking another word to Gunther. The treasure of the Nibelungs, left to her by Siegfried, was carried to Worms, and Kriemhild made use of it to win friends through the giving of charitable gifts. Hagen, distrusting her intent, then caused the hoard to be sunk in the river Rhine.

For thirteen years Kriemhild cherished her plans for revenge, chiefly against Hagen. Emissaries presently came from Etzel, king of the Huns, to pay court to her on the king's behalf. Filled with grief for Siegfried, she at first refused their overtures; not even Giselher, her favorite brother, who had always proved himself a friend to Siegfried, was able to prevail upon her to receive the king's suit with favor. But when she saw an opportunity to gratify her revenge, she gave consent. The wedding festival was held in Vienna, whence Etzel carried her to his own kingdom, the land of the

Huns (Hungary). Years passed by. At length she induced Etzel to invite her brothers and Hagen to pay them a visit. Hagen, thinking that he saw through her designs, advised against the proposed journey, but on Giselher's hinting at cowardice, Hagen forthwith determined to go; yet he persuaded Gunther to command all of his men to follow in their train. Kriemhild gave none but Giselher a welcome, and she let Hagen feel the brunt of her displeasure. Notwithstanding that Hagen had been warned by his old friend Dietrich of Bern, who was living in exile at Etzel's court, he nevertheless conducted himself in so defiant a manner as even to carry the sword Balmung before the very eyes of Kriemhild and to boast openly of the murder. The queen soon won to her cause Etzel's brother Blodel, who shortly declared open warfare against the Burgundians. Hagen countered by cutting off the head of Etzel's and Kriemhild's son Ortlieb, and by this act the Burgundians lost all chance of saving their lives. The queen, to be sure, made overtures of peace to her brothers on the condition that they would deliver Hagen into her hands; but even Giselher set his face against such treachery. A terrific battle ensued. Dietrich and his Goths finally put an end to the struggle. Gernot and Giselher fell, Gunther was taken prisoner and bound, and at length Dietrich disarmed Hagen himself and made him captive. Gunther at the command of Etzel was put to death; and Kriemhild herself thrust a sword into the breast of Hagen. At that Dietrich's old armorer Hildebrand sprang forward and, enraged at her cruelty, pierced her to

Heroic Legends

the heart. Another heroic poem, *Die Klage*, gives a brief account of the fate of those that survived. Uote died of grief. Brunhild, with her own and Gunther's son, was the last of the royal house of the Burgundians.

THE DEVELOPMENT OF THE LEGENDARY CYCLE OF THE VOLSUNGS

As already indicated, the legends of the Volsungs have been formed for the most part from events that happened among German peoples during historic times. The original home of the legends must have been Germany; the circumstance that they are to be found also in the North is not to be explained on the theory that the legends were the common property of Northern and German tribes before these tribes became distinct, but rather on the supposition that the legends migrated from Germany to the North. Just when this may have occurred is difficult to determine. Since the historical events have undergone considerable modifications in this heroic poetry, the German legends must have taken shape at a period measurably distant from the time of the death of Attila (453). On the other hand, the legends of the Volsungs were known in the Northern countries early in the Viking age; *Eiríksmál*, dating from about the year 950, mentions Sigmund and Sinfjotli,[1] and skaldic verses contain paraphrases based on the same legends. According to these evidences, the legends must have found their way

[1] See p. 165.

into the North at some time between the sixth and the eighth centuries. There was opportunity for an independent development of these legends during several hundreds of years among the various Germanic peoples; and herein lies the explanation of the great differences between the German and the Northern forms of the legends, as regards both their general scope and their details. To discover in just what shape the legends came to the North is well-nigh impossible, particularly inasmuch as the most circumstantial German version, the *Nibelungenlied*, dates from a comparatively late period, the twelfth century.

The Norse form of the story begins with Odin and his son Sigi, and follows the fate of the Volsungs down to the very days of the sons of Ragnar. The *Nibelungenlied*, on the contrary, deals only with the events from Siegfried's first appearance in Mainz to the fall of the Burgundians at Etzel's court. At the start, no doubt, the cycle did not embrace the huge mass of material which now is to be found embodied in the Norse versions. Both the German and the Norse redactions show a tendency toward combination of legends originally foreign to one another into a larger unified structure, and it is therefore necessary to try to determine by a process of comparison how much of the conglomerate belonged to the cycle at the beginning. When, for example, the *Nibelungenlied* permits the legends of Dietrich of Bern to crop up in the earlier part of the account of the destruction of the Burgundians, while the Eddic poems do not even admit Dietrich among the participating heroes, the probability is that he was not known in the legends of the Volsungs at the time when these legends made their way into the North.[1] In a like manner it is possible to cull out from the Northern versions a heap of legends of later origin. First of all, it appears quite clearly that the legend of Aslaug has no proper place in the Volsung cycle. Aslaug is not mentioned at all in the Eddic poems; and the report that she was the daughter of Sigurd Fafnirsbane is directly contradicted by the account given in the Eddic poems of the relations between Sigurd and Brynhild.[2] The situation is much the same in the case of the legend of Jormunrek. Jordanes, the first writer to deal with it, makes no mention of Sunilda's being the daughter of Sigurd, and he gives quite a different reason for Ermanaric's putting her to death than the one contained in the Northern poems.

In the first divisions of the cycle as well there are similar, and even more accidental cases of attachment. The legend of Helgi Hundingsbane, for instance, is an exclusively Northern story, which has been attached to the Volsung cycle through the device of making Helgi an elder half brother of Sigurd. Still weaker is

[1] The mention of Thjodrek (Dietrich) in the prose induction to *Guðrúnarkviða II* as the person to whom Gudrun makes her lament is of no consequence, since he does not appear in the poem itself; this induction proves only that the one who brought the poems together knew the German legends. In a similar way *Guðrúnarkviða III*, which deals with the relations between Gudrun and Thjodrek, rests upon earlier material which has found its way in from without. See G. Storm, *Sagnkredsene om Karl den Store og Didrik af Bern*, p. 87; G. Neckel, *Beiträge zur Eddaforschung*, p. 221.
[2] See note to p. 184.

the link binding together the Volsung legends and the legend of Helgi Hjorvardsson; this Helgi it was necessary to reincarnate as Helgi Hundingsbane. Even if all these additions be eliminated, the whole legendary series from Sigi down to Sigmund Volsungsson would still remain to identify the Northern redactions. How much of this material was ever a portion of legends other than the Northern is not easy to determine; but since the poem of *Beowulf* mentions Wæls, Sigmund, and Fitela, it is clear at any rate that Volsung, Sigmund, and Sinfjotli were once subject to poetic treatment among other Germanic peoples, so much the more since the remarkable name "Sinfjotli" is readily recognizable in the ancient Germanic man's name *Sintarfizilo*. Possibly the legend at first reached no farther back than to Volsung,[1] in which case the stories of Sigi and Rerir must be regarded as Norse legends added at some later time. Signy's relation to her husband Siggeir and to her brother Sigmund supports this view; for these relations are to such a degree reminiscent, even in details, of Gudrun's relations to Atli and to the brothers Gunnar and Hogni that it appears certain that one of these legends is an imitation of the other; and since the version found in the Northern legend of Gudrun (as will be made manifest later) probably is older than the German account of the fate of the Burgundians, likelihood points out the story of Siggeir's death at the hands of brother and sister as an imitation of the other story.

In those phases of the legend which are common

[1] See note to p. 159.

Heroic Legends

to German and to Northern literature there are a number of differences in detail, as will be evident from the foregoing brief abstract of the contents of the *Nibelungenlied*.

In the Northern version considerable importance attaches to the hoard of Andvari; this hoard, like Tyrfing in the *Hervarar Saga*, serves as a means of connecting the several elements of the legend, through the curse that clings to it. In the *Nibelungenlied*, on the contrary, Siegfried's hoard is practically inessential to the course of the action; his death has no connection with the treasure, but is merely a result of his relations to Brynhild. This may indeed be the more primitive set of circumstances. For it is to be noted that not even in the Northern version is Sigurd's death an immediate consequence of his having acquired the fateful treasure; in this version as well it is in reality his relation to Brynhild that brings about his death. The importance attaching to the gold in the Northern story can therefore hardly be regarded as a very ancient trait of the Sigurd legend.

Another difference between the Northern legends and the German lies in the relation between Sigurd and Brynhild. The *Nibelungenlied* knows nothing of an earlier association of the two, while nearly all of the Northern versions mention, or at least presuppose, a betrothal between them before the marriage of Brynhild and Gunnar. Just how the *Poetic Edda* presented their first meeting we do not know definitely, since unfortunately there is at this point a considerable lacuna in the manuscript. From various hints in other poems that have been preserved it is nevertheless evident that Sigurd had known Brynhild before the time when he visited her in Gunnar's stead. And the *Vǫlsunga Saga*, which in great part is based on older poems, gives a circumstantial account of their meeting at the court of Heimir; this meeting must therefore have been described in some one of the lost poems. When, however, the *Vǫlsunga Saga* also gives an account of a still earlier meeting between them, in that it identifies Sigrdrifa with Brynhild, this circumstance must be due to a later duplication of the original single legend. For the story of Sigrdrifa forms a finished episode in the *Poetic Edda; Sigrdrifumál* has nothing to say of a betrothal, and none of the other poems so much as suggests the identity of the Valkyrie and Brynhild, with the solitary exception of the *Helreið Brynhildar;* but this poem is so confused and apparently of so late an origin that no great value can be attached to it. It is possible, however, that the entire story of the betrothal between Sigurd and Brynhild had no proper place in the legend as first formed, but that it was wholly Northern in origin; for the *Nibelungenlied* makes no reference to it, and for that matter it is not necessary to an understanding of the fate of the hero. In the Northern version Brynhild determines upon his death in desperation at learning that he of all men, her lover and the hero of heroes, had a part in the deception practised upon her; it is jealousy toward Gudrun and bitter hatred of Sigurd that impels her to the deed. In the *Nibelungenlied* the motive for Brynhild's revenge is a feeling of indignation at being

Heroic Legends

duped; and her resentment at the imposture is increased by the thought that it was the impostor Siegfried who had prevailed over her, more especially since she had held the most eminent hero alone worthy of her love. The disposition of the narrative elements in both the Northern and the German stories is satisfactory; and it is hardly possible to determine priority of origin as between the two.

The last great difference between the *Nibelungenlied* and the Northern story is to be found in the narrative of the fall of the Burgundians. In the German poem, Kriemhild exacts vengeance for her husband; in the Eddic poems it is her brothers she avenges by the killing of Atli. In this particular the Northern account probably has the priority. It has already been mentioned that the story of the fate of the Burgundians rests on historical reminiscences, namely the defeat of the Burgundians at the hands of the Huns in the year 437; here then the Eddic poems have best preserved the historical situation in representing Atli as the foe of the brothers, while the Etzel of the *Nibelungenlied* bears them no grudge and is drawn into the conflict against his will. Besides, the Northern story has an antique, authentically Germanic coloring. Gudrun is the loving wife and the grieving widow but also the faithful sister; despite the great wrong done to her by her brothers, she proves herself in the final test to be true to the most sacred relationship known to the ancient Germanic peoples, namely the mutual love of brothers and sisters, fidelity to family ties.

HADDING

HADDING is mentioned in various connections in the ancient legends. At first the name seems to have been used to designate an entire royal house or royal family. Thus we read in the genealogies of princes of the olden time that Hadding, son of Raum, king of Hadding-jadal (Hallingdal), had a son by the name of Hadding; his son in turn was called Hadding; his son again bore the name of Hogni the Red; and after him came three Haddings in succession: in the retinue of one of these appears Helgi Haddingjaskati.[1] It is not difficult to understand how the name *Haddingr* might come to be applied to a man of noble birth: *haddr* signifies "long and fair hair", and among several of the Germanic royal houses (particularly among the Franks) it was customary to permit the hair to grow long, while the commonalty wore the hair short. Concerning one of these Haddings Saxo tells the following story, which no doubt has a Norse origin:

King Gram of Denmark had been killed by the Norwegian king Svipdag, who thereupon brought both Denmark and Sweden under his sway. King Gram left two sons, Guttorm and Hadding; their foster father fled with the boys to Sweden, where he entrusted them to the care of the Giants Vagnhofdi and Haflidi. Guttorm afterward let himself be persuaded by Svipdag to become his vassal king in Denmark. Hadding meanwhile, under the care of Vagnhofdi and his daughter Hardgreip, had grown up to be a youth of

[1] See p. 164 f.

Heroic Legends

uncommon parts and skilled in the use of all manner
of weapons; refusing to listen to any overtures of peace,
he bent all his thoughts toward avenging his father.
Hardgreip, loving him, prayed him to become her
husband, and he yielded to her entreaties. When not
long afterward he set forth in search of adventure, she
went with him dressed as a man and kept watch over
his safety with the utmost zeal. One night they found
lodging in the house of a husbandman who had just
died and who was still lying there in his shroud. Hardgreip declared her intention of summoning the dead
man back to life for a space in order that he might foretell their future; she accordingly scratched magic runes
on a chip of wood and got Hadding to lay it beneath
the tongue of the corpse. The dead man, waking to
life, foretold that she who had dared to disturb his repose was to suffer the punishment of falling into the
power of unearthly beings. The next night they spent
in a leafy lodge which they had raised over their heads
in the midst of a forest. In the course of the night
they were awakened by an immense hand fumbling
about in the lodge. Hardgreip, who was able to make
herself large or small at will, summoned her entire
Giant strength, seized upon the hand, and held it fast
until Hadding succeeded in striking it off. From the
wound flowed forth a liquor more like venom than like
blood. Hardgreip, having in this way played the
traitor to her own kindred, was promptly punished in a
most pitiable manner by being torn limb from limb
by Giantesses.

Hadding now found himself alone. Presently he

met an old one-eyed man (Odin), who persuaded him
to enter into sworn brotherhood with the Viking Liser.
Hadding and Liser then joined forces in making war
against Loker, king of Kurland, but were defeated and
put to flight. Once more Hadding met the old man,
who placed him on his own horse, led him to his own
house, and there refreshed him with a strengthening
draught. He foretold that his guest would be taken
prisoner by Loker and be cast before a wild beast
which it was Loker's custom to permit to tear his cap-
tives asunder; yet if he would bravely grapple with the
beast he would be able to conquer and kill it; whereupon
he was to eat the heart of the beast and thus grow far
stronger than he was before; during the night the old
man would then cause a deep sleep to fall upon the
watchmen so that Hadding might make his escape un-
seen. He now set Hadding again upon the horse,
wrapped a cloak of his own about him, and led him
once more to the place where he had found him. In
the course of the journey Hadding, peering through
the folds of the cloak, saw with astonishment that the
horse was trotting over the surface of the sea.

All happened as the old man had foretold. Hadding
was taken prisoner by Loker and thrown before the
wild beast; but he slew it, ate its heart, and made his
escape. Afterward he undertook many expeditions
to the east. On one of these he fell in with Svipdag
near Gotland, attacked him, and killed him. He now
hurried to Denmark, where he ascended the throne as
Gram's heir. But Asmund, son of Svipdag, mustered
an army against Hadding for the purpose of avenging

his father's death. A fierce battle ensued between them. Asmund's son Henrik was the first to fall. Hereat Asmund became so enraged that he slung his shield on his back, rushed into the very midst of Hadding's ranks, and struck down men on every hand. Hadding now called upon his foster father Vagnhofdi for aid. On Vagnhofdi's coming promptly to his support, Hadding succeeded in thrusting Asmund through the body with a hooked spear; but in the struggle he himself received a wound in the foot that lamed him for the rest of his life. Asmund's body was burned at Uppsala; his wife Gunnhild killed herself and was laid with him on the pyre.

Asmund's son Uffi now came forward to take vengeance for the death of his father and gave Hadding no respite whatever. Hadding bore arms against his new enemy in warfare lasting through five full years, in the course of which his army suffered such hardship that at length they were constrained to slaughter and eat their own horses; finally they even resorted to the eating of human flesh. Defeated in one of these battles, Hadding was driven to seek refuge in Helsingland. During his sojourn there a wild beast one day attacked him as he was bathing at the seaside; he slew it, but while he was carrying the carcass back to the camp as booty, he met a woman on the way who told him that he had slain one of the gods, who had assumed the guise of the animal, and that therefore misfortune would dog his steps until he had done penance for his sacrilege. Even as she had foretold it came to pass. He set sail for home, but a storm scattered his ships. Wherever he sought shelter, destruction fell upon the house. At last he had no other recourse than to offer up a solemn sacrifice of black animals to Frey; not till then did the curse lose its force. Thus he became the first to offer such a sacrifice, called the "Sacrifice of Frey."

Some time later, rumor told that a hideous Giant was attempting to force himself into the favor of the fair Norwegian princess Ragnhild. Hadding determined to defeat that purpose. Hastening to Norway, he slew the Giant but was himself severely wounded in the fray. Ragnhild herself healed him; but in order to be able to recognize him later, she inserted a ring into one of the wounds on his foot before it had closed. Soon the time came for her to wed. From her father she received permission to make her choice among a number of youths, one of whom was Hadding; but before she made her choice she insisted on feeling of their feet. In this way she identified Hadding and chose him for her husband. During Hadding's sojourn at that place a remarkable adventure befell him. One day, as he was sitting at meat, a woman rose up through the floor with her arms full of green herbs. On Hadding's expressing a desire to learn where such green herbs were to be had in the dead of winter, she wrapped her cloak about him, and together they sank down to the nether world. After wandering for a while through dense mists they came to a sunny meadow where they found the herbs in full growth. Before long they came to a river in which all kinds of weapons were floating; a bridge spanned the stream. On the other side they saw two hosts in combat; these were warriors who had

Heroic Legends

fallen in battle and who now after death were continuing the heroic actions of life. Their farther progress
was stayed by an insurmountable wall. The woman,
when she found that she could not climb over the bar-
rier, wrung the head off a cock and threw his body over
the wall, whereupon he at once came to life and began
to crow. When Hadding had returned from this journey to the nether world, he went to Denmark, taking
his queen with him.

In the meantime Uffi had published a proclamation
that he would give his daughter in marriage to the man
who should kill Hadding. This promise tempted
Tuning, lord of Bjarmiland, to undertake the combat.
Hadding sailed forth to meet him. On the coast of
Norway, as he passed close by a headland, he saw an
old man standing there and making signs with his
cloak to indicate that he wished to be taken on board.
Hadding took him into the ship; and by way of recompense the old man taught him a novel method of dis-
posing troops for battle in the shape of a wedge. When
battle was joined, the old man drew his bow and with
it shot ten arrows at one time, each arrow bringing
down its man. The men of Bjarmiland, being
skilled in magic, raised a terrific shower of rain that
beat into the eyes of Hadding's soldiery; but the aged
man, who was none other than Nikar or Odin,[1] dis-
persed the storm, and Hadding won the victory. The
old man then went on his way, with the prophecy that
Hadding was not to fall at the hands of his enemies
but that he was to take his own life.

[1] See p. 172.

Hadding at length succeeded in defeating and slaying Uffi. He buried his enemy with great pomp beneath a cairn and made Uffi's brother Hunding a vassal king in Sweden, wishing through magnanimity to gain the good will of those whom he had conquered. For a long time he now lived in peace and quiet among the mountains in the house of his wife; but at last, having grown tired of inaction, he sang lays, like those which Njord sang to Skadi, expressing his weariness of the mountains and of the howling of the wolves. Ragnhild made her response, as did Skadi before her, declaring that the sea and the clamor of the gulls were no less distasteful to her. But soon the call of battle came to him once more. A lawless man named Tosti, who had made himself master of Jutland, began the conflict. Hadding suffered defeat but saved himself by flight in a boat after having bored holes in the other vessels lying along the shore. Tosti made an attempt to overtake him but was compelled to abandon the pursuit when water began pouring into his ship. He nevertheless got hold of another seaworthy ship, and soon was on the point of closing with Hadding; but Hadding had outdistanced his pursuer so far that he could safely overturn his own boat and save himself by swimming. Tosti, believing him to be drowned, put his vessel about. Meanwhile Hadding hastily summoned men to his aid; and while Tosti was busied with the booty, Hadding attacked him and put him to flight. Tosti fled to Bretland, made common cause with the Viking Kolli, and launched a new attack against Hadding, but was killed by him in single combat.

Heroic Legends

Not long thereafter Hadding's wife Ragnhild died; but after her death she appeared before him and warned him to beware of their daughter Ulfhild. Ulfhild was married to a man named Guttorm, and him she sought to induce to betray Hadding. Guttorm let himself be prevailed upon, and it was agreed that a retainer at a signal from him was to murder the king. Hadding, however, was warned anew in a dream, and in the nick of time the would-be traitor was struck down. Meanwhile the rumor had spread abroad that Hadding had been killed, and so Hunding in Sweden made ready a great funeral feast in his honor. A large quantity of mead was brewed and poured into a huge vat. As Hunding was about to see that all was as it should be, he stumbled into the vat and was drowned. When the news reached Hadding, he could think of only one fitting means of returning the honor Hunding had meant to show him; Hadding accordingly hanged himself in the sight of all the people.

FRODI THE PEACEFUL AND HIS MILL

KING FRODI of Denmark was the son of Fridleif, who in turn was the son of Odin's son Skjold. During his minority the land was governed by twelve men of rank, with the brothers Koll and Vestmar at their head, but so badly governed that it sank into the utmost misery. The evil wife of Koll, Gautvor, abetted by his sons and Vestmar's sons, disturbed the peace of men's homes and of the court itself. Frodi was kept in a state of nonage; his own wife was tempted to unfaithfulness by Vestmar's son Greip, who at the same time had the hardihood to pay court to the king's sister Gunnvor. Two brothers, Erik and Roll (Roller, Saxo's *Rollerus*) from Rennesey in Ryfylke, learning how badly things stood in Denmark, sought to use the occasion to gain power in the land. Sailing to Denmark in three ships, they first of all slew Odd, the captain of Frodi's fleet. Then Erik landed from one of the ships on the coast of Zealand, intending to spy upon Frodi's court, and advanced inland with his brother Roll. Greip rode out to meet him and, as was his habit, overwhelmed him with terms of abuse; but Erik, being a wise man, gave him meet answer. When Greip realized that he was being worsted in the combat of words, he hastened home and erected a spite pole against Erik in order to keep him away. The pole, which was to be erected near a bridge, was surmounted by a horse's head. Erik, however, before leaving Norway had eaten of a magical dish, prepared by his stepmother Kraka, compounded of the venom of serpents; by this means he had become so sagacious as even to understand the language of beasts. Thus it was easy for him to conjure away the effect of Greip's witchcraft. He caused the horse's head to fall from the pole in such a manner as to bring about the death of the man who was carrying the pole. Erik now proceeded on his journey, even to the very court of Frodi, where he was received with all kinds of gross ribaldry, hootings, clamor, and insult; but he pretended to notice nothing at all. With him he carried a lump of ice, which he declared to be a present for the king; every

one supposed that it was a precious stone. He handed
his gift across the fire to Koll; but as the king's man
was about to take it, Erik craftily let it fall and then
maintained that Koll had been careless enough to allow
the gift to be lost in the flames. By way of punishment for his mistake, Koll was hanged. In ambigu-
ous terms Erik now told the king all that had befallen
him on the journey and ended his story by revealing
the secret understanding between Greip and the queen.
The queen confessed and begged for mercy. Greip
attempted to thrust Erik through the body; Roll,
however, anticipating his intent, killed Greip, who thus
came to the end his evil deeds deserved. Greip's
brothers challenged Erik to single combat, but by the
aid of trickery he succeeded in killing them all; their
mother Gautvor he defeated in a duel of words; and
finally he laid Vestmar himself low in a wrestling
match. When Erik through guile had induced Frodi
to promise his sister's hand in marriage, Frodi came to
the conclusion that matters were going too far, and so
Erik found that there was nothing for him to do but to
seek safety in flight; in advance, meanwhile, he had
loosened certain planks in Frodi's ships. As the
king set out in pursuit, his ships filled and sank; but
Erik promptly came to the rescue and pulled him out
of the water. Frodi at first felt so humbled by his
misfortune and disgrace that he begged Erik to take
his life; but Erik heartened him and, promising to devote all his wisdom to the service of the king, returned
with him to the court. There Erik wedded Gunnvor,
and Roll wedded the queen whom the king had put

away. Erik became the king's earl, cleansed the court of evil hangers-on, and restored order throughout the land. From this time forth, good fortune befell Frodi in all his undertakings: he became rich, mighty, and famous; he conquered the Slavs, the Russians, the Huns, the Britons, and the Irish, and subjugated the better part of Norway and Sweden. Advised by Erik, he made many excellent laws and saw that they were strictly enforced; above all, he rendered property inviolate, so that no man dared steal from another: on the heath of Jællinge in Jutland and on Frodi's Hill near Tunsberg hung gold rings that no one ventured to lay hands upon. Being sated with strife, he proclaimed universal peace throughout his far-flung empire. This armistice, called the peace of Frodi, endured for thirty years. Our forefathers, who gave full credence to these legends, associated the Peace of Frodi with the Roman Peace of Augustus, and regarded it as a mark of divine providence that tranquillity thus reigned both in the North and in the South at the birth of Christ.

Frodi was a good friend of king Fjolnir in Uppsala, the son of Frey. Once Frodi came as his friend's guest to a great banquet, where he bought two tall and strong bondwomen of Giant race, named Fenja and Menja; these he carried back with him to Denmark. Some time later Fjolnir visited Frodi and was received with the most lavish hospitality; but one night Fjolnir drank too much, fell into a huge tun of mead, and so met his death. Frodi set his bondwomen to grinding at a mill that had been given to him by a man named Hengikjopt. The millstones were so heavy that no man in Denmark had the strength to turn them; but they had the capability of producing anything that might be required of them. Fenja and Menja alone were able to turn Grotti, for so the mill was called; they were therefore assigned the task of grinding out for the king gold, peace, and fair fortune. He allowed them to rest only so long as it took them to sing a song. When they had ground for a while, they sang the so-called Grotti Song, which still is preserved: in it they voiced the wish that Frodi might be set upon and killed. And their wish was fulfilled. That selfsame night appeared the sea-king Mysing; he fell upon Frodi, killed him, and so put an end to the Peace of Frodi. Mysing carried off with him Grotti and the two sisters. He at once put them to work at grinding salt, and they ground till the ships sank in Pentland Firth; ever since that time there has been a maelstrom where the sea rushes in and out through the hole in the millstone.

HELGI AND ROLF KRAKI

THE Danish king Halfdan, son of Frodi the Brave, lost his life at the hands of his brother, an ambitious man also named Frodi. The slain man left three children, a daughter Signy, eldest of the three, and the sons Helgi and Roar. Signy was already the wife of an earl named Sævil; Helgi and Roar, being still small boys, were by their foster father Regin given in charge of an old man named Vivil, who had his dwelling on an island. Frod sought to find out, by questioning witches and wizards, where the boys might be, but in vain. At last he was advised to search Vivil's island; he did so, but could not find the boys, Vivil having given them instructions that when he called his dogs Hopp and Ho they were to hide themselves deep in an earth house he had made. Afterward, not daring to keep them longer, Vivil sent them in disguise to Earl Sævil; there they were put to work as shepherds. Not even Signy recognized them until one day, as she and her husband rode to a banquet at the palace and the two shepherd boys followed in their retinue, it so happened that Roar's cap fell off and she knew him by his fair hair. At the banquet the brothers succeeded by Earl Sævil's aid in burning the house down over Frodi's head, whereupon they took the rule into their own hands. Roar won for himself a kingdom in Northumberland, and governed there; Helgi ruled over Denmark, but spent most of his time in warlike forays. Earl Sævil and Signy had a wicked son named Rok, who after the death of his father laid claim not only to his patrimony but also to an heirloom of the family, a ring which now belonged to Roar. Rok made a journey to Northumberland and was kindly received by Roar. Once when the two were out together in a boat, Rok asked for the ring. Roar refused to give it up but allowed Rok to look at it, who, when he got hold of it, threw it far out into the sea. To punish him Roar caused his foot to be cut off; but Rok soon recovered from his wound, summoned men from his own earldom, fell upon Roar, and killed him. Rok meant to compel Ogn, Roar's wife, to marry himself, but

instead she sent messengers to Helgi to ask for aid.
He was at once ready to avenge his brother; attacking Rok, he took him captive and caused his arms and legs to be broken asunder. Ogn gave birth to a son named Agnar. Before he was twelve years of age he was able to dive down and fetch up the ring; many had tried to do so by all manner of devices, but without success.

On one of his Viking forays Helgi came to the land of the Saxons. The queen of the land bore the name Olof. He thought so well of her that without delay he began paying court to her, but she rewarded him with nothing but scorn. In revenge he later led his forces against her, took her prisoner, and kept her by him for a time; in due course she gave birth to a daughter who was given the name Yrsa. On a subsequent foray Helgi happened to meet Yrsa, not knowing that she was his own daughter; he took her to wife, and she bore him a son, who was named Rolf. Better revenge than this queen Olof could not desire, and after some years she revealed the true relationship. Yrsa now returned to her mother and was later married to king Adils in Uppsala. On learning the news Helgi journeyed to Uppsala for the purpose of carrying Yrsa away. Wishing to bring about a reconciliation between the two kings, she made a great banquet for Helgi; but Adils treacherously mustered an army in secret with which he attacked Helgi. After a brave defense Helgi was overpowered and killed.

Rolf, the son of Helgi and Yrsa, became king after

his father; he was an illustrious man, who gained signal renown in warfare and who assembled at his court in Leire the most celebrated warriors of the North. Helgi also left a daughter, Skuld, whom he had by an elfin woman; Skuld, who was by nature wicked and deceitful, wedded Hjorvard, one of Rolf's under-kings. Among Rolf's champions one of the most doughty was the Norwegian Bodvar Bjarki, who ever and anon took on the likeness of a bear. Another was Hjalti, who at first bore the name Hott, and who was a wretched being, the sport and butt of the other retainers until Bjarki took him in charge and got him to drink the blood of a ravening beast; thereafter he became a champion of champions and won the name of Hjalti the Proud. Still another of Rolf's men was Vogg. As a poor little boy he had come into the hall and stood staring at the king; on Rolf's asking what he was looking at, he answered that rumor had spoken falsehood in declaring that Rolf was so large a man, since he was in reality nothing but a *kraki* (a twisted sapling, a wretch). Rolf adopted the nickname Kraki and gave Vogg a gold ring. Vogg promised in return to kill any man who should slay Rolf, to which the king said with a laugh, "Vogg is pleased with very little." Rolf lived on the best of terms with his stepfather Adils; he lent certain of his own champions for a battle Adils fought on the ice of Lake Vänaren with the Norwegian king Ali the Uplander. Adils won the battle, and according to promise was to give Rolf by way of reward three of his most highly prized possessions, the helmet Hildegalt, the byrnie Finnsleif, and

Heroic Legends

the ring Sviagris; but he broke his promise, and Rolf, unwilling to let himself be cheated, went to Uppsala with twelve of his men to compel Adils to deliver up the treasures. Adils, receiving the visitor with seeming kindness, yet tried guilefully to take his life; he caused so much wood to be laid on the fire in the hall where Rolf and his men were sitting that their clothes were singed from their backs, and then he asked Rolf if it were true that he and his champions fled neither fire nor iron. Rolf replied:

"Let us mend the fire
On Adils' hearth;
He fears no fire
Who leaps over flames."

With these words he and his men threw their shields on the fire, sprang over it, each seized one of Adils' men, and hurled them into the flames. This done, they stormed out through the door; Yrsa in all haste gave Rolf a horn filled with gold, and Sviagris besides, and then he and his men rushed away over the Plains of Fyri. Adils at once took up the pursuit with a mighty host. Rolf, in imminent danger of being overtaken, saved himself by strewing the gold along the road and thus delayed the Swedes, who could not refrain from gathering it up. Adils nevertheless was on the point of closing in on Rolf. Rolf now threw Sviagris on the ground; Adils halted, stooped down, and picked up the ring on his spear. Rolf said, "Now I have made the first of the Swedes bow down like a swine!" With these words they parted.

After this inroad Rolf and his champions remained

for a long time quietly at home. But his downfall was near at hand. His wicked sister Skuld egged her husband Hjorvard on to rebellion against his over-king and kinsman, and Hjorvard at length fell in with her purposes. Having begged Rolf for permission to defer the payment of tribute for the space of three years, they used the money during this time to gather a large number of retainers in secret. Thereupon they advanced with a huge army against Leire and pitched their tents outside the walls of the stronghold. It was the Yuletide, and the thoughts of Rolf and his men were bent on naught but gayety and festival. The only man who surmised evil was Hjalti. Noticing that Hjorvard had in his train a suspicious number of men clad in byrnies, he made haste to warn the king. Rolf and his Berserks sprang to their feet, drank together for the last time, and sallied out to meet the enemy. Bodvar Bjarki alone was missing; but an immense bear kept close to the king's heels in the battle and crushed down all that came in his path. Hjalti at last found Bodvar and goaded him into taking part in the combat. The bear disappeared—it was Bodvar who had been fighting in the likeness of a bear—and from that time the greater loss of men fell on Rolf's side. Skuld, cunning in witchcraft, cast her magic arts into the balance, and finally Rolf and the eleven champions were laid low. Vogg alone survived. Saxo tells how Vogg kept his promise to kill the slayer of the king. Hjorvard desired the champion to enter his service, and Vogg was willing to do so; but as the king, intending to show him honor at a banquet, gave into his hand a drawn sword, Vogg thrust the giver through with it, and himself fell at the hands of Hjorvard's men.

STARKAD THE OLD

NEXT after Sigurd Fafnirsbane, the greatest champion of the heroic legends is Starkad,[1] to whom are attributed many supernatural qualities and deeds of prowess. His father's father is said also to have borne the name Starkad, with the surname of Aludreng; he lived at Alufoss (*Aluforsar*, Ulefoss), he owed his descent to Giants, he had eight arms, and he was capable of wielding four swords at one and the same time. The betrothed of the elder Starkad was named Ogn Alfisprengi; but once while Starkad was making a journey to the north across the Elivagar, she was carried off by Hergrim Sea-Troll. Hergrim's and Ogn's son was Grim, father of that Arngrim of Bolm [2] from whom Angantyr and Hervor were in their turn descended. On Starkad's return from his journey he challenged Hergrim to single combat and killed him; Ogn took her own life. Afterward Starkad carried off the fair Alfhild, daughter of king Alf of Alfheim; with her he had a daughter, Baugheid, who became the wife of Grim Hergrimsson. King Alf called upon the god Thor to restore Alfhild. Thor killed Starkad and brought Alfhild back to her father's house. Not long thereafter she gave birth to a son named Storvirk, a handsome, dark-haired child, uncommonly large and

[1] This is the correct form (see the note), not "Stærkodder".
[2] P. 131

strong. As the years passed he became a great Viking and was admitted as a member of the bodyguard of the mighty king Harold of Agder. Harold made him a leader of the yoemanry and gave him in fee the beautiful island of Thruma or Tromey off the coasts of Agder. There Storvirk made his abode, and thence he undertook great Viking forays. On one of these expeditions he carried off the daughter of an earl of Halogaland, whom he wedded and with whom he had a son named Starkad, the younger Starkad concerning whom the following legends have been handed down. The earl's sons took their revenge by burning the house down over the heads of Storvirk and all his household. Starkad himself, who was still a small boy, escaped with his life and was put under the care of king Harold as a member of his retinue. Harold had a son named Vikar, who was a little older than Starkad.

At this time there ruled in Hordaland a mighty king named Herthjof, a son of the famous Fridthjof the Brave and Ingeborg the Fair. Herthjof found occasion to attack king Harold, killed him, and subjugated his kingdom, but carried Vikar and the sons of the foremost men of the realm away as hostages. Among Herthjof's men was one named Grani, also called Horsehair-Grani, who lived on the estate of Ask on the island of Fenring (Askey); this man seized Starkad as a prisoner of war and took the boy to his home, Starkad being at the time only three years of age. With Horsehair-Grani he remained nine years, during which period he grew tall and strong as a giant but spent all his time lying among the ashes of the hearth, doing

Heroic Legends

nothing whatsoever. King Herthjof occupied himself for the most part in warlike expeditions, as a result of which his own realm was often harried in turn; in order to prevent these inroads he built beacons on the mountains and appointed Vikar to take charge of them in Fenring. Vikar made use of the opportunity to visit Starkad, raised him up out of the ashes, provided him with weapons and clothing, and agreed with him upon a means of taking vengeance on Herthjof. Getting hold of a ship, Vikar induced certain champions to become his followers; thirteen in number all told they fell upon Herthjof, who defended himself in a fortified fastness but at last was made to bite the dust. Vikar now took the rule of Herthjof's realm into his own hand, seized his ships, sailed away to his own hereditary domains of Agder and Jæren and was hailed there as king. Thus he gained suzerainty over all of southern Norway. Afterward he did many mighty deeds, and Starkad turned out to be one of the greatest champions in his army. Vikar won a marked victory at Vänaren over a king named Sisar, who fell before the prowess of Starkad; next he conquered Herthjof's brother Geirthjof, king of the Uplands, and Fridthjof, king of Telemark, and placed their kingdoms in vassalage to himself. King Vikar gave Starkad a gift of a gold ring weighing three marks. Starkad in his turn gave Vikar the island of Thruma. Starkad remained fifteen summers with Vikar.

It once happened that Vikar, sailing from Agder to Hordaland, was forced to seek shelter against high winds between certain islands. He and his men besought the gods in the usual way by means of the so-called sacrificial chips, and the answer came to them that Odin might be appeased through the sacrifice of a man from the army, whom they were to choose by lot and to hang. The lot falling on Vikar, they were all so terrified that they determined to do nothing until the next day. In the middle of the night Horsehair-Grani came to his foster son Starkad, awakened him, and bade that he go with him. Rowing across to another wooded island, they went ashore and passed into the forest to a clearing where a large number of people were met in assembly; eleven men were sitting each on his chair, the twelfth chair being vacant. On it Horsehair-Grani seated himself and was hailed as Odin by all those assembled there. So it turned out to be Odin who all this time had fostered Starkad and borne him company; the eleven others were the eleven chief deities. Odin bade them sit in judgment on the fate of Starkad. Thor at once spoke, saying: "His father's mother Alfhild chose a Giant as the father of her son instead of Asa-Thor; therefore Starkad shall have neither son nor daughter, and his race shall die with him." "In lieu thereof he shall live thrice as long as other men," said Odin. "In each of those spans of life he shall do the deed of a dastard," said Thor. "He shall possess the best of weapons and armor," declared Odin. "He shall possess neither grounds nor lands," rejoined Thor. "He shall have abundance of other possessions," said Odin. "He shall never think he possesses enough," replied Thor. "I shall make him victorious and ever ready for bat-

Heroic Legends

tle," said Odin. "In every combat he shall receive terrible wounds," answered Thor. "I shall dower him with poetic gifts so that lays shall flow from his lips as easily as the words of common speech," said Odin. "He shall not be able to recall the poems he has made," said Thor. "The bravest and best men shall hold him in honor," said Odin. "But all the common people shall hate him," said Thor. All these sayings the judges confirmed in passing judgment, and the assembly came to an end. It is not certain whether Starkad had most cause to grieve or to rejoice at what had been granted to him. Odin, or Horsehair-Grani, and Starkad again rowed across to the island. "Now you must repay me for the aid I have given you," said Horsehair-Grani; "you must despatch Vikar to me, and I will help you to do the deed." Starkad promised to carry out the command and Odin gave into his hand a spear which, he said, would have the outward semblance of a reed; moreover he taught him the proper mode of going about the task. The next day the king's counselors came to an agreement that they should offer up a mock sacrifice. Starkad told them how they were to proceed. Near at hand stood a fir tree; beneath it there was a tall stump, and far down on the fir there hung a slender branch. Starkad mounted onto the stump, bent the branch downward, and fastened to it the entrails of a newly slaughtered calf. "Now the gallows are ready for you, O king," said Starkad, "and it does not look very perilous." Vikar, who thought as much, ascended the stump, and Starkad laid the noose about his neck. Starkad then stepped down, thrust at the king with the reed, and quit his hold of the branch with the words, "Now I give you to Odin." The reed instantly turned into a spear that pierced the king's body, the stump toppled to earth, the entrails became a stout rope, the branch sprang upward lifting the king high in the air, and thus he lost his life. This was Starkad's first dastard's deed, which made him so hated of the commonalty that he had to flee from Hordaland. Deeply grieved at his own treachery, he fared to Uppsala, entered the service of the Yngling kings Alrek and Erik, and followed them to the wars. He grew moody and silent, and was compelled to listen to frequent reproaches from the twelve Berserks who served in the king's bodyguard.

When Alrek and Erik gave over their warfare, Starkad went out to do battle on his own account in the ship that Alrek had given him, manned with Norwegians and Swedes. He encountered many adventures. On one occasion he made common cause with the Norwegian Viking king Haki, who attacked king Hugleik in Uppsala, grandson of king Alrek, and won from him the whole realm of Uppsala. In Hugleik's armies there were two mighty champions, Svipdag and Geigad; Geigad bore hard upon Starkad and gave him a blow on the head from which he was never wholly healed. While Haki ruled peacefully over his realm in Uppsala, Starkad set forth on other Viking forays; he gained victories in Kurland and Samland, slew the Muscovy Berserk Visin (*Wisinnus* in Saxo), and afterward two other eastern champions, Tanni and Vasi. At length he suffered shipwreck on the coasts of Den-

Heroic Legends

mark and so lost all his men. Alone he came to the court of king Frodi the Brave, was well received there, and entered into the service of the king. As a warrior among the hosts of Frodi, Starkad took part in a memorable victory over the Saxons, who had undertaken to free themselves from the overlordship of Denmark; he joined battle with the greatest champion among the Saxons, Hami by name, and killed him but was himself also on this occasion badly wounded. Frodi was at length treacherously slain by Sverting, king of the Germans; his son Ingjald (Ingellus), Starkad's foster son, became king in his stead. Ingjald gave himself up to all manner of effeminate and luxurious practices and neglected the pursuit of warfare; in consequence he was despised and hated, and Starkad found service at his court so insufferable that he sought a place in the retinue of the Swedish king Halfdan. But when Starkad was gone, matters went from bad to worse; Ingjald so far forgot himself as to wed the daughter of Sverting and to permit a goldsmith to pay court to his own sister Helga. Starkad, on learning of these things, hastened back to Denmark with the purpose of bringing the wastrel king to his senses and of restoring his fallen repute. He went in disguise to the goldsmith's house, where the king's daughter happened to be at the time; and, seeing with his own eyes what liberties the suitor was taking with her, he drove the man away in disgrace. Thinking that he had done enough for the nonce, he returned to Sweden. Helga took a higher view of her own position and soon found a worthier suitor in the person of a Norwegian prince named Helgi, who had come in a splendidly fitted ship to ask her hand. Ingjald had nothing against their troth, demanding only that Helgi should make proof of his prowess by meeting in combat any rival suitor who might challenge him. At the spousal ale a challenge came from the doughty Angantyr, who for some time past had courted her in vain. Helgi took up the challenge and even offered to fight Angantyr and his eight brothers at one and the same time; but this promise was so daring that on the counsel of his betrothed he journeyed to Sweden to seek the aid of Starkad. Starkad gave willing consent and, asking Helgi to return to Denmark, he promised to follow in due season. Helgi set out on his journey, for which he used twelve days; Starkad started on the twelfth day, and yet he and Helgi passed together through the gates to Ingjald's court.

As the bridal ale was being drunk in the palace, Angantyr and his brothers heaped insult and contempt on the aged Starkad. When Helgi and Helga went to bed, Starkad stood guard outside their bower door. On the following morning the combat was to take place. Helgi wakened early, rose and dressed himself; but since daylight was not yet fully come, he lay down on the bed and fell asleep again. As the day dawned Starkad came in but did not have the heart to rouse Helgi; so he went off alone to meet the champions. He sat down on the slope of a hill facing the wind and took off his clothes for the purpose of hunting fleas, though both snow and hail were falling. Soon the nine brothers came up from behind and found Starkad snowed under up to his neck. He sprang to his feet, and when they asked him whether he chose to fight them singly or all together, he declared he would meet them all at once. The battle began, and he was soon able to do away with six of his enemies; but the other three he found it hard to defeat. At last he killed them all; but he had himself received seventeen dangerous wounds, and his entrails were hanging from a gash in his body. His strength failing, he crept to a stone and leaned against it to rest; long afterward men pointed out the impress of his body on the surface of the rock. Several people passed the spot and offered to give him aid, but he turned them all away; for one was a king's bailiff who lived on the sorrows of other men, another had wedded a bondwoman and was in the service of her master for the purpose of redeeming her, and the third was herself a bondwoman who should have been at home caring for her child: all of these he held in such contempt that he would have nothing to do with them. At length a peasant came driving by in a cart; from this man he accepted aid, allowing him to bind up the wounds with willow withes. The peasant carried Starkad in his cart to Ingjald's court. There Starkad went inside and made an uproar at the door of Helgi's bridal chamber. Helgi in the meantime having learned what sort of reception Starkad would like, rushed upon him and struck him a blow in the forehead. In this way Starkad was assured that Helgi was not afraid to risk his life in combat and that Helga might safely be left in his keeping.

Starkad now returned to Sweden; but rumors of

Ingjald's effeminacy brought him once more back to Denmark. He came in disguise to Ingjald's court bearing a large sack of coals on his back, and took a seat at the foot of the table. The German queen, Sverting's daughter, met him with the utmost contempt; but Ingjald, soon afterward returning home, at once recognized his foster father, and thereafter both he and the queen sought to make amends for her earlier insolence. But their efforts were of no avail. The luxuries of the table, the many alien customs, and the newfangled modes of living put Starkad in a great rage; he poured out his feelings in violent punitive lays, and at length egged Ingjald to such a pitch that he fell upon Sverting's sons and killed them. In the warmest and most vigorous terms Starkad commended his deed to the favor of fortune.

Starkad has also been associated with a certain king Ragnvald (*Regnaldus*), among whose warriors he took part in a great battle in Zealand, from which for the first time of his life he sought safety in flight. But Starkad is known in chief and above all as a retainer of the famous Viking king Haki.

Haki's brother Hagbard, who also was an eminent king of Vikings, came on one of his expeditions to the court of king Sigar in Zealand and there fell in love with Sigar's beautiful daughter Signy. She loved him in turn; but an enmity that arose between him and her brothers made it impossible for him to pay court to her openly. In the garb of a woman he accordingly gained entrance to her bower; and Signy, who knew her father's mind toward her lover, gave him the solemn

promise that she would not survive him if death should
be his portion. Hagbard being betrayed by a serving
maid, Sigar's men came upon him and in spite of his
brave resistance took him captive. Hagbard was
haled before the assembly and doomed to hang. When
Signy learned what was in store for him, she determined to set fire to her bower and burn it down over
the heads of herself and her maidservants, all of
whom offered to go to their death with her. Hagbard,
seeing his end draw near, craved assurance of her faith.
He therefore begged the hangman first to hang his
cloak up on the gallows. Those who were looking on
from afar thought it was Hagbard himself, and so
Signy kindled the fire in her house. When Hagbard
saw the flames rising from Signy's chamber, he burst
into pæans of praise for her constancy; soon he should
be united with her, and he longed for death. So he
ended his life. His brother Haki, intent on avenging
his death, set sail with a fleet of ships; but Starkad,
who had enjoyed the hospitality of king Sigar, would
not go with him. For this reason Haki did not have
the best of luck. He won a victory indeed and slew
Sigar; but Sigar's son Sigvaldi drove him out of the
island and destroyed a part of the army which he had
left behind. Haki was afterward attacked at Uppsala
by Jorund, king Hugleik's kinsman, and slain in battle.

Finally, Starkad is associated with the Norwegian
king Ali the Bold, an ally of the mighty Sigurd Ring.
Sigurd Ring was an under-king in Sweden subject to
his father's brother, the Dane Harold Hilditonn.
When Harold had become old and blind, it came to

his mind that he would rather die in battle than on a bed of sickness; he therefore sent a messenger to Sigurd Ring asking him to muster a strong force from the whole of his kingdom, Harold on his part undertaking to summon a force of his own, whereupon the two were to do battle against each other. There followed seven years of preparation for warfare. At the end of that time the two armies met at Bravalla in Östergötland; there the combat took place, doubtless the most famous battle in all the legendary history of the North. Harold Hilditonn had men from Denmark, Saxony, and the Slavic countries; Sigurd, from Sweden and Norway. Among Sigurd's warriors were Ali the Bold, Starkad, and many other champions. In Harold's army Ubbi the Frisian, the shield-maiden Vebjorg, and Haki fought most fiercely. Ubbi killed sixteen common soldiers and six champions before he fell pierced by the Telemark archers. Vebjorg, encountering Starkad, shore through his chin so that it hung down and he was able to hold it up only by biting his beard. She was later killed by Thorkel Thra. Starkad brought to earth many Danish champions and cut off the hand of the shield-maiden Visma, who bore Harold's standard. Afterward he engaged Haki, whom he found a hard nut to crack; he killed his enemy indeed, but in the combat he himself received grievous wounds, one in his throat through which a man might look into his body, one in the chest so that a lung hung from the gash, and one that shore off a finger. King Harold Hilditonn himself, sitting in his chariot of war, fought valiantly in spite of his

Heroic Legends

blindness; at last he fell beneath the stroke of a mace in the hands of his own servant Bruni, who was supposed to be Odin himself in disguise. The Danes then fled, and Sigurd Ring remained master of the field. Denmark he put under his own sway; Zealand and Fyn came beneath the rule of Ali the Bold. Some while later Sigurd Ring engaged in warfare against the Gjukungs, Sigurd Fafnirsbane being at the time still alive. Sigurd Ring sent against them his brothers-in-law, the sons of Gandalf of Alfheim, he himself being occupied in a campaign against Kurland and Kvænland. Starkad was a warrior in the army, and in the battle that now took place he encountered Sigurd Fafnirsbane in person. In him, however, Starkad found his master. Sigurd put him to flight, after striking him in the mouth so that two of his teeth were loosened.

Starkad continued to sojourn with Ali the Bold until the severe judgment passed upon him by Thor brought him new misfortunes. Twelve Danish chiefs conspired against the life of Ali and persuaded Starkad for 120 gold marks to murder the king. He came upon the king in his bath; at first he fell back before the sharp eyes of Ali, which no man had hitherto been able to endure; but Ali felt that his time had come and therefore, covering his eyes with his hands, made Starkad's task easier for him. Starkad thrust him through the body and so accomplished his third dastard's deed.[1] But being at once seized with remorse

---

[1] The first dastard's deed was the slaying of Vikar; of the second tradition has no record.

for his act, in his wrath he killed several of those who had misled him. Bent with sorrow he then wandered through the world with the money, the price of his treachery, bound about his neck; with his gains he meant to pay some one or other to wreak vengeance upon him. He was so old and feeble that he walked by the aid of two crutches, and yet he bore two swords at his side. At last he met with a young man of high lineage named Hader, whom he persuaded by means of gold and eloquent speech to sever his head from his shoulders. Starkad said that if the youth found it possible to jump between the head and the trunk before the body sank to the ground, he should thereafter be invulnerable. Here his old-time malice, the unhappy gift of Thor, expressed itself again. Hader promptly hewed off his head but did not attempt the leap, knowing very well that if he tried he should be crushed beneath the weight of Starkad's gigantic body. So fierce a champion was Starkad that his head, even after being severed from the trunk, bit at the grass.

Starkad sang his own praises in many a lay, and in this respect he had better fortune than Thor's judgment allowed him. Though he forgot his own lays, others remembered them; and thus it came about that the men of antiquity knew most of his songs, notably his ballad of the Battle of Bravalla.

Heroic Legends

ORVAR-ODD

ORVAR-ODD has been mentioned before, in the discussion of the legends of Tyrfing.[1] His father's father, Ketil Hæng (i. e.,"milt salmon"), was a son of Hallbjorn Sea-Troll and a grandson of Ulf Uarge. Ketil grew to man's estate on his father's farm on the island of Rafnista (now Ramsta) in Naumdølafylke. As a lad he was little liked by his father; he lay continually by the hearth, poking the fire and doing nothing useful. At length he gained his father's respect by a successful combat with a dragon and by other deeds of prowess. On an expedition to Finmark he killed the king of the Finns, Gusi, and got possession of his three arrows, which had the virtue of always hitting the mark and of returning of their own accord to the hand that sent them forth. These arrows later passed from father to son in that family. His son Grim Loddinkinn lived at Rafnista after his father and likewise did many wonderful deeds. He was wedded to Lopthœna, a daughter of the chief, Harold of Viken. Their son Odd was born on the farm Berrjod in Jæren, where his parents had gone ashore on a voyage to Viken. At Berrjod Odd remained under the care of his father's friend Ingjald together with Ingjald's son Asmund, who became his best friend. At an early age Odd was an expert bowman. A prophetess once foretold that his foster father's horse, Faxi, was to bring about his death after the space of three hundred years. To make the prophecy void, Odd killed the horse and buried it in a valley near

[1] P. 130 ff.

Berrjod.   Some time later he went with Asmund home
to his father's house and got from his father the arrows
of Gusi; the great feats he performed with them earned
him the name of Orvar-Odd (Arrow-Odd).   Odd
now traveled far and wide in search of adventure.   In
Bjarmiland he and his companions took a mass of silver
from a burial mound, but were hard pressed when the
men of the land came over them with superior numbers.
They were nevertheless saved by the valor of Odd, who
with his mace made great havoc among the hostile
ranks.   After many combats with Giants and Vikings
he at length came into conflict in Sweden with the Viking Hjalmar the Proud; the struggle ended with their
becoming sworn brothers, whereupon they stood by
each other loyally in many battles.   The most remarkable of these was the battle of Samsey against the
sons of Arngrim,[1] where Hjalmar fell.   Odd here killed
eleven of the brothers with his mace.   He had already
lost his friend Asmund on an earlier expedition to Ire-
land.   Odd avenged his death upon the Irish and prepared to carry the king's daughter Olvor off by force.
But she persuaded him to absent himself for a year; in
return she was to give him a shirt that iron would not
sunder, and that would afford protection against fire,
hunger, and other evils.   A year later Odd came back
again, received the shirt, and took the king's daughter
to wife for the space of three years; they got a daughter
whom they named Ragnhild.   After Hjalmar's death
Odd journeyed far and wide to the west and to the
south and far east into Russia as well.   In the south he

[1] See p. 131 ff.

allowed himself to be baptized and afterward wedded
the princess Silkesif, to whose father he had lent aid.
When he had grown old, he longed to see his father's
estate once more, and so sailed with two ships to Rafnista, where his daughter Ragnhild's son was then
living. On the return voyage he went ashore at Berrjod to visit his foster father's estate. There he came
across an old skull of a horse. "Surely, that cannot be
Faxi's skull!" said Odd, striking it with his sword.
At that a serpent crept out and stung him to death.
And thus the sibyl's prophecy was fulfilled.

NORNA-GEST

In the third year of the reign of Olaf Tryggvason a man
came into the presence of the king and asked to be
admitted to his bodyguard. He was uncommonly
tall and strong and somewhat stricken in years. He
said that his name was Gest and that he was the son of
a Danish man named Thord of Thinghusbit, who once
dwelt on the estate of Grøning in Denmark. Though
he had not been baptized but only signed with the
cross, the king gave him a seat among the guests.
One day king Olaf was presented with a costly ring
by one of his men; all the retinue admired it greatly,
with the exception of Gest, who let it be understood
that he had seen better gold before. What he said
proved to be true; for he produced a piece of what was
once a buckle of a saddle, and all those who saw it had
to admit that the gold in it was of superior quality.
On the king's asking him to tell how he got hold of the

ornament, Gest recounted many of the adventures he had passed through. He related how he had fared to the court of king Hjalprek in Frankland and there had entered the service of Sigurd Fafnirsbane; furthermore, how he had followed Sigurd in battles against the sons of Hunding [1] and against the sons of Gandalf.[2] The piece of ring Sigurd had given him once when Grani's chest harness had broken. After the death of Sigurd he had for some time attended the sons of Ragnar Lodbrok as they were about to set forth for Rome. Later he had sojourned with king Erik of Uppsala and with king Harold Fairhair. It was at the court of king Lodvi of Saxony that he had been signed with the cross. Finally he told how he had come by the name of Norna-Gest. While he still lay in the cradle, three wise women or Norns had come to his father's estate at Grøning and had foretold the child's destiny. The youngest of the Norns, deeming that the two others made rather light of her, determined to render void their promises of good fortune for the child; so she prophesied that his life was to last no longer than that of a candle standing lit beside the cradle. The eldest Norn at once quenched the candle and bade the mother hide it well. When Gest was grown to manhood, he got the candle in his own keeping; and now he showed it to the king. Gest afterward permitted himself, at the king's desire, to be baptized. When he had come to be three hundred years of age, the king asked him how much longer he wished to live. "Only

[1] See p. 171.
[2] See p. 233.

a short time," answered Gest. He then lighted his candle and made ready for death. When the candle had burned down, Gest's life was at an end.

ASMUND KEMPIBANE

IN Sweden ruled a mighty king named Budli. Before him once came two men who gave their names as Olius and Alius; they boasted of their superior skill as smiths, and the king therefore bade them forge for him one sword each, swords that would cut anything they touched. The sword made by Alius met all tests imposed by the king; but the edge of Olius's sword bent a little under trial. Budli accordingly bade Olius forge a better one; the smith did so, but against his will, and foretold when he had finished that the sword should be the death of the two sons of the king's daughter. The king in anger struck at him with the sword, but in a twinkling the two smiths had disappeared. Budli, intent on bringing the prophecy to naught, caused the swords to be sunk in Lake Mälaren near Agnafit.

King Hildebrand in Hunaland had a warlike son named Helgi, who paid court to Budli's daughter Hild. Budli looked with favor on his suit and later found in Helgi a staff for his old age in times when it was hard for him to defend his realm. Helgi and Hild got a son who was named Hildebrand; the boy, put under the fostering charge of his father's father, gave early promise of becoming a great warrior. Once while Helgi was absent at the wars in which he lost his life,

Budli's land suffered an inroad by enemies; the Danish king Alf with a large army entered Sweden and slew the old king. The king's daughter Hild was bestowed upon Alf's bravest warrior, Aki, as a reward for his valor; they had a son, Asmund by name, who even in early youth became known as a famous Viking. Asmund's half brother Hildebrand had by that time fared far and wide and by mighty deeds had earned the name of Hun-Champion. Having learned of the death of his mother's father Budli, he set out for Denmark to wreak vengeance upon Alf. Aki and Asmund chanced to be off on a Viking foray just when the king most needed their aid; for no one could resist the doughty Hildebrand. In Berserk rage he broke the ranks of Alf. The king himself fell in battle, leaving a daughter named Æsa. When Aki and Asmund returned, Hildebrand had already departed. All was now quiet for a time.

Asmund soon paid court to Æsa but found a powerful rival in Eyvind Skinnhall, a rich and mighty man. Æsa promised to wed that one who the next autumn should be able to show her the fairest hands. Eyvind during the summer took his ease and never removed his gloves from his hands; but Asmund spent the time in Viking raids that brought him both honor and booty. In the autumn they both presented themselves before Æsa for the purpose of showing her their hands. Eyvind's were white and fair: Asmund's, on the contrary, were filled with scars and gashes, but his arms were adorned with rings up to the very shoulders. Æsa decreed that Asmund had the fairer hands and

Heroic Legends

promised to wed him if he would avenge her father's death upon Hildebrand Hun-Champion. To do so, she said, he must find the sword that had been sunk in the waters at Agnafit, for this weapon alone would prevail against Hildebrand's. Asmund set forth on his quest; at Agnafit he met an aged peasant who still remembered the spot where the sword had been submerged, and with the old man's help he fetched it up from the deep.

In the meantime Hildebrand had brought the counts of Saxony to a sorry pass. Each year he bade his Berserks challenge the counts' men to combat, the penalty being a landed estate each time the Saxons were worsted. In this way they were losing both their men and their lands; at last they had but twelve estates left. In the nick of time Asmund came to their aid, promising to take up the battle against Hildebrand. When the day set for the combat drew near, Hildebrand sent one of his Berserks out against Asmund; but Asmund promptly shore him through the middle. The next day Hildebrand sent two Berserks out against him, but they met the same fate. Hildebrand gradually raised the number to eight, but Asmund continued to carry away the victory. In a fury of rage Hildebrand despatched against him the remaining eleven Berserks all at once; these too Asmund succeeded in cutting down. When this news reached Hildebrand, his Berserk madness came over him, so that he even slew his own son. Afterward he advanced up along the banks of the Rhine to meet Asmund himself, bearing on his shield the tally of all the men he had killed during his whole life. Asmund came out to the onslaught, and a long and fierce combat ensued. At last Hildebrand's sword was shattered on Asmund's helmet. Hildebrand himself, stricken with many wounds, then chanted a lay revealing to Asmund that they two were brothers, born of one and the same mother. Praying that he might be buried in Asmund's clothing, Hildebrand died. Little joy did Asmund take in what he had done. He at once returned to Denmark and there found that Æsa had a new suitor. She was glad to see him; and when he had laid his rival low, he took her to wife. In the course of time he added still more to his renown.

ROMUND GREIPSSON

A CERTAIN wealthy husbandman named Greip and his wife Gunnlod, a daughter of Rok the Black, had nine stalwart sons, of whom the most stalwart bore the name Romund. Once upon a time they all went out on a Viking expedition with king Olaf of Garder. Near the Wolf Skerries they encountered six warships under the command of a redoubtable Viking named Rongvid. A furious battle followed. The king's men were on the point of losing courage; but when Romund at length succeeded in felling Rongvid, the enemy was compelled to give in. Rongvid's brother, Helgi the Brave, accepted quarter from Romund and healing for his wounds; Helgi then went to Sweden and there joined the forces defending the land. After the victory king Olaf sailed westward to the Southern Isles, where his men landed and took booty. An old man, whose cattle they had seized, ridiculed their action as cowardly and mean, and directed them to riches that were really worth taking. He told them that a powerful Berserk named Thrain, who once was king of Valland, lay buried in a mound in the midst of a vast treasure; he was brooding over his wealth in the shape of a Sprite, but they might nevertheless be able to gain possession of it. Romund, having thanked him for his counsel and besought his guidance for the journey, sailed away for Valland. They found the cairn easily enough, but Romund alone had the courage to enter it. After a furious struggle with the Sprite, he emerged victorious from the cairn with untold treasure and with Thrain's sword Misteltein. Having won renown through this exploit, after his return home he cast his eyes on the king's sister Swanwhite. But his enemies spread such evil rumors about him that he and his brothers were finally forced to leave the king's body-guard and seek safety in flight.

Not long afterward king Olaf was challenged to a combat on the ice of Lake Vänaren by a Swedish king named Hadding, one of whose retainers at the time was Helgi the Brave. Swanwhite, mistrusting her brother's success in the struggle, sought out Romund in secret and begged him to come without delay to the aid of the king. Romund promised to do as she bade him. He and his eight brothers set forth at once. Over the heads of the Swedish hosts there flew a Troll woman named Kara in the likeness of a swan, who by her magic spells brought great harm to king Olaf's men;

she was Helgi's beloved. Helgi had the good fortune to slay all of Romund's brothers. At last Romund and Helgi met face to face; as Helgi lifted his sword, he happened to strike the swan on the foot so that it fell to earth dead. "Now your luck is at an end, Helgi!" Romund shouted, and therewith clove his enemy's head with Misteltein. Romund himself had suffered fourteen wounds; notwithstanding he continued the battle until his foes fled. Swanwhite sewed up his gashes and sent him to a husbandman named Hagal, whose wife, as it chanced, had skill in sundry arts and crafts. In their house he was healed of his wounds.

King Hadding had a counselor named Blind the Bad. Blind having learned that Romund was in hiding in Hagal's house, told the news to the king, who at once gave commands to seize the dangerous enemy. Blind made a search of Hagal's house, but his wife had hidden Romund under a huge kettle, so that Blind saw nothing of him. As the messengers were on their homeward way, it occurred to Blind that he had forgotten to look beneath the kettle, and so he promptly retraced his steps. But Hagal's wife, having foreseen something of the sort, had dressed Romund in the clothing of a woman and had set him to work grinding at the mill. Although Romund cast sharp glances at them while they searched for him, a spell was on them so that they failed to recognize him. Not before they were homeward bound once more did Blind realize who the handmaiden was; but he understood as well that he could not cope with the craft of the old woman and so returned home with his errand unfulfilled. The next year king Olaf again mustered an army to invade Hadding's realm, and Romund followed in his train. They surprised Hadding as he lay abed. Hadding was slain by Romund. Blind was hanged. Romund took Swanwhite to wife. From them famous families count their descent.

RAGNAR LODBROK AND HIS SONS

HERROD, earl of Gautland, had a fair daughter named Thora, with the surname of Borgarhjort. From her father she got as a present a small grass snake, which she kept in a box and under which she laid a bed of gold. As the snake grew, the gold grew too; but the snake at length became so large that it could no longer find room in her bower but curled itself in a circle about the house. It now showed such bad temper that no one dared approach it except the man who gave it food, and he was compelled to bring it an ox for each meal. The earl, thinking that matters were taking an ill turn, promised his daughter to any man who should kill it, and the gold besides by way of dowry; yet no man dared attempt the task.

King Sigurd Ring of Denmark had a son named Ragnar. He was tall and handsome, and distinguished at an early age for his valor and his deeds of prowess. Having learned of the earl's offer, he journeyed with his men to Gautland. Before setting out he equipped himself with a shaggy cloak and shaggy breeches that had been steeped in boiling pitch. Clothed in this raiment he went ashore early one morning and, making his way to the earl's house, thrust his spear through the serpent. Though the serpent spouted venom over him, Ragnar suffered no harm, being protected by his heavy garments. Having thus killed the serpent, he took Thora to wife and with her had two sons, Erik and Agnar. Thora died soon after, and Ragnar mourned her death so deeply that he forsook his kingdom and wandered about, continually engaged in warfare. One summer he came to Spangereid in Norway, and there lay at anchor in the harbor during the night. In the morning he sent his bakers ashore to bake bread. They found a little farm, where two people lived named Aki and Grima—the same two who had killed king Heimir and who now had in their keeping Sigurd Fafnirsbane's daughter Aslaug or, as she was called there, Kraka.[1] The bakers got help in their work from the fair Kraka. She had been out bathing, something that Grima had forbidden her to do, being unwilling that any one should discover the girl's beauty. Kraka had loosened her long hair, which had grown under the tarred hat she was compelled to wear; fine as silk, it reached down to the very ground when she stood upright. The bakers, who were to go about their work with her, lost their senses completely when they beheld her beauty, and so their loaves were burned. Ragnar, in seeking to learn the cause of their mishap, found out how fair a woman Kraka was. He sent his men to summon her into his presence; but wishing to make trial of her wit, he bade her come neither dressed nor nude, neither hungry nor

[1] See p. 190 f.

Heroic Legends

filled, neither alone nor in the company of another. Kraka removed her clothing, wrapped herself in a net, swathed herself in her own hair as in a garment, took a bite from a leek, and brought the husbandman's dog along at her heels. In this manner she met the difficult test, and Ragnar was so taken with her beauty and wisdom that he wanted to carry her away with him without further ado. But she would not go with him until he should have returned from a certain expedition which he was about to undertake; if by that time he had not changed his mind, she would consent to be his wife. Ragnar returned indeed in due season, and Kraka went with him aboard the ship, after telling her stepfather and stepmother that she knew of their evil deed but had no mind to take vengeance on them. They were married in state on Ragnar's returning to his own kingdom, and Kraka bore him sons who were named Ivar Lackbones, Bjorn Ironside, Whitesark, and Ragnvald. The three younger sons were stalwart and brave. Ivar, having cartilage instead of bones, was unable to walk; he had himself carried about in the company of his brothers, and since he surpassed them in shrewdness they always followed his advice. He was also the one among them who first thought of winning honor in Viking forays; he egged the others into making an incursion against Whitby, and they captured the town, but Ragnvald fell in the course of the attack.

In Sweden there ruled a king named Eystein, a man most zealous in offering sacrifices. In preference to all other deities he worshipped a cow, Sibilja, that walked before his army in battle, filling the enemy with fear. King Eystein and Ragnar Lodbrok were the best of friends and paid frequent visits to each other. Once upon a time, when Ragnar was feasting at the court of Eystein, Eystein's fair daughter filled the beakers for the kings; Ragnar's retainers persuaded him to make her his bride and to put away the humble peasant's daughter Kraka. King Eystein too favored the match, and so it was agreed that Ragnar was to return later to claim the princess. Ragnar bade his men say nothing about the plan to Kraka; but three birds revealed the secret to the queen, and when he came home she upbraided him with what he purposed doing. Not until that moment had she disclosed to him her true descent and her right name. She was about to give birth to a child, she told him, and it was to be a son who should be marked with the image of a serpent in his eye; this token would prove her to be the daughter of Sigurd Fafnirsbane. It all happened just as she had foretold, and the boy got the name of Sigurd Snake-In-The-Eye. But king Eystein's wrath was kindled because Ragnar had broken his troth with the princess, and from that time Eystein was Ragnar's enemy. Ragnar's eldest sons Erik and Agnar therefore mustered an army to carry the combat within the confines of Sweden, but luck was against them; Agnar fell, and Erik, who would not owe his life to Eystein, chose to die by being thrown upon a spear fixed in the earth. One of his men carried his ring to queen Aslaug, who without delay egged her sons on to avenge his death. With an army they sailed for Sweden and slew king Eystein in battle, Ivar Lackbones having succeeded meanwhile in killing Sibilja. After finishing this enterprise, they continued to make war throughout the south, gaining renown on every hand. They destroyed the powerful stronghold of Vivilsborg, captured Luna, and had no thought of halting their course until they should have reached Rome. From an old man who came to them in Luna they sought to learn how long was the road to Rome. He showed them a pair of iron boots on his feet and another pair slung across his back; both pairs, he declared, he had worn out on the journey from Rome to Luna. The sons of Lodbrok now realized that they would have to give up their plan of pushing on against Rome.

In the meantime Ragnar had remained quietly at home. He soon heard of the renown his sons were winning and determined not to be outdone by them. He gave orders for the building of two great merchant vessels, so large that with them he could transport a whole army overseas to England. Aslaug advised him to divide his host among several smaller ships so as to make landing more easy; but Ragnar would not heed her good counsel. She then gave him at his departure a shirt capable of protecting him against all kinds of wounds, and he set forth on his expedition. On the coasts of England, however, his two ships ran aground; although he effected the landing of his men, he was thus cut off from retreat. Ella was king in England at the time. When the news of Ragnar's invasion reached him, he gathered a large army and with it destroyed the enemy by force of numbers.

Ragnar himself was taken prisoner and cast by Ella's orders into a den of serpents. But the shirt protected him from their stings; only when it was stripped from his back did he succumb to their venom. Before he died he sang a lay, in which were these words: "The pigs would grunt if they knew what pains the boar suffers."

Ragnar's sons having meanwhile returned to Denmark, Ella sent couriers to acquaint them with the death of their father, with instructions to note carefully how each of them received the tidings. The messengers found Ivar sitting in the high seat, while Whitesark and Sigurd were playing chess, and Bjorn was busied in shaping a spear shaft. As the heralds were delivering their message, Bjorn shook the shaft till it broke in two, Whitesark crushed a chessman in his hands so that the blood sprang from under his nails, while Sigurd, who was paring his nails, cut his finger to the bone without giving the least sign. Ivar alone questioned the messengers closely and spoke quietly with them, the only mark of his agitation being a change of color, from flushed cheeks to paleness. When Ella was told all these things, he said, "Ivar we have to fear, and none other." The brothers now deliberated on taking vengeance for their father; but Ivar lifted his voice against such a course, advising instead that they accept wergild from Ella. The others, incensed at his speech, mustered an army. Although Ivar went with them to England, he led no armed force and took no part in the battle, in which the brothers were defeated. He sought the presence of

Heroic Legends

Ella by himself to demand a small forfeit for his father: only as much land as he might be able to encompass with an ox hide. Ella deemed this a most reasonable demand; but crafty Ivar cut a softened hide in strips, by means of which he encompassed a large plain. There he built a house and a stronghold and gave the place the name of Lundunaborg (London). He had bound himself by an oath not to make war against Ella; but he used his patrimony to entice the mightiest men of the land away from Ella. When he judged that all things fitted his purpose, he sent word to his brothers that they should muster a large army. They did as he bade them and crossed over to England. Ella found himself unable to put a sufficient force in the field because his liege men had forsworn their faith. In a decisive battle he was taken captive, and at Ivar's orders the bloody eagle was carved on his back. Thus he died. Ivar now permitted his brothers to maintain their sway over Ragnar's realm; he took England for himself and ruled there until his death. Whitesark was taken prisoner on an expedition to the shores of the Baltic, and chose as his mode of death to be burned on a pyre of human skulls. Bjorn later ruled in Sweden, and Sigurd Snake-In-The-Eye in Denmark.

HJORLEIF AND HALF

TRADITION relates that in the time of Vikar, who is mentioned in the legend of Starkad, there lived as ruler of Rogaland a king named Hjorr. His son Hjorleif in his turn held dominion over both Rogaland

and Hordaland. Hjorleif, by reason of his many marriages, got the nickname of "woman-lover". First he was wedded to Æsa the Bright of Valdres; some time later, on a voyage to Bjarmiland, he took to wife Hild the Slender from Njardey (now Nærøy) near Namdalen. He became after a season a fast friend to Heri in Kongehelle, a son of Reidar, king of Zealand. Reidar invited Hjorleif to visit his house, and the sojourn ended with a marriage between Hjorleif and the king's daughter Ringja. On the voyage to Norway Ringja fell sick and died; her body, sunk into the sea, drifted back to her father's shipyard. There Heri found the coffin and came to the conclusion that Hjorleif had put her to death. That same autumn two fishermen, having caught a merman, brought him before Hjorleif. The king saw to it that the merman was well treated by the royal retinue, but no one could draw a word from his lips. Once queen Hild had the mischance to spill a horn filled with liquor over Æsa's cloak; when the king struck her, she laid the blame on the dog Floki, that had come in her way, and the king likewise beat the dog. The merman burst into laughter; on the king's asking him why, he answered: "Because you have played the fool; these two shall in good time save your life." The king promised him liberty if he would only make other prophecies of like import; and as they walked down toward the sea, the merman chanted verses foretelling that before long the king of Denmark would make his appearance, bringing bloody battles with him. Hjorleif now sought to gather an army; but Reidar, intent on avenging his daughter, came upon Hjorleif by stealth during the night and surrounded the house. Floki began to bark as was his wont when he sensed danger. Hjorleif rushed out and hurled a spear at his enemies which brought Heri to earth. Hjorleif escaped to the forest but had to stand looking on while his estates were burned. Reidar carried off the two queens and much booty. Afterward during the same autumn Hjorleif stole alone into Reidar's house, where he asked his own wife Æsa to help him in taking his revenge; but she, having no love for him, betrayed his design to Reidar, who ordered him to be hung up by his own shoe strings between two fires. In his worst need his other wife Hild came to his aid. She moderated the heat by pouring ale on the flames; and when Reidar had fallen asleep over his cups, she loosed the bands with which Hjorleif was bound. Hjorleif then killed his enemy and hung the body up in the same cords from which he himself had been saved. He now returned home with his two wives. The people assembled in judgment doomed Æsa to a death by drowning in a morass; but Hjorleif contented himself with sending her home with her dowry to Valdres. King Hjorleif lost his life on a Viking foray. His son by Æsa was named Oblaud; by Hild he had two sons, Hjorolf and Half.

Hild later wedded a king named Asmund, under whose tutelage her two sons grew up. When Hjorolf had reached thirteen years of age, he was taken with a desire to try his luck as a Viking. He gathered about him as many men as he could find; but he took account of numbers alone and paid no heed to whether his retainers were able men or fitly armed. Soon he met with misfortune and had to return home in disgrace.

The following spring Half reached his twelfth year, and he too determined to seek his fortune as a freebooter. He had but one ship; but it was new and uncommonly well provided, and he was most hard to please in the choosing of his men. No man was to be younger than eighteen years, and to be accepted he had to be able to lift a huge stone that lay in the courtyard; no man was to complain or to move a muscle in case he happened to be wounded. Half's foremost counselor was Stein, a son of earl Alf the Old of Hordaland. This Stein had a brother, twelve years of age, of the same name; but he was too young to be one of the warriors. Stein's cousins, Rok the White and Rok the Black, were among the champions, the number of whom all told was only twenty-three. On the first evening that they lay in harbor, a hard rain was falling, wherefore Stein meant to raise the tents; but the king put him aback with the words, "Are you still going to raise tents, as if you were at home?" Thenceforth Stein bore the nickname of In-Stein. The next day, as they were rounding a headland in a stiff gale, they saw some one standing there making signs that he wanted to be taken aboard ship. They granted his wish but, so the king decreed, only on his promising to man the rudder until evening. The stranger looked with favor on the proposal, since in that case he would have his station near the king. It soon appeared that it was the younger brother

Heroic Legends

Stein who had boarded the ship; he was dubbed Out-Stein.

Half's men, who were called Half's Champions, never numbered more than sixty. They were governed by strict laws. No one of them was to bear a sword of more than two feet in length, since they had orders to close with the enemy at short range. They were forbidden to carry off women or children. No man was to bind up his wounds before a day had passed. They were not to raise their tents aboard ship. They were never to reef their sails in a storm; if they were compelled to lay by, they were not to seek harborage but to ride out the storm, even off the most forbidding headlands. With champions such as these Half led his Viking life for eighteen years, always victorious. Once upon a time when they encountered a terrific gale, they agreed to cast lots to determine which of them was to leap overboard to lighten the ship; but the lots were never cast, for the men vied with one another in jumping into the sea, with the shout, "There is no straw outside the gunwales" (that is to say, they should not die on beds of straw if they dived over the side). Half then sailed to Hordaland, where his stepfather king Asmund acknowledged him as overlord, swore fealty, and then invited Half and one half of his force home for a festival. In-Stein had no faith in Asmund; having dreamed foreboding dreams, he begged Half to take all of his men with him; but the king, refusing to listen to this prudent counsel, went off with only one half of his band. It was a most splendid feast, and the drink was so strong that

Half's Champions fell asleep. King Asmund promptly set fire to the hall. One of Half's Champions waked and cried out, "Smoke wreathes the hawks in the king's hall." Then he lay down to sleep again. Another waked and called out, "Wax drips from our swords" (an intimation that the wax used in the setting of the swords was melting with the heat). Finally In-Stein waked and shouted to Half. The king rose and roused all of his men, and they all ran together against the wall with such force that the corner timbers sprang apart, and they made their escape. But Asmund's greater numbers bore them down, and Half himself fell. The men from the ships now rushed into the fray, and In-Stein kept up the battle till nightfall; then he fell, and by that time many of Half's Champions had met a like fate. Out-Stein was wounded, but recovered and fled to Denmark; he and Rok the Black later killed Asmund and thus avenged their liege lord. Half's son Hjorr now became king of Hordaland.

FRIDTHJOF

KING BELI in Sogn had three children, two sons named Halfdan and Helgi, and a daughter named Ingeborg. Over against king Beli's castle of Syrstrand lay the farm Framnes, where the king's good friend, the chieftain Thorstein Vikingsson had his abode. Thorstein's son was called Fridthjof; by reason of his skill in all manner of manly pursuits he had won the surname, the Brave. Beli's queen died at an early age, and Ingeborg was accepted as a foster daughter by a

Heroic Legends

mighty farmer of Sogn, named Hilding. Since Fridthjof also was under his tutelage, the two foster children
soon became very fond of each other. When Beli had
grown old, Thorstein and Fridthjof were his chief
support; and as the king noted the approach of death,
he urged his inexperienced sons to put their faith in
these tried and true friends. Not long afterward
Thorstein died, having prayed his son to be governed
by the wishes of the princes, for they were above him
in lineage. In accordance with his wish he was laid in
a barrow just opposite to the burial mound that
housed his old friend Beli.

Fridthjof soon won a name for himself by his courage and his amiability; the youthful princes, on the
contrary, were not well liked, and therefore bore him
no good will. Their ill will grew when they discovered
that Ingeborg looked upon him with favor; and when
Fridthjof in due course asked for her hand, they returned a curt refusal. Fridthjof then declared that
they need expect aid from him no more, and they soon
found that he was in earnest. Rumors of the increasing disagreement between the kings and their chief
retainer came to the ears of the mighty king Ring of
Ringerike. He accordingly sent messengers to Sogn
demanding that the brothers recognize him as their
overlord and pay him tribute. They gave him, to be
sure, a defiant answer and armed their forces to meet
him in Jæren; but finding themselves deprived of
Fridthjof's aid, they quailed before Ring's greater
numbers and composed their differences with him
rather than risk the issue of battle. They were com-

pelled to bow to Ring's demands and to promise him the hand of Ingeborg in marriage. At Baldershagi, not far from Syrstrand, there was a place of sacrifice where many gods were worshipped, Balder most of all; this temple had the utmost sanctity. The kings, therefore, before they took their departure, placed Ingeborg there to keep her in safety from Fridthjof. Notwithstanding, Fridthjof, holding the love of Ingeborg far above the anger of the gods, rowed across the fjord to visit her. They now repeated their vows to each other; Fridthjof gave Ingeborg a precious ring, an heirloom from his father, and from her he received another ring in return. When the kings came home from Jæren and heard all that had taken place, their wrath was kindled; but they dared not attack him, since he had gathered his men about him. They sought therefore to be rid of him by guile. They sent Hilding to him with the proposal that he should make a voyage to the Orkneys to demand the tribute that earl Angantyr had withheld since the death of Beli; by way of recompense they promised him their pardon. Fridthjof was willing to undertake the mission provided only that his lands and chattels were left unmolested during his absence. But no sooner had he set out on the voyage than the kings burned his estates and seized his goods; moreover, they bought the services of two witches, who were to bring upon him such a storm that he could not but perish. In the meantime Fridthjof and his men had sailed out of the Sognefjord on his splendid ship Ellidi, which had the virtue of being able to understand the speech of men. Near the Sulen Islands so violent a storm broke over them that even Fridthjof himself gave up all hope of safety. Presently he caught sight of a whale that had bent itself about the ship in a circle and on the back of which sat two witches. He now bade his ship sail straight over the whale. Ellidi obeyed his command and broke the back of one of the women; Fridthjof himself killed the other. Therewith the evil spell was broken, the storm was stilled, and they made land in Evjesund in the Orkneys. Earl Angantyr, an old friend of Thorstein Vikingsson, received Fridthjof with great hospitality and promised to give him a sum of money; he might call it tribute if he were so minded. They sojourned at the house of Angantyr during that winter. Meanwhile king Ring, according to arrangement, had come to Sogn and there celebrated his marriage with Ingeborg. When he saw Fridthjof's ring, he forbade her to wear it; so she gave it to Helgi's wife with the request that it be returned to Fridthjof. Ring thereupon carried his wife home and loved her with a great love.

The following spring Fridthjof, on coming home again, found his estates burned to the ground. Learning that the kings were about their sacrifices at Baldershagi, he determined on vengeance. He gave orders to his men to cut holes in the bottoms of all the ships lying in the harbor, while he went alone into the temple, where he found the kings sitting over their beakers in the company of a small number of their retainers. Men and women were sitting there anointing the images of the gods and drying them with cloths; others were warming the images over the fire. Fridthjof stepped up before king Helgi, and said, "Would you not like to receive your tribute?" With these words he struck the king in the face with the purse so hard that two teeth fell from his mouth. Helgi toppled from his high seat bereft of his senses, and Halfdan had to grasp hold of him to prevent his falling into the fire. As Fridthjof was about to walk out, he caught sight of his ring on the finger of Helgi's wife, who sat warming the image of Balder at the fire. He seized her by the hand so that the image fell into the flames, and dragged her toward the door for the purpose of taking the ring away from her. Halfdan's wife took hold of her on the other side to draw her back; at that the image she was holding likewise fell among the coals. Both of the anointed images began to burn, and the whole house burst into flames. Fridthjof in the meantime had regained his ring and so sailed away; but when the kings set out in pursuit, they found themselves unable to make use of their ships. They now declared Fridthjof an outlaw. Halfdan rebuilt Framnes and made his own abode there; Helgi remained at Syrstrand.

Fridthjof now spent three years as a Viking, gathering much booty. At the end of that time he left his men in Viken and made his way to the Uplands, to the court of king Ring, for the purpose of seeing Ingeborg again. Disguised as an old man, he drew a broad-brimmed hat over his face, and thus apparelled entered the palace and took his station at the lower end of the hall. Ring asked who the old man might be. "Thjof is my name; I dwelt with Wolf last night; I am the foster son of Anger",[1] the stranger answered Ring was surprised at the enigmatic reply, bade the man draw near, and inquired where he made his home. "My wish brought me here, and my home is nowhere," answered the singular guest, adding that he was by calling a cooker of salt. "You have spent the night in the forest," said Ring; "for there is no husbandman in the neighborhood by the name of Wolf. Since you say that you have no home, it may be that your desire to visit us surpasses your longing for home." The queen offered him a seat among the guests, but the king asked him to take a place at his own side. The stranger did so, and in a trice stood before them splendidly dressed, with a sword by his side and a large ring on his finger. On seeing the ring, the queen became red as blood, but said never a word. The king said in merry mood, "You must have cooked salt a long while for a ring like that." Thjof sojourned there during the whole of the winter and gained the good will of all men. The queen seldom addressed him, but the king always spoke with him in friendly fashion.

Once upon a time Ring and his queen set forth to lend their presence to a festival, and Fridthjof attended them. Against Fridthjof's counsel they chose to drive across certain dangerous reaches of ice. Presently it broke beneath them; but Fridthjof pulled both horse

---

[1] A play on words, since the term may mean both "sorrow" and "fjord". It is probably an allusion to a definite fjord region —a region of salt works, from which the people of Ringerike in ancient times were in the habit of securing salt—namely, Sande in Vestfold, where the fjord in an earlier day bore the name of *Angr*. Cf. M. Olsen in *Studier tillägnade Esaias Tegnér* (Lund, 1918), pp. 214–22.

and sleigh out of the water while the king and the queen still sat in their seats. "You have a strong arm, Thjof!" said Ring; "even Fridthjof the Brave himself could not have taken hold with greater power had he been in your place." Of the banquet itself there is nothing remarkable to tell.

One day the king bade his retinue go with him out into the forest so that he might gladden his heart amidst the beauty of nature. It so befell that king Ring and Fridthjof found themselves alone together. The king said that he was drowsy and wished to lie down for a while to sleep. "Turn homeward then, king!" said Fridthjof; "that were more seemly." The king refused, and lay down to rest; soon he gave signs of being fast asleep. Thjof, seated near him, drew his sword from the scabbard and hurled it far away. The king presently rose and said: "Is it not true, Fridthjof, that many thoughts even now coursed through your mind, and that you gained mastery over them? You shall henceforth remain with me and enjoy such honors as I can bestow. I knew you the first night, as soon as you stepped into the hall." "I must take my leave ere long," answered Fridthjof. When they returned home, it was promptly noised abroad that it was Fridthjof the Brave who had sojourned there throughout the winter.

Early one morning a knock came at the door of the chamber where the king and queen lay asleep. The king asked who was there, and got the answer that it was Fridthjof, who was on the point of taking his departure. He came into the room and thanked them for the kind treatment he had received at their hands;

finally, handing his ring to Ingeborg, he asked her to wear it. The king smiled and said: "In that case she gets more thanks than I, though she has shown you no greater friendship." They drank to each other, and then the king said: "It would please me if you were to remain here, Fridthjof; for my sons are small, and I am an old man, little fitted to undertake the defense of the realm if need should arise." Fridthjof regretfully declined. Ring now offered him all that he possessed, and the queen into the bargain; for, he declared, he felt the approach of death. Fridthjof could no longer refuse; he was dubbed an earl and clothed with authority to rule the kingdom until Ring's sons should be grown to man's estate. King Ring lived but a short while thereafter. His death brought great grief to the land. His funeral ale was drunk with the utmost pomp, and at the same time Fridthjof and Ingeborg celebrated their marriage. But king Helgi and king Halfdan were filled with ire to think that the son of a local chieftain should wed their sister. So they mustered a large army against their new kinsman; but he defeated them both and slew Helgi. To Halfdan he made offers of peace provided only that Halfdan would acclaim him as overlord; and Halfdan had no other choice. Fridthjof thus became king of Sogn, where he continued to govern after Ring's sons had taken over the rule in Ringerike. Later he brought Hordaland as well under his sway. Among the children of Fridthjof and Ingeborg mention is made only of the sons Gunnthjof and Hunthjof. Hunthjof had three sons, named Herthjof, Geirthjof, and Fridthjof; but the family is not often referred to in the ancient annals.

III

THE WORSHIP OF THE GODS

OF TEMPLES, OF SACRIFICES, AND OF DIVINATION

IN later pagan times a great number of temples and other places of sacrifice were to be found throughout the North. During this period a considerable advance had been made beyond the state of affairs described by Tacitus, according to whose account the ancient German tribes worshipped under the open sky in groves or forests. Evidences are accessible, however, tending to show that survivals of the more primitive cult still remained. From Iceland reports have come down to us that in the early days of the settlement of the island there were men who worshipped supernatural beings living in stones and waterfalls; and in the ecclesiastical ordinances of the Gula assembly appear certain prohibitions directed against putting faith in "Land-Sprites dwelling in cairns or cataracts."

The common designation for a house of sacrifice or temple was *hof*. Besides, mention is made of *hǫrgar*, which at the beginning of our historical epoch seem to have been very small buildings, used for sacrifice but less elaborately equipped than the *hof*. Originally, as the name suggests, they must have been stone altars open to the heavens; on this point, compare Norwegian dialectal *horg*, "rocky knoll", "mountain top"; Swedish dialectal *harg* (*harj*), meaning among other things, "rocky height"; and Icelandic *hörgr*, a term used to denote uneven ground. In its oldest signification, that of stone altar, *hǫrgr* appears still to have been used in one of the Eddic poems (*Hyndluljóð* 10), where reference is made to a *hǫrgr* dedicated to Freyja. There is no reason, however, to believe that the *hǫrgr* was employed in the worship of goddesses alone; in Sweden, on the contrary, occur such place names as *Odinshargher* and *Thorshargher*.[1]

A more comprehensive signification seems to have attached to the term *vé* (Anglo-Saxon *wīh*, related to Gothic *weihs*, "holy", and to Old Norse *vígja*, "to consecrate"). The best rendering for the word is perhaps "sanctuary". It was used to designate the hallowed ground set apart as the inviolate meeting place for the legal assembly, which as such was enclosed within *vé*-bounds (*vébǫnd*). One who desecrated the spot was denominated *vargr i véum* (a miscreant in the sanctuary) and declared an outlaw.

In the older literature occur several descriptions of these *hofar* and their furniture. Mention is made of great buildings, splendidly equipped, containing magnificently adorned carven images of the gods. The deities were here figured in the likeness most familiar to the imagination of the people: Thor in his wagon,

---

[1] On the *hǫrgr*, see M. Olsen, *Hedenske kultminder* I, p. 285 ff. Those *horgar* which have left reminiscences in the Icelandic place names *Hörgsdalr* and *Hörgsholt*, have been excavated by Björn M. Olsen and Daniel Bruun (see *Árbók hins íslenzka fornleifafjelags* 1903, p. 1 ff.). At the place first named the existence of an oblong, four-cornered building (9.7 x 6.3 meters, interior dimensions) was demonstrated, which was certainly roofed over and which by means of a wall 60 centimeters in height was divided into a small room to the north and a room twice the size of the first to the south. At Hörgsholt the *hǫrgr* measured only 5.3 x 1.6 meters, with a cross wall toward the northern end; it was probably a sanctuary open to the sky.

The Worship of the Gods

holding Mjollnir in his hand; and Frey riding on his boar. Certain of these descriptions, however, are not reliable. The best of them is the account given in the *Eyrbyggja Saga* of the *hof* erected by the Norwegian chieftain Thorolf Mostrarskegg at Breidafjord in Iceland; and the accuracy of this description, as will appear later, has been substantiated in various important particulars by recent excavations of *hof* sites in Iceland.

Thorolf had carried with him from his home on the island of Moster in Sunnhordland the timbers of the *hof* dedicated to Thor that he had had there, and also earth from the mound on which the image of Thor had stood in the old temple. Not far from his new farm in Iceland he accordingly erected "a *hof*, and a large building it was; it had a door in the side wall, nearer to one end of the house than to the other. Within were placed the pillars of the high seat, in which were fixed certain nails, the so-called *regin*-nails (nails of the gods). Inside those walls was high sanctuary. At the innermost end of the *hof* there was a little house like the present choirs in churches. In the middle of the floor was a stall or stand, used as an altar, on which lay a ring, unjointed and weighing twenty penny-weight;[1] by this ring all oaths were to be sworn, and the high priest was to wear it on his arm at all solemn assemblies. On the stand there was also to be placed a bowl (*hlaut-bolli*) for the sacrificial blood, and in it a brush (*hlaut-teinn*) with which the blood from the bowl, called *hlaut*, was to be sprinkled over the wor-

[1] In the Norwegian text: *ører.*—Translator's note.

shippers; the blood was taken from the beasts offered as a sacrifice to the gods. Round about the stand the gods were stationed in their order in the inner sanctuary. To this *hof* all the men of the assembly district were obliged to pay a tax, and they were also obligated to make all required journeys with the chief priest . . . ; but the priest himself was charged with maintaining the *hof* at his own cost, so that it should not fall into neglect, and with performing his ministry at the sacrificial feasts."

As to the environs of the *hof* we read further in the saga:

"To the land between Vigrafjord and Hofsvag, Thorolf gave the name of Thorsnes. On the headland rises a mountain; to it Thorolf attached such sanctity that no man was to let his eyes rest on it without first having washed himself; and on the mountain itself it was forbidden to lay violent hands on either men or beasts, until they had descended from it of their own accord. This mountain he called Helgafjall ("holy mountain"), and into it he believed that he himself and his kin were to enter after death. At the point of the headland, where Thor (that is, the image of Thor on one of the pillars of the high seat) had drifted ashore, he caused all judicial proceedings to be held, making it the place of legal assembly for the district. This spot he elevated likewise to such high sanctity that he would in no wise permit the slope to be defiled, either by the shedding of blood through violence or by the evacuations of the body."

Our forefathers probably knew no other form of sacrifice than that of blood, either of beasts or of men.

The Worship of the Gods

To offer sacrifice was called *at blóta*, and the offering itself was known as *blót*.[1] We have the best account of the procedure at this kind of sacrificial feast (*blót-veizla*) from Snorri's description in the *Saga of Hakon the Good* (chapter 14); certain details in this description have likewise been confirmed through investigation of the sites of ancient Icelandic temples. The description runs as follows:

"It was an old custom, when sacrificial offerings were to be made, that all the farmers should gather at the spot where the *hof* lay, bringing with them supplies of food sufficient for the entire period of the festival. At this feast all men were to have ale; a large number of the lesser animals [2] and of horses were killed; the blood that flowed from the slaughtered beasts was called *hlaut*, and the bowls in which the blood was collected were called *hlaut*-bowls; and besides there was something called a *hlaut-teinn*, made in the form of a brush or broom, with which it was customary to color the stands red and likewise the walls of the *hof* within and without, and in addition, to sprinkle the blood over the assembled men; the flesh was cooked to provide meat for the banquet. There were to be fires on the middle of the floor of the *hof*, above which kettles were to be hung. Beakers were to be borne

---

[1] This word has no connection with the word "blood". The term *at blóta* comprised prayers and spoken formulas, and therefore the word is used also of cursing. It was not customary to use the locution *"at blóta* to Thor", but *"at blóta* Thor". The Anglo-Saxons had the word as well; from it is derived the Anglo-Saxon *bletsian*, "to bless" (Old Norse *bleza*, "to bless", is borrowed from the Anglo-Saxon).

[2] Especially sheep.

round about the fire. The man who gave the festival and held authority there was to consecrate the beakers and all the flesh of the sacrifice; first he would dedicate a beaker to Odin—this was pledged to the rule and victory of the king—and afterward a beaker to Njord and a beaker to Frey, for plentiful harvests and for peace. It was common practice thereafter to drain a beaker to the honor of Bragi;[1] likewise, to drink to departed kinsmen, 'the cup of remembrance'." In a subsequent passage from the saga (chapter 17) we read the following story of king Hakon's action at a sacrificial feast at Lade: "The next day, as men gathered at the table, the countrymen crowded about the king and demanded that he should eat horseflesh. The king would not. Then they bade him drink of the broth, but he would not. Then they bade him to eat of the fat; he would not do this either. . . Earl Sigurd now asked him to place his open mouth over the handle of the kettle, where the steam from the broth of horseflesh had deposited a film of fat. Then the king stepped forward, laid a linen kerchief across the handle of the kettle, and opened his mouth over it." (From Gustav Storm's translation).

It is only in Iceland, so far as we know, that the *hof* has left traces to this day. Among the many *hof* sites the location of which can with greater or less probability be demonstrated, one has recently been minutely investigated by Daniel Bruun and Finnur Jónsson.[2]

[1] See note to p. 18, line 12.
[2] The results have been presented in *Aarbøger for nordisk oldkyndighed* 1909, p. 245 ff.

The Worship of the Gods

This excavation—on the farm of Hofstaðir near Mývatn in the district of Southern Thingey—revealed what in this instance must have been a stately, longish building comprising two rooms: a festival hall (36.3 meters in length and 5.85–8.25 meters in breadth) and an annex (*af-hús*) (6.2 ca. 4 meters). The festival hall comprised a central nave and two aisles, formed by rows of pillars resting on stones. Along the middle of the floor burned long fires, and beside the long walls were seats, probably with movable tables before them. In this hall the sacrificial banquet was held; the flesh of the slaughtered animals was prepared on hearthstones that are still visible; within the *hof* were found the bones of sheep, goats, oxen, swine, and horses, and of haddock as well. The hall was separated from the annex by a wall, not too high for the assembled worshippers to see what was taking place in the annex, the holy of holies, where the images of the gods stood and where the temple ring lay on the stand. To each of the rooms there was a door: to the festival hall, it was, as the account runs in the *Eyrbyggja Saga*, "on the side wall, nearer to the one end than to the other"; while to the smaller room there was a private door through which only the priest had access.

Three great sacrifices were held yearly: "At winter-day (October 14th) sacrifice was offered for a good year; at mid-winter (Yule) for a good harvest, and at summer-day (April 14th) for victory."[1] According to *Gísli Súrsson's Saga* (chapter 15), the autumnal sacrifice was offered to Frey, "to bid welcome to winter."

[1] *Ynglinga Saga*, chapter 8, cf. p. 276.

Norse Mythology

There were in existence both public *hofar* (chief *hofar*) and private *hofar*. It was in the chief *hof* that oaths were taken in cases of judicial procedure. The consecrated ring that lay on the stand was on such occasions colored red with the blood of the sacrificial animals, and the person who was to swear an oath by the ring made use of the formula: "So help me Frey and Njord and the almighty god" (no doubt Thor).

The chieftain who ruled over a public *hof* had the title in Iceland of *hof-goði* or *goði*;[1] women also were qualified to superintend such a *hof*, and in that office bore the title of *hofgyðjur* (singular, *gyðja*). Any one who chose to do so was at liberty to offer private sacrifices; we thus hear of women who in their own homes offered sacrifice to the Elves. In Norway the dignity of priest was doubtless commonly joined with that of the secular chieftain of a district, the *hersir*. Since the title of *hersir*, as it happened, was the most esteemed and the most frequently employed title, the designation of *goði* seldom occurs in Norway. In Iceland, on the contrary, where titles such as *hersir*, earl, and king were under a ban, the appellation of *goði* came to be the usual title for the officiating head of the temple. In Iceland as well they were not merely officials of the temple, but also secular chieftains and judges; and these combined offices, called *goðorð*—of which there were, in the second half of the tenth century, thirty-nine in number, connected with an equal number of *hofar*—passed down through certain families in hereditary succession.

[1] Gothic *gudja*, derived from the word for "god".

The Worship of the Gods

Our forefathers were accustomed, like all other pagan peoples, to seek at sacred ceremonials to learn the will of the gods in matters of importance. This procedure they called "to make interrogation" (*ganga til fréttar*); it was done most commonly by means of "cutting sacrificial chips", as the practice was denominated. The details of this ceremony are not disclosed in the sagas; but Tacitus describes the custom as it prevailed among the German tribes, as follows: From a tree bearing fruit they selected a branch, which they then cut up into small chips, each of which they marked with a sign; thereupon they scattered them at random upon a white cloth. The priest, in matters affecting the general weal, or the head of the house in matters of family concern, offered up prayers to the gods and then with upturned eyes picked up the chips one by one; this ritual was thrice repeated, and the meaning of the incised marks was interpreted.[1]

Another procedure, when information about future events was desired, was to appeal to soothsayers or magicians. Particularly women, the so-called *vǫlur*, occupied themselves with soothsaying and sorcery. There were two types of sorcery, *galdr* and *seiðr*. *Galdr* is supposed to have been first practised and spread abroad by Odin; it was regarded as more permissible than *seiðr*, and probably consisted for the most part in magic chants and formulas,[2] to some extent in combination with the cutting of runes.

[1] There can be no thought of runes in this case, since runic writing was unknown in the time of Tacitus.

[2] *Galdr*, related to *at gala*, "to crow", "to cry".

Seiðr, on the other hand, owes its origin and diffusion to Freyja. Women especially were instructed in this lower type of magic, considered disgraceful to men. Nevertheless *seiðr* continued in some measure to be practised by men, as late as the beginning of the Christian era; even men of high lineage were practitioners, as for example Ragnvald Rettilbeini, the son of Harold Fairhair. A *seiðr*-man or wizard (*skratti*), as he was also called, was no less feared than hated and despised by reason of the offensive ceremonies and oaths that pertained to this sort of sorcery.

THE PRINCIPAL TEMPLES IN THE NORTH

THE sites of the pagan worship we know partly from ancient written accounts in the Norse tongue and in Latin, and partly from names of places.[1] In the present section a survey will be made of the most important testimony from older literature as to the sites of prehistoric worship; in the nature of the case, the main concern will be with the principal temples of the North.

Two of these are mentioned in closely connected passages from ancient literature. Snorri refers, in the *Ynglinga Saga*, chapter 5, to one such located at Sigtuna, in the following words: "Odin made his abode near Lake Mälaren, at a spot now called Old Sigtuna, and there established a great *hof* and place of sacrifice, after the manner of the Æsir." In chapter 10 he gives the following account of a notable

[1] As to the Norwegian place names containing reminders of the pagan cult, information will be found in the Norwegian text, § 86.

The Worship of the Gods

temple at Uppsala, dedicated to Frey: "Frey erected at Uppsala a great *hof* and there established his chief seat, to which he added all his rents, lands, and chattels. This is the origin of the Uppsala-domain,[1] which has been ever since an appurtenance of the crown." As to the furniture and appointments of the temple at Uppsala, we gather further details from the account given by Adam of Bremen.[2]

Denmark also, according to a foreign writer, had a principal temple, situated at Leire.[3] The German chronicle writer, Thietmar of Merseburg, writing about the year 1000, records the following narrative (Book I, chapter 9): In the chief town of the kingdom, Lederun (Leire) in the province of Selon (Zealand), all the people were accustomed to assemble each ninth year in the month of January for the purpose of sacrificing to their gods ninety-nine human beings and the same number of horses and of dogs, and—in lieu of hawks—cocks. He adds in a later passage that king Heinrich Vogelfänger was the first to compel the Danes to abandon this particular cult (about the year 930). Danish sources, meanwhile, are wholly silent on the subject.

Several well-known principal temples are mentioned as existing in Norway. Such a one was located, for example, at Throndenes on the island of Hinney (*í Qmð á þrándarnesi*), where in all likelihood the ancient kings of Halogaland had their seat. Concerning Si-

---

[1] The royal domain of Sweden; *auðr*, "riches", "property".
[2] See pp. 117–18.
[3] Norse form, *Hleiðrar*.

gurd Thorisson, brother of Thori Hund, Snorri relates
the following story, in the *Saga of Olaf the Saint* (chapter 117): "Sigurd dwelt at Throndenes in Omd. . .
So long as paganism endured, he was in the habit of
holding three sacrifices during each winter, one at win-
ter-night, one at mid-winter, and one toward summer.
When he embraced the Christian faith, he continued
to give banquets in much the same manner: in the autumn he made a great festival for his friends; at Yule
another festival, to which he asked a large number of
guests; and a third time at Easter, on which occasion
also he had many folk in his house." As is well
known, the sagas make further mention of great temples at Lade near Trondhjem and at Mære in Sparbu.
Legendary sources contain accounts also of a principal
temple in Viken, at Skiringssal (now Tjølling), where
kings were said to officiate at the sacrifices.

In addition to public *hofar* such as these, there were
in Norway many private temples erected by powerful
farmers and chieftains on their estates. In Iceland all
of the *hofar* were in reality private, being the property
of the priests; but since the priests, as explained above,
were the bearers of hereditary jurisdiction, the *hofar*
thus took on a public character, so that they may properly be juxtaposed with the public *hofar* in Norway.

BIBLIOGRAPHY

In the Preface to the Norwegian original Professor Olsen gives the following list of the more important works in the field of Norse and Germanic mythology:

CHRISTIANSEN, REIDAR TH., *Veiledning* in *Maal og Minne* 1917; also issued as a separate pamphlet.

CRAIGIE, W. A., *The Religion of Ancient Scandinavia*, London 1906.

FEILBERG, H. F., *Danmarks folkeminder* (5. Bjœrgtagen. 10. Sjœletro. 18. Nissens historie).

GOLTHER, W., *Handbuch der germanischen Mythologie*, Leipzig 1895.

GRIMM, J., *Deutsche Mythologie*, 4. Aufl., Berlin 1875–78.

HOOPS, J., *Reallexicon der germanischen Altertumskunde* (I–IV, 1911–19).

JIRICZEK, O. L., *Die deutsche Heldensage* (Samml. Göschen).

JÓNSSON, F., *Goðafrœði norðmanna og íslendinga eftir heimildum*, Reykjavík 1913.

MEYER, E. H., *Germanische Mythologie*, Berlin 1891; and *Mythologie der Germanen*, Strassburg 1903.

MEYER, R. M., *Altgermanische Religionsgeschichte*, Leipzig 1910.

MOGK, E., *Germanische Mythologie*, 2. Aufl. 2. Abdr., Strassburg 1907 (also in Paul's *Grundriss der germanischen Philologie* III); and *Germanische Religionsgeschichte und Mythologie*, 2. Aufl., 1921 (Samml. Göschen).

DE LA SAUSSAYE, P. D. CHANTEPIE, *The Religion of the Teutons*, Boston and London 1903.

SIJMONS, B., *Heldensage* (in Paul's *Grundriss* II, 1).

Works by SOPHUS BUGGE, V. GRØNBECH, K. HELM, KAARLE KROHN, K. LIESTØL, W. MANNHARDT, AXEL OLRIK, HENRY PETERSEN, GUDMUND SCHÜTTE, and C. W. VON SYDOW will be found mentioned in the notes and in the index.

To the above may be added the following titles:

The Poetic Edda, translated, with an introduction and notes, by H. A. BELLOWS, The American-Scandinavian Foundation, N. Y., second printing, 1926.

[279]

Norse Mythology

The Prose Edda, translated, with an introduction, by A. G.
BRODEUR, second printing, The American-Scandinavian
Foundation, N. Y. 1923.

OLRIK, AXEL, *The Heroic Legends of Denmark*, translated and
revised, in collaboration with the author, by L. M. Hollander, The American-Scandinavian Foundation, N. Y. 1919.
BUGGE, SOPHUS, *The Home of the Eddic Poems*, translated by W. H.
Schofield. (The "Grimm Library", no. XI), London 1899.

TRANSLATOR'S NOTE

The title page of the Norwegian work here presented in translation reads as follows: "Norrøne Gude- og Heltesagn. Ordnet og fremstillet av P. A. Munch. Tredje utgave, efter A. Kjær's bearbeidelse, ved Magnus Olsen, Professor. Kristiania, P. F. Steensballes Boghandels Eftg. (H. Reenskaug) 1922." Munch's original volume was published in 1840; the second edition, revised by Kjær, appeared in 1880; the third edition, from which the translation is made, was revised by Professor Magnus Olsen and published in 1922.

According to the Norwegian preface to the second edition, Kjær made few changes in the body of the text; his most important alterations affected the sections entitled in English "Corruption", "Ragnarok—The Twilight of the Gods", and "On the Mythology of the *Eddas*". He added the following new sections: "German Legends Dealing with Siegfried and the Nibelungs", "The Development of the Legendary Cycle of the Volsungs", "Orvar-Odd", "Norna-Gest", "Asmund Kempibane", "Romund Greipsson", "Ragnar Lodbrok and His Sons", "Hjorleif and Half", and "Fridthjof". The first edition contained only brief discussions of Orvar-Odd and of Ragnar Lodbrok. Kjær also revised the original notes.

Professor Olsen, according to his own statement in the preface to the third edition, made use of newer readings of the ancient texts, harmonized the narrative style throughout, rewrote the sections entitled "On the Mythology of the *Eddas*", "Introductory Remarks" (to the Heroic Legends), and "Of Temples, of Sacrifices, and of Divination", added an appendix dealing with the reminiscences of the ancient mythology in Norwegian place names, and made a thorough revision of the critical notes.

The English translation includes the whole of the third edition of the original, text and notes, with the exception of the Appendix on Norwegian place names. The critical commentaries appended to the various sections of the Norwegian text have in the translation been grouped below. The numbered footnotes, on the other hand, have been retained as such. A few translator's notes have been added; these are in all cases clearly identified.

No attempt has been made in the punctuation of the English text to distinguish between the first Norwegian edition and its successive revisions. Certain marks of punctuation in the origi-

[281]

Translator's Note

nal have therefore been changed or omitted in the translation, and some of the parentheses have been relegated to the foot of the page.

In the body of the English text, proper names are given without the old Norse accents. For the most part the names are spelled as in Old Norse, with the following principal exceptions: initial *h* has been omitted before consonants other than *j*, and final *r* has been omitted after another consonant; thus Rimfaxi, not *Hrím-faxi*, and Hermod, not *Hermóðr*. The Old Norse ð has been rendered as *d; þ* as *th*. Orthographical deviations from the above rules affect cases where an English spelling has become conventional or where considerations of euphony have suggested themselves. The Norwegian word *Norrøn*, both in the title and in the text, is translated as "Norse"; *Nordisk* as "Northern".

The bibliography from the preface to the Norwegian third edition will be found in full; to it have been added some titles of particular use to English and American readers.

S. B. H.

NOTES

INTRODUCTION

Page xvii, *line* 10—An instance may be cited here of the apprehensiveness with which the Catholic clergy regarded survivals of the pagan past. The zealous Icelandic bishop, Jón Ogmundsson (about the year 1110), would not even permit the days of the week to be designated, as was the old custom, according to the names of the gods (Wednesday, Thursday, etc.), but instead introduced the designations "Second Day ", "Third Day," etc. These names are still used in Iceland (*þriðjudagr*, Tuesday; *fimtudagr*, Thursday, and the like); among us, as is well known, the earlier names are still in vogue.

The pagan myths afforded substance not only for poetry but for the pictorial arts. Thus the powerful Icelandic chieftain, Olaf Pá (about the year 970) employed scenes from the mythical stories in the interior decoration of his own house. With these pictures as a subject the skald Ulf Uggason composed a long poem, the *Húsdrápa*, fragments of which still exist. We may read strophes of the poem which deal with the struggle between Loki and Heimdal for the necklace of the Brisings, with the fishing of Thor and Hymir, and with Balder's funeral pyre. Besides, we find representations of myths and heroic legends on runic stones and, at a somewhat later date, on the portals of churches and on church appurtenances; see note to p. 203.

Page xviii, *line* 14—The collection of early poems has been erroneously named *Sæmund's Edda* and the *Poetic Edda* because Icelandic traditions of long standing pointed to the learned Sæmund Sigfusson as the author of the poems or at any rate as the person who had collected them and put them in writing. Sæmund (born in 1056, died in 1133) traced his descent in the direct line to the Scylding, Harold Hilditonn; in his youth he traveled abroad and pursued his studies in France; according to a tradition current in Iceland, he even studied the mystic sciences. He lived at Oddi in the south of Iceland, and was one of the leaders in the land. He revised Ari Frodi's celebrated *Íslendingabók*, and through the school established on his own estate he exerted a great influence on the development of letters; for these reasons the authorship of various

[283]

Norse Mythology

literary works has in recent times been ascribed to him. His son Lopt married Thora, daughter of king Magnus Barefoot; one of their sons was the learned Jón Loptsson, foster father of Snorri Sturluson.

The poems contained in this collection are the following: *Vǫluspá*, or the Sibyl's Prophecy; *Hávamál*, or the Sayings of the High One (a gnomic poem, combined from sundry sayings ascribed to Odin); *Vafþrúðnismál*, or the Duel of Questions between Odin and Vafthrudnir (see below, p. 100); *Grímnismál*, or the Tale of Grimnir (see p. 102); *Skírnismál*, or Skirnir's Journey (p. 15); *Hárbarðslióð*, or Harbard's Abuse of Thor (p. 105); *Hymiskviða*, or Thor's Visit to Hymir (p. 65); *Lokasenna*, or Loki's Flyting (p. 86); *Þrymskviða*, on Thor's recovery of his hammer from Thrym, king of the Giants (p. 76); *Alvíssmál*, a poem containing interpretations of various words; *Vegtamskviða* or *Baldrs Draumar* (p. 80); *Rigsþula*, an allegorical poem dealing with the origin of the various estates or classes of society; *Hyndluljóð*, an historico-genealogical poem; thereafter come the historical lays, of which the greater number have to do with the Volsung cycle: *Vǫlundarkviða*, *Helgakviða Hjǫrvarðssonar*, *Helgakviða Hundingsbana I* and *II*, *Grípisspá*, *Reginsmál*, *Fáfnismál*, *Sigrdrífumál*, a fragment [1] of a *Sigurðarkviða*, *Guðrúnarkviða I*, *Sigurðarkviða in Skamma*, *Helreið Brynhildar*, *Guðrúnarkviða II* and *III*, *Oddrúnargrátr*, *Atlakviða*, *Atlamál*, *Guðrúnarhvǫt*, and *Hamðismál*. [2]

[1] Just before this fragment several leaves are missing in the principal manuscript, the *Codex Regius;* to this lacuna is due the loss of several of the poems. Their contents, however, are known through the *Volsunga Saga*, the writer of which had access to a complete manuscript of the *Edda*.

[2] The later and most useful editions of Sæmund's *Edda* are the following: *Norrœn Fornkvœði*. Islandsk Samling av folkelige Oldtidsdigte om Nordens Guder og Heroer, almindelig kaldet *Sæmundar Edda hins fróða*. Udg. af Sophus Bugge. Christiania 1867.—*Die Lieder der älteren Edda (Sæmundar Edda)* herausgeg. von K. Hildebrand. Paderborn 1876 (*Bibliothek der ältesten deutschen Literatur-Denkmäler*. Bd. 7).—The same. Völlig umgearbeitet von H. Gering. 3 Aufl. 1912. (Among the critical apparatus is to be found an exhaustive account of the treatment of the text by earlier editors.)—*Eddalieder*. Altnordische gedichte mythologischen und heroischen inhalts herausgeg. von Finnur Jónsson. I. Halle 1888. II. 1890 (*Altnordische Textbibliothek*. No. 2. 3).—*Die Lieder der Edda* herausgeg. von B. Sijmons und H. Gering. I. Text. Halle 1888–1906. II. Wörterbuch. 1903 (*Ger-*

Notes

The ascription of the so-called *Younger* or *Prose Edda*, or at any rate great parts of it, to Snorri, rests on traditional testimony and also on definite evidences in the ancient work itself. Its contents are as follows: (1) *Gylfaginning* (i. e., the Hoodwinking of Gylfi), a survey of mythology, in the form of questions and answers; the questioner is king Gylfi, who visits Asgard in disguise; and those who answer are the three supreme gods, here called *Hár, Jafnhár,* and *Þriði*. (2) *Bragarœður*, Bragi's explanations to Ægir of the origins of the art of poetry. (3) *Skáldskaparmál*, a list of the most important poetic paraphrases and of the ancient legends which provide a means of understanding the paraphrases. (4) *Háttatal,* a set of poetic principles, with appropriate examples. This work alone properly bears the name of *Edda;* the common designation of the old collection of poems by the same title was originally due to a confusion of the two works. [1]

manistische Handbibliothek. VII).—*Sœmundar-edda. Eddu-kvæði.* Finnur Jónsson bjó til prentunar. Reykjavik 1905.—*Edda.* Die Lieder des Codex Regius nebst verwandten Denkmälern herausgeg. von G. Neckel. Text. Heidelberg 1914 (*Germanische Bibliothek.* 2 Abteil. Bd. 9).

Of more recent translations the following may be noted: *Den ældre Edda.* Norrøne oldkvad fra vikingetiden 9–11 aarh. e. Chr. oversatte av G. A. Gjessing. Christiania 1899.—*Eddakvæde.* Norrøne fornsongar. Paa nynorsk ved Ivar Mortensson. I. Oslo 1905. II. 1908.—*Den ældre Edda.* Ny Oversættelse ved Olaf Hansen. Copenhagen 1911.—*Sämunds Edda* översatt från isländskan av Erik Brate. Stockholm 1913.

[Translator's note.—Vigfusson and Powell's *Corpus Poeticum Boreale* contains translations into English prose. For an English metrical translation, see H. A. Bellows, *The Poetic Edda*, The American-Scandinavian Foundation, second printing, New York 1926.]

[1] Snorri's *Edda* was edited in Copenhagen in the 17th century by Resenius. The most important later editions are the following: *Edda Snorra Sturlusonar.* Tom. I–III. Hafniae 1848, 1852, 1880–87 (with a Latin translation). *Snorri Sturluson: Edda.* Udg. av Finnur Jónsson. Copenhagen 1900. *Edda Snorra Sturlusonar.* Finnur Jónsson bjó til prentunar. Reykjavik 1907. (Translation): *Snorre Sturluson: Gylfaginning.* Den gamle nordiske Gudelære (første Del af Snorres Edda) oversatt av Finnur Jónsson. Copenhagen 1902.

[Translator's note.—Selections from the *Edda* of Snorri have been published in English translation by A. G. Brodeur. *The Prose Edda.* The American-Scandinavian Foundation, second printing, New York 1923.]

Norse Mythology

THE CREATION OF THE WORLD—THE GIANTS—THE ÆSIR—MEN AND WOMEN—DWARFS— VANIR—ELVES

Page 4, *line* 7—Our forefathers thought of the earth as a round disk or plate, which had been lifted up by the sons of Borr in such a manner that it swam on the surface of the universal ocean. Round about along the coasts of this sea lay Jotunheim, the home of the Giants, separated from Midgard by huge mountains. It is for this reason that the Giants were also called Cliff-Ettins. Jotunheim was a cold and dreary realm; thence the name Rime-Thursar. These beliefs rested on the more primitive supposition that mountains in general were the habitat of Giants or Mountain-Trolls, who harassed neighboring human beings, robbed them of their cattle, enticed persons into the mountain fastnesses, and the like (see p. 39). The earliest form of the name of the Giants, or Jotuns, seems to have been *"etuna-"*, related to the verb *eta*, to eat; the original meaning would then appear to be "big-eater" (cf. C. W. von Sydow, *Jättarna i mytologi och folktradition*, in the periodical *Folkminnen och Folktankar* VI, Lund 1919; cf. also VII, 1921, p. 136 ff.). In Anglo-Saxon the name had the form *eoten*. A Jotun woman was called in ancient times a *gýgr*, and to this day the mountain-troll's wife is designated as *"gygr"* or *"gyvr"*.— The later, Christian conception of the Jotuns has been thoroughly dealt with by K. Liestøl in an article, *Jøtnarne og joli (Maal og Minne* 1911).

As the geographical horizon of the Northern peoples gradually became more extended, Ginnunga-gap was moved farther and farther outward. As early as the 13th century, Bjarmiland in Northern Russia was supposed to stretch far to the north and west until it joined the boundaries of Greenland. "Trollebotn" now came to occupy the spaces formerly assigned to Ginnunga-gap in the Arctic Seas (cf. p. 40) and according to one theory Ginnunga-gap was placed at the outermost edge of the ocean between Greenland and Vinland, while Vinland was thought to touch the boundaries of Africa. See Gustav Storm's article, *Ginnungagap i Mythologien og i Geografien (Arkiv för nordisk filologi* VI, 1890, pp. 340–50).

Audhumla (a later form has -*humbla*) was no doubt imagined to be a cow without horns, since in Scottish dialects "humblecow" still has that meaning (adjective *homyll, hummilt*, "polled"); it is uncertain whether the first syllable of the name is the adjective

Notes

auðr, "waste", or the substantive *auðr*, "riches" (referring to the wealth of milk); probably it is the latter. Polled cows—which are excellent milkers—are mentioned by Tacitus (about 100 A.D.) as a characteristic feature of the agricultural economy of the Germanic tribes. The explanation of Audhumla as meaning "the rich polled cow" was put forward by P. A. Munch (1854). This etymology has recently been justified independently by A. Noreen, in his article, *Urkon Auðhumla och några hennes språkliga släktingar*, in the periodical *Namn och Bygd* VI, 1918, pp. 169–72.

Manigarm is not mentioned in the *Poetic Edda*, the omission being due to Snorri's misunderstanding a passage in the Eddic poem *Grímnismál*. According to this poem, both Skoll and Hati are the pursuers of the sun. The basis for the notions about them is to be found in the so-called mock suns (variegated beams of light caused by the sun's rays breaking through clouds); in Norway and Denmark these phenomena are known as "solulver" (sun-wolves), and in Sweden as "solvargar" (sun-wolves). See Axel Olrik, *Aarbøger for nordisk oldkyndighed* 1902, p. 189 ff.

Lidskjalf, from *hlið*, "gate", "portal", and *skjálf* (*skjǫlf*), a word known from place names (Skjelve, Skjelver) and from the Anglo-Saxon *scylf*, "point", "tower" (cf. E. Björkman, *Namn och Bygd* VII, 1919, p. 174 f). The word then probably has the meaning "gate-tower".

The name Æsir (Modern Norwegian singular "ås") is the Old Norse form, derived from a theoretical **ansuz*, Gothic **ansus;* thus even the ancient Gothic author Jordanes relates that the Goths, before they accepted Christianity, worshipped "*Anses*". The ancient *ans-* has become, in our language, "ås", just as *anst-* (love) has become "åst" (cf. the feminine name Åsta), and as *gans-* has become "gås". In German the form *ans-* remained. In Anglo-Saxon, on the other hand, it was contracted to *ōs*, plural *ēse*. In Sweden and Denmark it appears in the mutated form *æs-*. Evidences of these facts occur particularly in the numerous personal names with *Ans-*, *Ōs-*, *Æs-* or *Ås-*, for example, German "Ansmund", Anglo-Saxon "Osmund", Danish and Swedish "Æsmund", Norwegian "Åsmund". The celebrated missionary's German name "Ansgar" corresponds to the Danish "Æsger", the Norwegian Åsgeir. It is thus easy to see that the name of the Æsir, contrary to a common supposition, has nothing to do with Asia.—The meaning of the word "anser" or "æser" is not certain.—From "ås" is derived the feminine form "åsynjer",

[287]

Norse Mythology

a designation for the goddesses (in Old Norse *ásynja*, plural *ásynjur*).

Page 4, line 27—Among scholars the opinion is general that the warfare between the Æsir and the Vanir is the reflection of a struggle between an earlier, more naturalistic cult and a later cult introduced from without. In this connection stress is laid on the circumstance that the worship of Odin appears to have come from the south into the North at a relatively late date. Cf. Henry Petersen, *Om Nordboernes Gudedyrkelse og Gudetro i Hedenold*, Copenhagen 1876; Kaarle Krohn, *Skandinavisk mytologi*, Helsingfors 1922, p. 93 ff.

In many localities the Elves are still a subject for familiar discussion. In Sweden they are known as *älvor* (cf. "älvkvarnar", a term used to designate saucer-shaped hollows in stones [rock engravings], in which the Elves up to a recent time were accustomed to accept offerings in kind), in Denmark as *elver* or *eller;* and many legends are current concerning elf-maidens and elfin kings. According to popular belief, they lived on hills or in barrows (Danish, elf-hills), in forests and thickets, particularly in copse wood (Danish "elle-krat").[1] Although they are described as beautiful ("fair as an elfin woman"), they may often be very malicious (cf. Norwegian "alvskot", a term applied to various illnesses; see Nils Lid, *Um finnskot og alvskot*, in *Maal og Minne* 1921). Among the Anglo-Saxons the word was *ælf* (English "elf") among the Germans, *alp;* but in modern German the word "Alp" has another meaning (see note to p. 47), and the term commonly used at present, "Elfen", was not introduced before the 18th century, when Wieland took it over from English.—On the position of the Elves in the history of religion, see note to p. 47, toward the end.

The word Alfheim implied in part a dwelling place of the gods, and in part an entire world. In the minds of our ancestors there were several such principal worlds (*heimar*) namely *Godheim* (home of the gods), *Vanaheim, Alfheim, Mannheim* (home of men), *Svartalfaheim, Jǫtunheim, Hel(heim)*, and *Niflheim*.

[1] The notion that the Elves ("ellefolket") lived in elf thickets ("ellekrattet") is due to popular etymology based on a similarity in sound between two words originally quite different. The same similarity led Herder to render "ellekonge", in the Danish ballad *Elveskud*, into German as "Erlkönig"; thence the word passed on into Goethe's famous ballad.

Notes

THE PLAINS OF IDA—VALHALLA—YGGDRASIL

Page 5, line 21—Vingolf in all probability means "friend-floor", "friend-hall", from *vinr*, "friend". Although Vingolf was the domain of the goddesses, the Heroes received entertainment there. Valhalla comes from *valr*, i. e., "the men who lie slain on the field of battle." *Einherjar* (the Heroes) is connected with *herr*, "army", and means "eminent, excellent warriors". Bifrost means "quivering roadway", *rǫst* being "way".

Page 7, line 3—The ash Yggdrasil is a symbol of the structure of the entire universe, which is at once illimitable in extent and closely conjoined. The warfare of Evil against Good and against the whole of Creation is represented by the serpent Nidhogg (that is, "he who strikes with malice, with bitter enmity or spite"), and the continual flux and transitoriness of created things find an emblem in the ever-perishing tree. So run the verses of *Grímnismál:* "Yggdrasil's ash is afflicted, no man knows how sorely; the stag crops its crown, the trunk rots away, Nidhogg gnaws at the root."

Scholars have long suspected that the Yggdrasil myth has come under the influence of Christianity. They have pointed to a series of strophes in the *Hávamál*, where the following words, among others, have been ascribed to Odin: "I know that I hung on the wind-swept tree for three full nights, pierced with a spear, and dedicated to Odin; I to myself, on the tree whereof no man can tell from the roots of what tree it springs" (strophe 138). Here the reference is plainly to "Ygg-drasill", that is, Odin's (Ygg's) horse, a poetical paraphrase for the gallows (cf. "Hagbard's horse"= the gallows, p. 231 and note.) Odin on the gallows, so the argument proceeds, corresponds to Christ on the cross. For this opinion Sophus Bugge has endeavored to present conclusive proofs in his famous *Studier over de nordiske Gude- og Helte-Sagns Oprindelse* (1881–89); and students of folklore have definitely allied themselves with Bugge inasmuch as they have extended the limits of the enquiry, and have brought forward and systematized a mass of fresh materials; see Kaarle Krohn, *Skandinavisk mytologi*, p. 105 ff. Yet the scholars who derive the myth of Odin on the gallows from the story of Christ on the cross, and Yggdrasil's ash from the cross as the tree of life, have at the same time maintained that ancient pagan faith and cult had become ingrained in the Norse myth. This point will be more fully discussed in the following section dealing with Odin.

Norse Mythology

ODIN

Page 10, *line* 18—Snorri says (*Ynglinga Saga*, chapter 6) of Odin that his aspect was as terrifying to his enemies as it was blessed to his friends. Therefore according to the testimonies of Christian writers he appears as a crafty, malicious, old one-eyed man who was always busy with some mischief or other; they actually believed that Odin existed, and that after the introduction of Christianity he was the head and front of all devilry. Even those who worshipped the Æsir did not always think of Odin as magnanimous and gracious; occasionally they represented him as moody, cruel, unjust.

Both the deity and his name were known among other peoples than the Northern; in Anglo-Saxon he is *Wōden*, and in Old German, *Wuotan*, *Wōtan*. The name doubtless is connected with Old Norse *óðr*, "raging", and German *wüten*, "to rage". This designation presents him as a god of death riding through storm at the head of the "raging army" (German, *wütendes Heer*) of the dead. Cf., among others, A. Olrik, *Dania* VIII, p. 139 (*Odinsjægeren i Jylland*).—On the comparatively late introduction of the cult of Odin into the North, see particularly, Henry Petersen's fundamental work cited above, note to p. 4. On the worship of Odin itself, see, among others, Chadwick, *The Cult of Othin* (London 1899).

Among the ancient Germans, Odin is mentioned also under the Latin appellation *Mercurius*, with whom he had in common the function of being captain of the dead. Corresponding to the day of Mercury (French *mercredi*) we thus find Old German *Wōdenestag*, Anglo-Saxon *Wōdnesdæg* (English *Wednesday*), Old Norse *Óðinsdagr* (Modern Norw. *onsdag*). This day, however, in Norway was formerly sometimes called *miðvikudagr* ("mid-week-day"), whence in Norwegian dialects *mekedag, møkedag*.

On Odin as the god of poetry, see p. 99 (on the skaldic mead). Odin was also the god of sorcery and runic magic, as we know especially from the magic formulas of the *Hávamál;* on these in particular Snorri drew for his account of Odin in the *Ynglinga Saga*, chapter 6 f.

THOR

Page 12, *line* 18—The name Thor is not, as the verbal similarity might seem to indicate, derived from *þora*, "to dare", but is a contracted form of the Germanic word for "thunder", Old Ger-

Notes

man *donar* (now *Donner*), and Anglo-Saxon *þunor*. In both of these languages the word is known both as the name for a god and as a designation for thunder. On the form of the word itself (early **þunra-*, rather than **þunara-*) see Hj. Lindroth, *Namn och Bygd* IV (1916), p. 161 ff. As the god of strength, Thor is the father of *Þrúðr*, originally a word meaning "strength" (cf. the son's name, Magni, as compared with *megin*, "might"), and so rules over Thrudvang or Thrudheim.—*Ake-Tor* is the correct form in Modern Norwegian; "Auka-Tor", as some would have it, gives no sense.—References to literature dealing with Thor will be cited in the notes to the several myths dealing with Thor (pp. 56–78).

Just as Odin corresponds to the Mercurius of the Romans, so Thor corresponds to Jupiter. Thence *þórsdagr*, Thursday (Old German, *Donarestac*, Modern German *Donnerstag*, Anglo-Saxon *þunresdæg*, English *Thursday*), = "Jupiter's day" (French *jeudi*).

As the enemy of the Trolls, legendary folklore first substituted for Thor Olaf Tryggvason and later his successor, Saint Olaf. Cf. K. Liestøl, *Norske trollvisor og norrøne sogor* (Christiania 1915), p. 45 ff.

BALDER

Page 13, *line* 8—Balder is no doubt the same word as Anglo-Saxon *bealdor*, "lord", "prince". The name of the god has entered into the composition of the name of a plant: *balder(s)brå* (i. e., "Balder's eyelash"), *pyrethrum inodorum*. On this point Snorri's *Edda* contains the statement: "A plant, the whitest of all, has been likened to Balder's eyelashes".

NJORD

Page 14, *line* 29—Noatun means "ship-yard", and Thrymheim means "storm-home".—For further information on the cult of Njord, see note to p. 16.

FREY

Page 16, *line* 25—Frey means literally "he who is foremost", "the lord" (cf. Gothic, *frauja*, "lord"), and thus at first was not really the name of a god. His cult shows great similarity to the worship of Njord (*Nerþuz*), concerning which antiquity has brought evidence from the hand of the historian Tacitus. In the

Norse Mythology

Germania (chapter 40), he gives the following account of seven small confederated tribes on the peninsula of Jutland:

"These people join together in the common worship of Nerthus, that is, mother earth (*Terram matrem*), who they believe takes part in the migrations of men. On an island in the sea there is an uncontaminated grove, within which stands a consecrated wagon, covered with a pall. The priest alone is permitted to touch it. He perceives on which occasions the goddess is present in her sacred concealment (that is, the wagon); and when she sets in motion the vehicle, which is drawn by cattle, he escorts her with the most profound veneration. These are seasons of gladness, during which festivals are held at such places as she honors with her sojourn; men do not go to war or even so much as take a weapon in their hands; all things made of iron lie hidden under lock and key; quiet and peace are then the only aims of desire, until such a time as the goddess no longer wishes to visit the children of men, and the priest accordingly brings her back to the hallowed spot. Thereupon the wagon and the palls and—if such a thing be susceptible of belief—the goddess herself, are bathed in a secret lake. This service is performed by thralls, whom the water immediately swallows up. Hence come the mysterious fears and the devout uncertainties regarding that something which no man is permitted to see until he knows his death to be at hand."

Reminiscences of a similar worship of Frey are to be found in the romantic story of Gunnar Helming in the *Flatey Book* (I, 338): Men believed that the image of Frey was alive; and a young and fair woman was dedicated to the god as his priestess and given the title of his "wife". With her the god actually led a wedded life. She ruled, together with Frey, over the temple and all that appertained to it. During the winter Frey, dressed in the habiliments of men, rode in his wagon through the several parishes; the priestess accompanied him, and he was everywhere received as a welcome guest. Frey and his priestess—like Nerthus and her priest—represented the fertility of nature; wherever they appeared, good weather and bountiful harvests followed in their train. (In still a third source the wagon is to be met with; see just below).

Even in more recent popular customs the pagan pair, deities of fruitfulness, have maintained their ancient prerogatives: the fructifying power of Spring is personified in various ways, as a

Notes

young birch decked with wreaths and with feminine apparel, as a
young girl crowned with a chaplet of leaves, as a young boy (cf.
the "May-Count" in Denmark), or finally as a "May bride and
groom" (cf. the "St. John's Bride" of certain localities in Norway).

As before mentioned, Frey is also called *Yngvi, Yngvifreyr*
(more correctly *Ingv-*), and *Ingunarfreyr*. With these names
may be compared *Ing* in a verse from the Anglo-Saxon: "Ing
was first seen of men among the East-Danes, until later when he
shaped his course eastward over the waters, and the wagon rolled
in his wake." Just as many given names have been formed from
Frey (Frøidis, Frøistein, etc.), so the element *Ing (v)-* is discov-
erable in numerous names, such as Ingeborg (*Ingibjǫrg*), Yngvild,
Inge, Inga, and the like.

In the saga of Rafnkel, Priest of Frey, occurs the story of the
horse consecrated to Frey, named Frey's-Mane. Rafnkel had
forbidden others to ride the horse; a manservant who defied the
prohibition paid for his disobedience with his life.

A kind of worship of horses, of which evidence presents itself
in the *Vǫlsa þáttr* (in the saga of Olaf the Saint, *Flatey Book* II,
331 ff.) no doubt has a close connection with the god of fruitfulness, Frey. *Vǫlsi*, who here appears as the symbol of fecundity,
is strongly reminiscent of the ancient Graeco-Roman cult of
Priapus.

On the worship of the wedded divinities of fertility, see, among
others, K. Krohn, *Finnisch-ugrische Forschungen* IV, p. 231 ff.
Cf. A. Olrik, *Danske studier* 1907, p. 62 ff.; M. Olsen, *Maal og
Minne* 1909, p. 17 ff., *Det gamle norske ønavn Njarðarlǫg (Kristiania Videnskabsselskabs forhandlinger* 1905), *Hœrnavi* (ibid.
1908); Lundberg and Sperber, *Hœrnavi* (Uppsala 1912); A. Olrik,
Danmarks heltedigtning II (Copenhagen 1910), p. 249 ff.

The basic work on the lower divinities of fertility is Wilh.
Mannhardt's *Wald- und Feldkulte* I–II, 2nd ed., Berlin, 1904–05).
A number of such lower beings have been incorporated in, or have
been collected about, the gods of fruitfulness; an example is Frey's
servant, Byggvir (p. 87), originally a supernatural being whose
special function was watching over the growth of barley (cf. M.
Olsen, *Hedenske kultminder i norske stedsnavne* I, 1915, p. 106 ff.).
Another instance is that of Roskva, the girl who served as hand-
maid to Thor (note to p. 65). It should also be remembered
that the Elves have a close connection with Frey; on p. 43 the

Norse Mythology

Elves are reckoned among the great troop of lower divinities who bear the common title of Sprites.

In other cases the servant of a god may be endowed with a name which really seems to have been a sobriquet of the god himself. So *Skirnir* (from the adjective *skirr*, "shining") was no doubt thought of as originally a name for Frey, "who directed the beams of the sun" (Snorri).

TYR

Page 17, line 9—Toward the close of the pagan era, the worship of Tyr had fallen off very much, particularly because Odin had become the god of War. In earlier times Tyr doubtless held, among several of the Germanic peoples, the eminence as supreme deity; his name also is known from Old German, *Zio*, and from Anglo-Saxon, *Tiw*, *Tig*. This name at first appears to have expressed the very idea of divinity. There exists, as a matter of fact, a plural of *Týr*,—namely *tivar*—which in the ancient poetic phraseology is used as a common noun meaning "gods" (for instance, *valtivar*, gods of battle; and in the singular, *Hangatýr*, "The God of Hanged Men", and *Sigtýr* (p. 8), which has come to be a name for Odin. A parallel case is Latin *divus*, "divine"; and both the Germanic and the Latin words have entered into the formation of a common Indo-European word for "heaven" and for "heavenly god",—Sanskrit *Dyāus*, Greek *Zeus* (from *Djeus*), Latin *Jupiter*, genitive *Jovis* (from *Djov-*, with the addition *pater*, "father").

Tyr has given his name to one of the days of the week: *Tý(r)sdagr*, "Tuesday", Old German *Ziestac*, Anglo-Saxon *Tiwesdæg* (English *Tuesday*). This word is formed after the model of the Latin *Martis dies* (the day of Mars, God of War), French *mardi*. On the occurrence of Tyr in place names, see § 86 of the Norwegian original.

HEIMDAL

Page 18, line 5—Heimdal is also called *Heimdǫllr* (gen. *dallar*). On the origin of the name, see E. Hellquist, *Arkiv för nordisk filologi* VII, p. 171 f. The *Prose Edda* contains references to various legends about him; but many of these are to us nothing but dark sayings. The skalds sometimes call him

Notes

"Loki's enemy" or him "who seeks the jewel of Freyja" (cf. p. 79). Heimdal's head is called "sword"; the story runs that he was pierced through with the head of a man; with this subject is concerned the lay of *Heimdallsgalder*, according to which the head is designated as "Heimdal's death". Heimdal is the master of Goldtop; he is also the one who "shapes his course for Vågaskjær and Singastein", where he fought with Loki for the Necklace of the Brisings; another name for him is Vindle. Ulf Uggason in the *Húsdrápa* made many verses on the subject of this story, according to which the two contestants were transformed into seals. Heimdal's nine mothers are mentioned by name in the Eddic poem, *Hyndluljóð*, as follows: Gjalp, Greip, Eistla, Eyrgjafa, Ulfrun, Angeyja, Imd, Atla, and Jarnsaxa. In the so-called "Saga-Fragment" which deals with Ivar Vidfadmir and Harold Hilditonn, king Gudrœd, Ivar's paternal uncle and Ingjald Illradi's son-in-law, is compared to Heimdal, who is here designated as the most stupid of the Æsir (*Fornaldar Sǫgur* I, 373). Curiously enough, a ram is sometimes called "Hallinskidi", for what reason has not been explained.

BRAGI

Page 18, line 12—The statement in Snorri's *Edda* according to which poesy has received the title *bragr* after the name of the god, is based on a misapprehension. The truth of the matter is just the reverse; the ancient language has a word *bragr* which means not only "minstrelsy", "poetry", but also "the foremost" (for instance, *bragr ása*, "the foremost of the Æsir", *bragr kvenna*, "supreme among women"). How the relationship between the god Bragi and the earliest named skald, Bragi Boddason, is to be understood, is a moot question. Sufficient grounds have not been advanced for the opinion that the god in reality is nothing more than the human poet elevated to rank among the gods. There are various statements in literature to the effect that at banquets it was a custom to drain a beaker, *bragarfull* (also, but less correctly, *bragafull*), and in so doing to make a solemn promise to perform some deed of note. This word is not derived from the god name *Bragi* but from the common noun *bragr;* accordingly, this was the beaker of him who was foremost (a hero-beaker).

Norse Mythology

FORSETI

Page 18, *line* 20—Forseti literally means "he who has the first seat" (in a tribunal). The name is much like the name of a Frisian divinity, *Fosite*, which occurs, for example, in the combination *Fositesland* (Helgoland), and various scholars have supposed that Forseti is a relatively late adaptation of this foreign name.

HOD—VALI—VIDAR—ULL

Page 19, *line* 20—Hod is originally an ancient term for war or battle; it is found in masculine names among the various Germanic peoples (Old Norse *Hǫðbroddr;* Old German *Hadubrand, Haduberht;* Anglo-Saxon *Heaðubrond, Heaðubeorht,* etc.).

On Vali's mother Rind, see p. 95. There also appears the story of how Odin got his son Vali.

Ullr is the same word as Gothic *wulþus,* "glory". The name no doubt designates him as an ancient god of the heavens; perhaps he was at first identical with Tyr. Place names indicate that the worship of him was general [1]. The name of his dwelling, Ydalir (i. e., "yew-dales"), harmonizes well with the attribution to him of skill as a bowman; bows were frequently made of yew, and the term for yew (*ýr,* from **iwa-,* Anglo-Saxon *īw, ēow,* English *yew;* cf. German *Eibe*) is often found in our ancient literature as a designation for the bow.

HŒNIR—LODUR

Page 21, *line* 5—In a Faroese lay (*Lokka Táttur*), published by V. H. Hammershaimb in his *Færøiske Kvæder* I, 1851, p. 140 ff., Hœnir is mentioned together with Odin and Loki; he is here called the master of the swans. Likewise he appears with Odin and Loki in the story of Thjazi (p. 53) and in the story of Oter, brother of Regin the Smith (p. 169). All this may mean that Lodur, who is referred to in connection with Odin and Hœnir, is only another name for Loki.

LOKI AND HIS CHILDREN

Page 25, *line* 7—Loki was a sort of counterpart of the devil of Christendom. Sophus Bugge therefore has supposed that this figure shows the influence of Christian ideas (*Loki,* from the devil's

[1] See § 86 of the Norwegian original.

Notes

name, *Lucifer*). Axel Olrik (in the *Festskrift til Feilberg* [= *Maal og Minne* 1911] p. 548 ff.) has examined the problem of Loki from other angles, among them that of folklore, since later popular beliefs have preserved reminiscences of a nature divinity named Loki (in sputtering flames, in atmospheric heat waves, and the like; cf. note to p. 37). With reference to higher mythmaking, he distinguishes between Loki as the associate of Odin ("Odins-Loke"), Loki as the companion of Thor ("Tors-Loke") and Loki as the devil of the Æsir faith ("den onde Loke"); but traces survive which point back to a mythical paternal character, a benefactor of men who spreads the benefits of culture, a sort of Prometheus (the inventor of the fish-net, cf. p. 92, and the fire-bringer, Olrik's explanation of the myth of the Necklace of the Brisings, p. 79).

Most of the names of Loki's relations are difficult to explain. E. N. Setälä (*Finnisch-ugrische Forschungen* XII, 1912, p. 210 ff.) has contributed toward a solution by references to Finnish legendary materials which he ascribes to loans from Northern myths; cf. also A. Olrik, *Danske studier* 1912, p. 95 ff. Certainly the name Angerboda may be interpreted as "she who 'bodes', warns of, misfortune or sorrow." Jormungand is "the mighty staff"; more common is the term Midgard Serpent, which no doubt is to be considered the original name of the monster.

The designations for material objects connected with the myth of the Fenris Wolf are no easier to explain; moreover, these names are not identical in the various manuscripts of Snorri's *Edda*. In the *Gylfaginning* (Snorri's *Edda* I, 106 ff.) mention is made not only of *Gleipnir*, but of the two links that were broken, here called *Lœðingr* and *Drómi*. Here occur also the designations *Lyngvi* (an island) and *Ámsvartnir* (a lake). Furthermore, there is a reference to *Gelgja*, a rope attached to the chain; this rope is thrust through a slab of rock, *Gjǫll*, while over the slab lies the stone *þviti*. Finally, the name of the river formed from the slaver of the Wolf is recorded by name, *Ván* (after it Fenrir is sometimes called *Vánargandr*).—In one of the manuscripts (Snorri's *Edda* II, 431) occurs a somewhat different terminology and also several other names than those listed above: *Siglitnir*, a barrow or hillock on Lyngvi; *Gnjǫll*, the hole in the stone *þviti*, to which the Wolf is bound; through this hole is drawn the rope *Hræða*, while *Gelgja* is the bar or stake that is placed before the hole. Here are mentioned also two rivers that run from the

Norse Mythology

mouth of the Wolf, namely *Ván* ("hope") and *Víl* ("despair").
The legendary motive used in the story of the Æsir's stronghold
and its builder is well known. It is localized, among other places,
in a large number of churches (the cathedrals of Lund and Thrond-
hjem, etc.); and the reward may be, for instance, the sun or the
moon or a person's soul, and the builder may be the devil or a
Giant. See C. W. von Sydow, *Studier i Finnsägnen och besläktade
byggmästarsägner* (*Fataburen* 1907, p. 65 ff., 199 ff., 1908 p. 19 ff.).

HERMOD—SKIRNIR

Page 25, line 19—The name Skirnir is formed from the adjective
skírr, "sheer", "shining". The term was originally probably a
cognomen for Frey himself (cf. note to p. 16). Hermod (*Hermóðr*)
means "he who is brave in battle".

THE GODDESSES—FRIGG—JORD—FREYJA

Page 27, line 29—Frigg was known also among the Germans.
Thus the historian of the Longobards, Paulus Diaconus, gives us
to understand that this people worshipped Odin's wife by the
name of Frea (more correctly *Fria*, which is to be met with elsewhere as the phonetic equivalent of *Frigg*). We read that when
the Longobards at one time were making war upon the Vandals,
Wodan promised the victory to that one of the contending tribes
upon whom his eyes first fell at the rising of the sun. Gambara,
the foremost woman among the Longobards, prayed Frea,
Wodan's wife, for aid; and Frea made answer advising the Longobard women to draw their hair down at both sides of their faces,
bind it under their chins after the fashion of beards, and thus
arrayed to take their station outside the casement through which
Wodan was accustomed to look forth toward the East; so doing
they would be certain to come within range of his vision. Wodan
caught sight of them and asked, "Who are these Longbeards?"
Whereupon Frea bade him keep his promise and award the victory
to the Longobards (the "longbeards"; cf. German *Bart*).

It is only Snorri who calls Frigg the daughter of Fjorgynn. He
seems to have misunderstood a passage in the Eddic poem
Lokasenna, in which Frigg is denominated *Fjǫrgyns mær*, that is,
"Fjorgyn's maiden". This expression is probably to be rendered
"Fjorgyn's beloved", in which case *Fjǫrgynn* is a name for Odin.

Notes

Linguistically the name of the god, *Fjǫrgynn*, is closely related to the name of the goddess, *Fjǫrgyn* (mother of Thor) = Jord (Odin's wife). The name of Thor's mother is related to the Lithuanian *Perkúnas*, who like Thor, is a god of thunder. All this points to the probability that the supreme deity had an earth-goddess to wife; in other words, that Frigg originally was identical with Jord (Fjorgyn). It is a general opinion that the goddess name *Fjǫrgyn* was the more primitive, and that the god name *Fjǫrgynn* was a relatively late derivation from the other. Besides *Fjǫrgyn*, Thor's mother also had the name *Hlǫðyn* (so understood by Finnur Jónsson; other scholars give it as *Hlóðyn*). According to Snorri's *Edda*, Jord is the daughter of Anar, or Onar, and Night.

Frigg (Old German *Fría, Fríja*) has been connected with the verb *frjá*, "to love". Her name thus designates her as the beloved of the supreme divinity, and so the same relationship appears here as that between the primal heaven-god Tyr and "Mother Earth" (*Nerthus*, Njord, see note to p. 16). These divine pairs are identical in nature, and with them is associated also a divine pair of whom the wife has been called Freyja. Freyja originally had the meaning "housewife", "mistress"; the name has been formed from the word for "lord" which is known in the name of the god Frey (see note to p. 16). It is thus not the word *frue* (housewife) which is derived from Freyja, as Snorri says; just the reverse is the case.

In addition to Frigg and Freyja, we know from place names (Swedish *Hærnavi*, that is Hœrn's *vi*, or sanctuary) also a third feminine divinity, namely *Hǫrn* (Hørn?), which according to Snorri is another name for Freyja. Possibly this name for a goddess is derived from the word for "flax" (*hǫrr*), in which case we are concerned with a goddess of fertility who is designated after a particular function. These goddess names open for us a vista into most primitive conditions: The goddess of earth or of fertility is the only one of the feminine divinities who was the object of general, public worship. She was worshipped under a number of different designations, locally circumscribed in use. The situation was another with reference to the masculine divinities. They were more numerous, and they were more widely known in that the public worship of them was connected with central localities.

The cult of Freyja was popular, if we may believe the evidence of a large number of place names.[1] She is regarded as a mighty goddess; like Odin she chooses those who are to fall and to come to her in Folkvang (that is, "the field of the warriors"), where she inhabits the hall Sessrymnir ("which has many seats"). Moreover, tradition relates that Freyja was a great sorceress; she practiced a lower form of sorcery (Modern Norw. *seid*), which was considered beneath the dignity of a man. The name Freyja does not occur outside the Northern countries. Among the Germans and the English the names corresponding to Freyja are *Fria*, *Frig*, the counterpart of the Venus of the Romans. Thence Old German *Friatac* (our "Friday"), Anglo-Saxon *Frigedæg*=Latin *Veneris dies* (French *vendredi*).

As to the subordinate goddesses little information can be given. *Hnoss* and *Gersemi* are words well known in the ancient language, having the meaning "treasure", "jewel". *Hlín* occurs also as a name for Frigg herself. The name of Gna's horse, *Hófvarpnir*, means "one who tosses his hoofs" (feet). *Sjǫfn* is connected with *sefi* and *sjafni*, "love". Snorri explains *Lofn* as having to do with *lof*, "leave", "permission", because she permits the lovers to win each other; but the word has a closer relationship to Gothic *lubains* or with Old Norse *ljúfr* (German *lieb*), "dear".

SAGA—EIR—GEFJON—VAR—VOR—SYN—SNOTRA

Page 29, line 14—None of these goddesses seems to have been the object of independent worship, with the possible exception of Gefjon (see, as to her and her plowing, Axel Olrik's article in *Danske studier* 1910, p. 1 ff.). The name Gefjon is connected with the verb *gefa*, "to give", or even more closely with Gothic *gabei*, "riches", *gabeigs*, "rich"; cf. Old Norse *gǫfugr*, "excellent", in Norwegian dialects *govug*, "liberal". Corresponding divinities have been pointed out as having been found among the Germans; in Latin inscriptions from the lower regions of the Rhine occur related names of goddesses: *matronae Gabiae, Junones Gabiae*.— The myth concerning Gefjon and the origin of Zealand and Mälaren is to be met with both in the *Heimskringla* (*Ynglinga Saga*, chapter 5) and in the introduction to *Gylfaginning* in Snorri's *Edda*. In both of these passages occurs a quotation from

---

[1] See § 86 of the Norwegian original.—Translator's note.

Notes

a verse of Bragi the Old: "Gladly Gefjon drew the increase of Denmark (Zealand) from generous Gylfi, so that smoke rose from the swift-moving beasts of burden."

IDUN—NANNA—SIF

Page 30, line 11—*Idunn* is connected with *ið-*, "again"; she is the one who "renews", "rejuvenates". The myth concerning her apples seems to have been derived from the classic myth of the Apples of Hesperides; see Sophus Bugge, in *Arkiv för nordisk filologi* V, p. 1 ff. It is not certain whether traces of the cult of Idun are demonstrable in place names (cf. A. Olrik, *Danske studier* 1910, p. 23 ff., on the name of the Danish island *Ithænø*, now *Enø*). *Nanna*, connected with *nenna* (Gothic *nanþjan*). is linguistically "the brave", "the persevering". *Sif* is the same as the common noun *sif* (see above), Gothic *sibja*, Anglo-Saxon *sib*, German *Sippe* (whence *Sippschaft*).

In the *Skáldskaparmál* of Snorri's *Edda* (I, 556) there is a list of the goddesses. Here are named Frigg, Freyja, Fulla, Snotra, Gerd, Gefjon, Gna, Lofn, Skadi, Jord, Idun, Ilm, Bil, "Njorun", Lin, Nanna, Noss, Rind, Sjofn, Sun, Saga, Sigyn, Vor, Var, Syn, Thrud, and Ran. Two of the number, Ilm and Njorun, are not known otherwise except in skaldic paraphrases, which are not very enlightening. Ilm is more likely to be a Valkyrie than a goddess.

THE NORNS

Page 31, line 2—The Norns are mentioned in countless passages in our ancient literature, and faith in them lingered long after the introduction of Christianity. Thus a runic inscription in the timber church at Borgund runs as follows: "The Norns have done both good and evil".

Of the Norns, according to *Gylfaginning*, there are, besides the three who are definitely named, also others, who come to each person at his birth, to determine his destiny. Some of them are of the race of the gods, others of the Elves, and others again of the Dwarfs.

The very names of the three principal Norns designate their function as rulers of fate. *Urðr* (having close affinities with *verða*, "to take place") is an ancient word for "fate", to be found also in Old Saxon *wurth* and in Anglo-Saxon *wyrd*. Only at a relatively late period, and only among our forefathers, have *Verðandi* (present participle of the verb *verða*) and *Skuld* (connected with *skulu*, "shall"; cf. *skuld*, "duty", "obligation") come into being to form a trinity representing past, present, and future. It is reasonable to assume that the three *Parcæ* of classic mythology have had something to do with this development. The word *norn* is frequently compared with Swedish dialectal *norna*, *nyrna* "to communicate in secret", "to forewarn", and with older English *nyrnen*, "to utter". The word corresponds fairly to Vulgar Latin *fata*, "goddess of destiny", which comes from Latin *fatum*, "fate", more literally "that which is uttered" (whence French *fée*, which through the medium of fairy tales has come into German and into Norwegian: *fe*).

FAMILIAR SPIRITS—ATTENDANT SPIRITS

Page 32, line 6—*Hamingja* really means: one who shows himself in a certain "shape" (*hamr*) or likeness different from his own; the fundamental word *hamr* may at times have the same signification. Sometimes the notion of external form is wholly set aside, so that the supernatural being may be called simply (a person's) "idea" or thought (*hugr*). When the tutelary spirits of a given family were thought of as a group, the names *kynfylgjur*, *ættarfylgjur* (*kyn*, "kin", "family") were often used. At times these spirits would appear in dreams, as the so-called *draumkonur*. They might also be designated as *spádísir* (on *dís*, see p. 33), in which case the emphasis rested on their prophetic function. It was frequently the tutelary spirits of deceased relatives who thus revealed themselves to the living kindred; hence the mention of "departed women" (*konur dauðar*).—As instances of the belief in Attendant Spirits may be mentioned the following: The Icelander Einar Thveraing foretold the death of his powerful brother Gudmund on the basis of a dream; he had seen an immense ox pace up through the parish of Eyfjord to Gudmund's farm and fall dead at the very high seat itself; this ox, said Einar, was the Attendant Spirit of some man or other (*Ljósvetninga Saga*, chapter 21). Harold Gormsson once sent a Finn in the likeness of a whale to Iceland to spy out the land with hostile intent, but he was driven away by the Land-Sprites who thronged all the mountains and mounds (cf. p. 42), and by the foremost chieftains' Attendant Spirits: a bellowing bull, for Thord *gellir* (that is,

Notes

"the bellower") in Breidafjord; a great bird with a large number of smaller birds, for Eyolf of Modruvellir in Eyfjord; a dragon, accompanied by serpents and toads, for Brodd-Helgi in Vapnafjord; a Cliff-Ettin armed with an iron staff, for Thorodd the Priest of the Southland (*Heimskringla* I, 316 ff.).

THE VALKYRIES

Page 33, line 27—Ancient Norse literature contains many accounts of the Valkyries. In *Njál's Saga* there is a picturesque story indicating the notions our forefathers entertained about the Valkyries as paganism was waning away. A farmer named Darrad, living in Caithness, Scotland, was said to have had a vision on the very day of Brian's bloody battle at Dublin in the year 1014. Twelve women came riding through the air and disappeared in a mound; through an aperture the man peeped within and saw them weaving a web of human entrails, using a sword for a weaver's beam and arrows for shuttles. They were singing meanwhile a song, the Song of Darrad (*Darraðarljóð*), which the saga recites at length. The saga further explains that they were weaving a web for the battle which was about to be fought; the struggle was to be sanguinary, a king was to be victorious, but another king and with him many great leaders were to fall. Among the women weavers mentioned by name are Hild, Hjorthrimul, Sangrid, and Svipul, all of them Valkyries. When they had finished their web, they tore it asunder, whereupon six of them rode off with the one piece toward the north and six with the other toward the south.—In Eyvind Skaldaspillir's splendid verses on Hakon the Good (*Hákonarmál*) it is said that Odin sent forth the Valkyries Gondul and Skogul to choose which king was to be the guest of Odin. They rode away on horseback, armed with helmet, spear, and shield, found Hakon, and conveyed him to Valhalla.—Warfare and battle had numerous designations after the Valkyries; "Hild's Game" is especially common. The name Hild is still used, alone and in a large number of combinations, such as Ragnhild (from *ragn* or *regin*, "the ruling powers"; see p. 6); Gunnhild (from *gunnr*, "battle"); Alfhild (from *alfr*, "elf"); and others. The word *dis* also is very common in feminine names, such as Halldis, Herdis, Hjordis, Thordis, and the like.—The legend of Thidrandi, son of Sidu-Hall (*Fornmanna Sögur* II, 192 ff.) informs us how different, mutually hostile Disir might be attached to certain families. A short time before the introduction of Christianity into Iceland, a promising youth named Thidrandi, contrary to the prohibition of the sorcerer Thorhall, went out after a winter night's merrymaking to see who had knocked at the door; thrice he had heard knocking at the door after the inmates of the house had lain down to sleep. Thidrandi saw nine women dressed in black come riding out from the north and other nine, dressed in white and mounted on white horses, riding up from the south; the sable-clad women bore in upon him and left him lying wounded to the death. He was discovered outside the door in the morning; and before he died, he told what he had seen. Thorhall interpreted the vision as portending a change in the ancient faith of the fathers. Both bands of women, so he read the tokens, were Disir, familiars of the household; but those garbed in black had loved the olden faith, now inclining to its fall, and had willed to demand a sacrifice or a tribute from the household before they parted from it forever. The women in white, on the contrary, were to remain alone as Disir of the family under the new dispensation; and these had sought in vain to keep the young man from harm. (In this legend are employed both the terms *fylgjur* and *dísir;* cf. p. 31 and note, and note to p. 47).

Of the literature on the Disir may be mentioned the following titles: L. Levander, *Antikvarisk Tidskrift för Sverige* XVIII, no. 3; M. Olsen, *Hedenske kultminder* I, p. 184 ff.; K. F. Johansson, *Skrifter utgifna af K. Humanistiska Vetenskaps-Samfundet i Uppsala* XX, no. 1.

The most complete catalog of Valkyries is to be found in Snorri's *Edda* II, 490: "*Hrist, Mist, Herja, Hlǫkk, Geiravǫr, Gǫll, Hjǫrþrimul, Guðr [Gunnr], Herfjǫtur, Skuld, Geirǫnul, Skǫgul ok Randgníð, Ráðgríð, Gǫndul, Svipul, Geirskǫgul, Hildr ok Skeggǫld, Hrund, Geirdriful, Randgríðr ok Þrúðr, Reginleif ok Sveið, Þǫgn, Hjalmþrimul, Þrima ok Skalmǫld.*"

THORGERD HŒLGABRUD AND IRPA

Page 34, line 20—The account in ancient sources of a temple erected to Thorgerd by Earl Hakon at Lade may have an historical foundation; but there is probably no solid historical basis for the description of the temple and the image of the goddess as it is found in *Sigmund Brestesson's Saga*. The like is the case with the

Notes

story in *Njál's Saga* concerning a temple which Earl Hakon is supposed to have had together with Dale-Gudbrand: here we have Thor sitting in his chariot, Thorgerd wearing a head kerchief, and with them Irpa, all of them adorned with arm rings of gold.—In the naval battle against the Joms-Vikings, Earl Hakon went ashore and sacrificed to Thorgerd his own son Erling. Whereupon she sent down from the north—the home of the Trolls —a terrific hailstorm accompanied by thunder and lightning; those among the enemy who were gifted with second sight then saw on board of the Earl's ship first a Troll, and thereafter two (Thorgerd and Irpa) engaged in hurling a shower of arrows, "as if an arrow were flying from each finger", against the Joms-Vikings; who then, and not until then, fled the field. (Here we meet with notions of the same kind as those which have given occasion for the discussion of the divinities mentioned in the paragraph next below).—Cf. Gustav Storm's article, *Om Thorgerd Hølgebrud*, in *Arkiv för nordisk filologi* II, p. 124 ff.; K. Liestøl, *Norske trollvisor*, p. 48 ff.

THE FORCES OF NATURE—ÆGIR

Page 37, line 3—Ægir is originally an old-word for "sea", connected with Gothic *ahwa*, Old Norse *á*, "river"; cf. the ancient name of the river Eider, *Egidora*, Old Norse *Ægisdyr* ("the door to the sea"). Ægir was also called *Gymir*, and the sounding of the waves "Gymir's Song". Hence we read in Thjodolf's lay on that king Yngvar who was buried in a mound on the shores of Estland: "The East Sea sings Gymir's song to pleasure the Swedish king".—The names of Ægir's daughters were Himinglæfa ("the translucent one who mirrors the heavens"), Dufa ("one who pitches or dips"), Blodughadda ("the bloody-haired"), Hefring, Unn, Ronn (*Hrǫnn*), Bylgja, Drofn (this word and the one preceding are different names for "wave"), and Kolga ("the coal-black"). (Snorri's *Edda* II, 493.)

Of Fornjot and his kindred we read in the legendary works, *Hversu Noregr byggðist* and *Fundinn Noregr* (*Flatey Book* I, 21 ff.; 219 ff.). Here Thorri, king of Finland and Kvænland, has three children: the sons Nor and Gor and the daughter Goe. Goe is stolen away, and the brothers go out to hunt for her. Gor goes by sea along the coast of Norway, and Nor goes by land. In this way Norway came to be discovered and inhabited, both the coast with its islands and the interior. Goe proved to have been carried off by Rolf of Berg (in Hedemark), son of the Giant Svadi (cf. *Svaðubú*, a part of the Ringsaker of our day). After Thorri, we read further, our fathers called the first month of winter Thorri, and the following month Goe, after Goe (Gjø); this is the reason why our almanacs long carried the headings "January or Thor's Month" and "February or Goe's Month". A piece of childish doggerel runs as follows:

> Torren med sit skjegg
> lokkar borni under sole-vegg.
> Gjø'i med sitt skinn
> lokkar [eller: jagar] borni inn.

> Thor with the beard
> Calls children to the sunny wall.
> Goe with the pelts
> Calls [or: chases] children in.

The meaning seems to be that during Thor's Month there was hard frost and sunshine, while during Goe's Month heavy weather and snowstorms were common. Cf. S. Bugge, *Arkiv för nordisk filologi* IV, p. 126.—It is a moot question what Fornjot really means (cf. E. Hellquist, *Arkiv* XIX, p. 134 f.). If it was a word for "giant", it may be explained as signifying "the consuming one", "the destroyer"; cf. Old High German *fir-niozan*, "to consume". The same mythical name seems to be found in the Anglo-Saxon *Forneotes folme*, "Fornjot's hand".

There are indications that Loki has assumed certain qualities of a fire being (cf. note to p. 25); in Iceland, chips and refuse are still called *Loka-spænir*, "Loki's chips"; *Loka-daunn*, "Loki's vapor", is a term for subterranean sulphur fumes. In Norway, when flames crackle, it is said that Loki is whipping his children.

Eldir means: "he who kindles fire"; *Fimafengr:* "he who is clever at providing ways and means."

NIGHT—DAY

Page 37, line 23—Night drives before Day because our forefathers were in the habit of beginning the twenty-four hours with the night. Therefore they also invariably reckoned time by nights, not as we do now, by days. When a person had sojourned somewhere six days, he would say, "I have been there six nights".

Notes

HEL

Page 39, *line* 4—*Hel* is a very old word for the kingdom of death, the nether world (Gothic *halja*, Old High German *hella*, Anglo-Saxon *hell*). Related words expressing the same thing appear to occur far outside of the boundaries of the Germanic languages; cf. E. N. Setälä, *Finnisch-ugrische Forschungen* XII (1912), p. 170 ff., and H. Güntert, *Kalypso* (Halle 1919).—It is, however, only among the inhabitants of the Scandinavian North that we find the Germanic word for the realm of death used for the personification of that realm: the feminine ruler of the kingdom of the dead. —A word into the composition of which *Hel* enters is *helvíti*, "hell", literally: "punishment (*víti*) in the nether world"; Old High German, *hellawízi;* Anglo-Saxon, *hellewíte.*

THE GIANTS

Page 41, *line* 3—Various Giant women were said to have ridden on the backs of wolves, for which reason the skalds sometimes refer to the wolf as the "Dark-Riders' horse".—In the ancient Eddic poem dealing with Helgi Hjorvardsson we learn of a Giantess who turned into stone at the rising of the sun. Helgi and his shipmate Atli craftily detained her in talk until morning; as the sun rose, Atli said: "Look to the East, Rimgerd, and see if Helgi has not struck you with death-runes . . . Now day is risen, and Atli has made you tarry and has put an end to your life; a laughable sea-mark you seem, standing there in the figure of a stone."—A similar story is told of the voyage of king Olaf during which he created the sound lying between Hornelen, on Bremanger, and Marøy. The king bade the cliff cleave asunder; just then a Giant woman came forward and called out to him: "Tell me, man with the white beard, why you split my rocky wall in twain?" Olaf answered: "Stand there, Troll, always in stone; and no man more shall make his moan!" And it happened according to his word: a figure of stone stands there to this day.— Many legends relate how a Mountain-Troll, pursuing a human being, is overtaken by the rays of the sun and turned to stone. Other legends deal with Trolls who have made compacts with Olaf to build churches, just as in the case of the owner of Svadilfari (see p. 24 and note to p. 25).

On the warfare of the Giants against one another and against

Norse Mythology

Christendom, legends are to be found in almost every parish; as examples may be mentioned the story from Gudbrandsdalen of Jutulberget and Vågå church, and from Ringerike of Gyvrihaugen. The Giants are so firmly established in the credence of the people that the legends connected with them cannot easily perish; they belong, with the Brownie, the Huldre, and the Nix, to that group of supernatural beings with which the countryman in Norway, even down to the present day, has believed himself surrounded. In very recent times new legends have sprung up, after the fashion of the older. See, for instance, in Asbjørnsen's *Huldreeventyr, The Jutul and Johannes Blessom,* and others of a similar tenor.

As was the case with Ginnunga-gap, so Jotunheim was removed to greater and greater distances according as the geographical knowledge of the Northern regions increased among our ancestors. Moreover, influences emanating from southern legends of the felicity of the Hyperboreans, or Dwellers in the Uttermost North, no doubt contributed toward placing the home of the Giants in vaguely remote confines; in the imagination of most people, Glæsisvoll and the neighboring Udainsaker (the Land of the Immortals) took the form of an earthly Paradise, where men were permitted to live in eternal bliss. Among the Roman stories of the Hyperboreans there is one to the effect that those who became sated with living, ended their days by throwing themselves over the edge of a high mountain. Something of the same kind is to be found in a romantic Norse saga (*Gautrek's Saga*), in which however the scene is not the same; according to this story there is in Götaland a beetling cliff, *Ætternisstape* ("the ancestral crag"), where the ancients sought death by hurling themselves down from the summit.

According to Kaarle Krohn (*Skandinavisk mytologi,* p. 58 ff.), the original notion of the Giants was that they were primeval folk who had taken refuge in the waste places of the land. They are different from the lower orders of the spirit world, the Sprites (*vettir*, p. 42), in that the Giants received no sacrifices. Nor were they originally among the beings who lived and moved in the darkness of the Yuletide season; see Liestøl's article, cited above, note to p. 4. On the more or less close identification of the Giants with natural forces, see C. W. von Sydow's article mentioned in the same connection.

Notes

THE DWARFS

Page 41, line 25—Of the king of the Swedes, Svegdi, Snorri tells in the *Ynglinga Saga* that he was decoyed into a stone, from which he never emerged. So firmly fixed was the faith of the fathers in the actual presence of these beings within the mountain sides, that they designated the echo as *dvergmáli*, that is, "the speech of the Dwarfs". In the romantic *Bosa Saga* (*Fornaldar Sǫgur* III, 222) occurs the line, "Sigurd played upon the harp so loudly that the speech of the Dwarfs resounded through the hall." In several localities in Norway we find *Dvergstein* as the name for a farm,[1] and P. A. Munch has pointed out that more than one mountain top bears the name "Dvergemål-kletten" ("Dwarf-speech-summit").

Among the chief examples of the work of Dwarf artisans may be mentioned the Necklace of the Brisings, Mjollnir, Gungnir, Draupnir, Sif's golden hair, and the swords Tyrfing and Gram.

The Norwegian word *dverg* is known also in Old German (*twerc*, German *Zwerg*) and in Anglo-Saxon (*dweorg*, English "dwarf"). A Dwarf woman was in old Norse called *dyrgja*. The connotation of the term is uncertain.

THE VETTIR

Page 47, line 27—To the word *vættr* corresponds the German *Wicht*, and German legends are much occupied with beings called *Wichtlein, Wichtelmännchen*. Here belongs also the well-known German word *Bösewicht*. In Anglo-Saxon the word was *wiht*, whence the English "wight", a term occurring frequently in ballads. Originally the word *vættr* and its variants had a more general meaning (e. g., "a thing"), a signification that still appears in *ekkivætta*, in Modern Norwegian dialects *ikkje* (*inkje*) *vetta*, "nothing". The compound form (*eit*) *godvette*, "guardian spirit", persists in present usage; in Nordland (*ei*) *godvetter* (*-vetra*) is practically equivalent to Huldre, "Hill-Lady". (Mountain names such as Vettaåsen, Vettakollen are, on the other hand, to be connected with *viti*, "a beacon-fire".)

The notes to p. 32 record instances in which the Land-Sprites of Iceland and the Attendant Spirits of mighty chieftains join in the protection of the land against hostile strategems. In

[1] See § 86 of the Norwegian original.—Translator's note.

Norse Mythology

the story of the seer Thorhall and the kin of Sidu-Hall, of which an excerpt is given in the note to p. 33 occurs also the following account: One day shortly before the coming of Christianity Thorhall lay in his bed looking out through a window; he smiled, and his host, the powerful Sidu-Hall, one of the first men who accepted baptism, asked him what he was smiling at. Thorhall answered: "I am smiling to see many a mound opening up and all living beings, great and small, packing their belongings and moving elsewhere." From these examples it is clear that there was no important distinction between the Vettir and Disir (Attendant Spirits) of the country and those of the individual family.

The narrative of Egil Skallagrimsson and his libel-pole is of importance for the illustration of the ancient runic magic; see M. Olsen, *Om troldruner* (*Fordomtima* II, Uppsala 1917) p. 19 ff. (=*Edda* V, p. 235 ff.)—On procession days, cf. Joh. Th. Storaker, *Tiden i den norske Folketro* (*Norsk Folkeminnelag* II), Christiania 1921, p. 97.

In certain localities, for example in Telemark, a distinction is made between Goblins or Hill-Goblins (*tusser* or *haugtusser*) and Jutuls; the Goblins are not larger than men, while the Jutuls are tall as mountains. The Vettir of this district are the same as the Hidden Folk; they are no larger than a child of ten, and dressed in gray clothing and black hats; their cattle are called *huddekrœtur*, "Huldre cattle", and their dogs *huddebikkjer*, "Huldre curs".

The name of the Huldre or Hill-Lady, *huldr*, probably comes from *at hylja*, "to hide", "to cover". The Germans are conversant with a somewhat similar being, *Holle*, *Frau Holle*, *Mutter Holle* or *Holde*, whose name appears at an early period to have been associated with the adjective *hold*, Old Norse *hollr*, "kind", "amiable", "friendly". Frau Holle sometimes takes the role of a severe and industrious spinner, who rewards the diligent and punishes the indolent; but usually she is described as having a hideous appearance and as riding about in the company of witches. Our Huldre, on the contrary, bears a name which linguistically has always been kept distinct from the adjective *hollr*.—In the *Sturlunga Saga* (Kålund's edition, II, 325) we read of a *Huldar Saga* ("of a great Troll woman") which the Icelander Sturla Tordsson told to king Magnus Lawmender and his queen; this saga is no longer extant. Cf. K. Maurer, *Abhandlungen der königlichen bayerischen Akademie der Wissenschaften* I Cl. XX, 1, 2.

In Denmark, popular belief is concerned more particularly with

Notes

Elves, and in Norway with the Hidden Folk (cf. note to p. 4). Both classes of beings show a decided preference for the alder and for the twigs of the alder, perhaps through association with the name, since *hulder* is like *older*, just as the Danish word *ellefolk* ("elves") approaches in sound the Danish name for the alder: *elle*.

The Nix (*nykr*) is called in Swedish *necken* and also *strömkarlen* ("the man of the stream"), who no doubt comes nearest to the Norwegian *fossegrimen* ("the water-sprite"). In German the Nix is called *Der Nix, Nickel, Nickelmann;* the Nix woman is called *Nixe, Wassernixe*. The Nix is said to apportion his instruction according to the gifts he receives. One who gives him bread he teaches to tune the fiddle; but one who gives him a ram he teaches to play perfectly. Of several peculiar, wild melodies it is told that the Nix has taught them to the fiddlers. In older times people also imagined the Nix as having the form of a dapple-gray horse; now and then he would come forth from the water, and it even happened that he permitted himself to be used for some work or other during the day. Concerning the prophecies of Mermen or Mermaids, various legends have been current, such for examples as the one in *Half's Saga* about the Merman who exercised his gift of prophecy for king Hjorleif the Woman-Lover (p. 252).

Formed in the same manner as *marmennill* "merman" from *marr*, "sea" and *maðr*, "man") is the Old High German *merimanni*, "mermaid". As early as the period of Old High German this word took the form *meriminni* (*minni* means "love", "the beloved", and in the language of children, "mother"). From the German comes the Danish *mareminde*, a word which later was erroneously applied to the Nightmare. According to the description in the *King's Mirror*, the Mermaid (*margýgr*) is not beautiful and winsome as Mermaids are usually represented; to be sure, she is a woman above the middle and a fish below the middle, but her hands are large and webbed between the fingers, and her features have a terrifying aspect, with sharp eyes, broad forehead, large mouth, and wrinkled cheeks. She makes her appearance only as a harbinger of great storms. On such occasions she emerges above the water holding fishes in her hands. If she eats the fishes or throws them in a direction away from the ship, the sailors have hopes of weathering the storm; but if she plays with them or tosses them toward the ship, the signs indicate misfortune.

Norse Mythology

With the Brownie may be compared the German *Kobold*, who also is a kind and good-natured domestic fairy dressed in a red cap; further, the English Puck or Robin Goodfellow. The Swedes do not use the name *Nisse* but *tomtegubbe, tomtekarl,* "brownie"; in Norwegian occur the similar terms: *tuftekall, tomtegubbe (tomtvette, tuftvette),* sometimes shortened to *tufte, tomte.* The notions on which these designations are based may be illustrated by corresponding terms current in western Norway: *tunvord (tunkall), gardvord,* ("the guardian of the yard or the farm"). *Nisse* is really a diminutive pet name for Nils (Nicolaus). This relatively modern designation has come to Norway from Germany, where Nicolaus, Niclas, Nickel, Klaus are used to denote a being who appears in disguise on St. Nicholas' Day (December 6) to distribute rewards or punishments to children; it is also used of a little imp.

In German the Nightmare is called *Alp,* the same word as Norwegian *alv.* In many countries legends prevail concerning people who were able to show themselves in a guise different from their own natural shape. We shall meet with several examples of this sort of thing in the Heroic Legends: Bodvar Bjarki fought at Rolf Kraki's side in the likeness of a bear (p. 220); Sigmund and Sinfjotli cloaked themselves as wolves (p. 156); and Valkyries appeared in the semblance of swans (p. 126). German legend abounds with stories of beautiful maidens who turn into swans as soon as they put on an enchanted ring or belt. In like manner the Werewolves were able to assume their alien guise as wolves through the aid of ring or belt. The myths of the gods also have something to tell of such metamorphoses (Freyja's feather-coat, p. 76); Odin above all others was skilled in the arts of transformation (*Ynglinga Saga,* chapter 7).

All the various beings of Northern superstition who may be brought under the common designation of Vettir (Elves, Hidden Folk, Underground Folk, and the like) were, according to Kaarle Krohn, departed spirits who had become attached to certain localities ("localized spirits or sprites"); see his exhaustive array of evidence in *Skandinavisk mytologi,* p. 36 ff. One link in his argument has to do with the inability of these Vettir to beget children with each other. Radically different from such Vettir are the Giants, who according to Krohn were prehistoric men who had migrated into waste places.

Notes

THE HEROES AND LIFE OF VALHALLA

Page 49, *line* 11—"To visit Odin in Valhalla" was a common expression, meaning to fall in honorable combat. When champions challenged each other to an island duel to the death, they were in the habit of invoking for each other a journey to Valhalla (cf. p. 9, for the throwing of spears over the heads of a hostile army). When a warrior had fallen and had been laid in his barrow, he too was dedicated to Valhalla in the course of an oration delivered beside the grave. The saga recounts expressly such a ceremony in the case of Hakon Adelsteinsfostri's burial. Many of the ancient lays bear witness to the reception accorded the Heroes by Odin in Valhalla. Of Helgi Hundingsbane we read that Odin took him into his counsels; and at once Helgi turned toward his quondam enemy Hunding and bade him do the service of a thrall:

> Thou shalt, Hunding,
> Wash the feet
> Of every man,
> Kindle the fire,
> Bind the dogs,
> Herd the horses,
> Give swine their swill,
> Ere thou sleepest.

In the old lay on Erik Bloody-Axe, *Eiríksmál*, we learn that it was a matter of great moment for Odin to give Erik an honorable reception on his coming to Valhalla in the company of five other kings:

> What mean these dreams? (said Odin)
> I dreamed I rose before day dawned,
> To prepare Valhalla
> For fallen warriors;
> I woke the Heroes,
> Bade them arise,
> Strew the benches with straw,
> And scour the vessels;
> Bade Valkyries bear wine
> Meet for a prince.
> From the earth yonder
> I wait the coming
> Of highborn heroes;
> Glad now is my heart.

Norse Mythology

Bragi, seized with wonder at the clatter and commotion, guesses that it is Balder who is about to return to the halls of Odin. But Odin says that such talk is folly; the roads are already resounding with the advance of Erik's company. Then Odin commands Sigmund and Sinfjotli to go out to meet the king. Bragi asks why Odin looks for Erik rather than for other kings. "Because he has harried so many lands and borne a bloody sword", answers Odin. Yet Bragi has still more questions to ask: "Why did not Odin grant victory to such a warrior?" "It were safer for the gods to have such a hero in their own midst as a bulwark against the Fenris Wolf," is Odin's reply. Thereupon Erik is bidden welcome and invited to enter the hall. "Who are the princes that come with you from the battle?" "They are five kings—I name them all by name for you—I am myself the sixth." With this speech ends the portion of the poem that has been preserved to our time.

According to the *Hákonarmál*, a poem composed by Eyvind Skaldaspillir to the honor of Hakon Adelsteinsfostri, Odin sends the Valkyries Gondul and Skogul to choose from among the Yngling kings those who were to visit Odin. They see Hakon throw off his byrnie, fighting desperately; him they choose, and Gondul says: "Now the retinue of the gods will increase, since they have asked Hakon to join their company with a great army." Hakon inquires of the Valkyries why the battle has taken such a turn: "We were surely worthy of the victory." "It lay in our hands," answered Skogul, "that you kept the field and that your enemies fled."

> Now shall we ride,
> Quoth mighty Skogul,
> To the gods' green home;
> We bring Odin tidings
> That soon the prince comes
> Himself to see him.

Odin bids Hermod and Bragi go forth to meet him and invite him to enter. Bragi invests him with the rights that pertain to the Heroes and promises him sojourn in Valhalla: there await him eight brothers who have gone before him.

> All of our armor,
> Quoth the good king,
> We will hold in our keeping;

Notes

Helmet and byrnie
No man lays aside;
It is well to be ever ready.

Further may be mentioned the *Krákumál*, a much later poem (from the 12th century) attributed to Ragnar Lodbrok. Ragnar recites the verses, celebrating one of his victories, in a den of serpents not long before his death. At the close we read: "I know that the benches of Balder's father (Odin) always stand ready for the banquet; forthwith we shall drink ale from the horn; the hero will not bewail his death in magnificent Odin's hall; I will not enter Odin's home with words of fear on my lips. Now am I fain to end my lay; for the Disir (Valkyries) whom Odin has sent to me from Valhalla bid me come into his home, even to himself. Gladly shall I drink ale with the Æsir in the high seat; all hope of life has fled, and laughing I go toward death."

Vingolf is mentioned as the resort of Heroes in only one passage in Snorri's *Edda* (I, 84); otherwise it is the hall of the goddesses. It is not mentioned at all in the Eddic Poems.

Of the names for the rivers which according to Snorri's Edda flow forth from the antlers of the hart, the greater number connote roaring or rapid streams, or cold or deep streams: Sid, Vid, Soekin, Eikin, Svol, Gunntro, Fjorm, Fimbulthul, Gipul, Gopul, Gomul, Geirvimul,—all these run through the domain of the Æsir; the others are: Thyn, Vin, Tholl, Holl, Grad, Gunnthrain, Nyt, Not, Nonn, Ronn, Vina, Vegsvin, Thjodnuma. *Grímnismál* records still others by name.

CORRUPTION

Page 50, line 19—Of the "three mighty Thursar maidens" nothing can be said with certainty; nor of Gullveig. There are conjectures pointing to the Norns and to a personification of the corrupting influence of gold. See Finnur Jónsson's explanation of the connection between passages in the *Vǫluspá*, in his brochure, *Vǫlu-spá, Vǫlvens spådom* (*Studier fra sprog- og oldtidsforskning.* no. 84), Copenhagen 1911.

THE RAPE OF IDUN

Page 56, line 11—The myth of Thjazi and Idun seems to have been widespread and well-known (cf. note to p. 76). The skalds sometimes refer to Idun as "Thjazi's booty", and to gold as the

Norse Mythology

"Giants' mouth-reckoning" or as the "Giants' words". According to Snorri's account in the *Ynglinga Saga*, Skadi became thoroughly tired of Njord and later wedded Odin; their son was Sæming, ancestor of the Haloigja family.

It is not certain just which stars were supposed to have been formed from Thjazi's eyes. In the opinion of J. Fr. Schroeter (*Maal og Minne* 1919, p. 120 f.) they are the two stars β and γ in Ursa Minor.

THOR'S UNLUCKY JOURNEY TO JOTUNHEIM

Page 65, *line* 18—The Swedish student of folklore, C. W. von Sydow, has subjected this myth to exhaustive scrutiny in his article *Tors färd til Utgard* (*Danske studier* 1910, pp. 65–105, 145–82). He reaches the conclusion that the most important components of the myth are to be traced to borrowings from the Celtic, presumably during the Viking era, but prior to the composition of the Eddic poems *Lokasenna* and *Hárbarðsljóð* (in which occur allusions to the episode of Skrymir), or in other words, before the tenth century. Sophus Bugge had at an earlier date expressed a similar opinion (*Populær-videnskabelige Foredrag*, Christiania, 1907, p. 19 f.). Bugge laid particular stress on the word "*gres*-iron" (rendered above as "troll-iron"), used of the bands with which Skrymir bound up the bag; this word is not Northern, but Irish: "*grés* in Irish means 'art', and is especially employed of the arts used by a smith in making iron sharp, hard, and shiny." Scholars have, however, also found in the myth ancient domestic motives (von Sydow, with others). Among these, particular interest attaches to Thor's youthful followers, Thjalfi and Roskva. The latter name (*Rǫskva*, *earlier *Vrǫskva*, related to Gothic *wrisqan*, pronounced *vriskv-*, "to bear fruit") points to a feminine divinity of fruitfulness (cf. note to p. 16) who once must have been closely allied with Thor; there are indications that Thor, notably in Sweden, ruled over seasons and harvests (see p. 118). Thjalfi is found in ancient myths of Thor as the retainer of this god; see Axel Olrik's article *Tordenguden og hans dreng* (*Danske studier* 1905).

THOR'S VISIT TO HYMIR

Page 69, *line* 31—The myth of Thor and the Midgard Serpent is known also from skaldic poems: Bragi the Elder's *Ragnarsdrápa*

Notes

and Ulf Uggason's *Húsdrápa*. The subject is treated also in a figured stone recently discovered in Sweden. On the presumed Christian prototype of the myth (Christ catching Leviathan on a hook), see, among others, K. Krohn, *Finnisch-ugrische Forschungen* VII, p. 167 ff. From the side of folklore certain phases of the myth have been investigated by C. W. von Sydow, *Jätten Hymes bägare* (*Danske studier* 1915 [= *Folkminnen och Folktankar* 1914] pp. 113–50). Among scholars no agreement prevails as to the relationship between Tyr and Hymir.

THOR'S VISIT TO GEIRRŒD

Page 72, line 22—This myth we know from Snorri's *Edda*, which in great measure bases its story upon a still partially extant skaldic poem, the *Þórsdrápa* of Eilif Godrunarson. An account of Geirrœd, certainly derived from a Northern source, occurs also in Saxo (see Axel Olrik, *Kilderne til Sakses oldhistorie* II, 1894, p. 133 ff.; cf. K. Liestøl, *Norske trollvisor*, p. 53 ff.):

A Danish king named Gorm had heard an Icelandic ("Thulanian") myth about Geruth's (Geirrœd's) farmstead. Determined to pay a visit to Geirrœd, he set out, accompanied by the widely traveled Thorkel Adelfar, with three ships and three hundred bold men. They sailed northward, but just off Halogaland they encountered head winds so that their provisions were presently exhausted. After many adventures they finally reached land, where they discovered such large herds of cattle that they could not refrain from slaughtering, to supply themselves for the voyage, more than they needed at the moment, in spite of the warnings of Thorkel. During the night they were attacked by a rout of hideous Giants, and they were not permitted to depart before they had delivered over one man from each vessel by way of ransom. Thereupon they continued their course to Bjarmiland, where they found continual winter, murky forests, and no end of monsters. Here they landed. Thorkel forbade them all to speak a single word to the inhabitants of the land, on pain of inevitable harm. A gigantic man came down to the shore to bid them welcome, naming each of the voyagers by his right name; Thorkel said it was Gudmund, Geirrœd's brother, who was in the habit of looking after all strangers. He asked Thorkel why they all remained silent, and Thorkel replied that they were dumb from shame at not knowing any other language than their mother tongue.

[317]

Gudmund invited them to go with him, and they consented;
Thorkel meanwhile bade them not to touch anything or anybody
and not to taste meat or drink; else they would lose all memory
of their earlier life. Gudmund was amazed at the king's not
eating a morsel of food, although his own twelve fair daughters
waited at the board; but Thorkel always found some excuse or
other. Now Gudmund sought to entice the newcomers, offering
his daughters in marriage; and four of their number, allowing
themselves to be hoodwinked, lost their reason. Once more,
but in vain, Gudmund tempted the king with the lovely flowers
in his garden. Not until all of his arts had come to naught did
he guide them on their way and across a stream so that they
might reach Geirrœd's estate. Presently they descried a hideous,
ruinous, filthy town; on the walls many severed human heads
stood fixed on stakes, and savage dogs lay on guard outside the
portals. Thorkel heartened his traveling companions, and
quieted the dogs by letting them lick a horn smeared with fat.
They had to climb over the gates by means of ladders, and now
they saw that the town was teeming with horrible black shapes;
fearful odors filled the air. They walked on, Thorkel meanwhile
repeating his warnings. Finally they reached Geirrœd's house;
it was black with soot and the floor was alive with snakes; spears
occupied the place of rafters, and a frightful stench filled the
room. On the benches along the wall sat Trolls as rigid as stones,
while near the door the watchmen leaped about in goatish antics.
First the travelers had to pass through a block of stone split in
twain; having done so, they caught sight of Geirrœd, an aged
man with a pierced body, sitting in the high seat, and beside him
three women with broken backs. The block of stone, said
Thorkel, had been split by Thor with the same bolt of iron with
which he transfixed Geirrœd; it was Thor too who had broken
the backs of the women. Here three men of the company yielded
to their desire to touch certain of the treasures, and promptly
fell dead. The rest meanwhile passed on into an adjoining room,
where treasures of such fabulous value met their gaze that even
Thorkel lost command of himself and seized upon a splendid
cloak. Instantly all the Trolls raised an outcry, surged in upon
the strangers, and killed all who were not able to defend themselves by means of arrows or stones. Only the king, Thorkel, and
twenty others escaped. They hurried back whence they had
come; in their retreat, however, one of their number succumbed to

Notes

temptation, married one of Gudmund's daughters, and in consequence lost his wits. Finally the rest reached the ships once more and sailed home.

In this story we meet again the daughters of Geirrœd, with broken backs; here, however, they are three, not two as in Snorri's *Edda*. Instead of the iron pillar we have here the sundered boulder. In general, the *Prose Edda's* description of the halls of Hell on the Strand of Corpses (see p. 38) seems to have occupied the saga writer's thoughts while he penned his account of Geirrœd's domain.

Echoes of the myth dealing with Geirrœd occur furthermore in the romantic Icelandic story of Thorstein Bœjarmagn (*Fornmanna Sǫgur* III, 174–98), dating from the 14th century. One of Olaf Tryggvason's bodyguard, named Thorstein Bœjarmagn, while on an expedition to the east, fell in with prince Godmund of Glæsisvoll, who was on a journey for the purpose of paying homage to Geirrœd of Risaland. Thorstein bore him company across the boundary river Hemra to Geirrœd's hall. Here he gave Godmund and his men assistance through occult arts in certain competitive games and trials of strength with Geirrœd and his retainers. At last he brought down upon the hall a rain of immense sparks which in the end blinded and killed Geirrœd, whereupon Godmund took sway over the whole of Geirrœd's kingdom.

Snorri relates in his *Edda* that Thor may sometimes in skaldic phrase be designated as the "Killer of Geirrœd", and Loki as "Geirrœd's Guest" or "Geirrœd's Shroud".

THOR'S COMBAT WITH RUNGNIR

Page 76, line 20—This myth Snorri learned to know from the poem *Haustlǫng*, the author of which was Harold Fairhair's Skald Thjodolf of Hvin. The same lay deals also with Thjazi and Idun (p. 53 ff.). The general opinion identifies Aurvandil's Toe with Orion. It is worth noticing that both of the myths providing material for the extant fragments of *Haustlǫng* have to do with the astronomical notions of our forefathers.

The masculine name Aurvandil, which obviously is of literary origin, occurs also among the ancient Germans: *Auriwandalo* in Longobard sources, *Orentil* in Frankish and Bavarian sources; furthermore, *Orendel*, in a Middle High German epic poem, half legend, half romantic tale, of the same name. A corresponding

[319]

Norse Mythology

common noun appears in Anglo-Saxon, *ēarendel*, glossed with Latin *jubar*, meaning "effulgence" and "morning-star". These circumstances seem to point to a legendary hero named Aurvandil (cf. the addition "Frœkni": the brave), concerning whom, however, no accurate information is available. He has nothing but the name in common with *Horvendillus* (a tributary king in Jutland, father of Amleth [*Amlóði*, "Hamlet"]; killed by his own brother Fengi) in Saxo, the hero of an islet duel in the Viking manner. A. Heusler (*Reallexikon der germanischen Altertums-kunde* III, p. 372 f.) summarizes his conception of the Aurvandil story as follows: "A mythical Aurvandil has left memorials among the Germanic peoples, both the southern and northern, and a star has taken its name from him; it is not certain whether he had a place in heroic literature, and whether the High German epic, supplied with materials from sources so numerous, had any other connection with him than that of the name."

THRYM STEALS MJOLLNIR

Page 78, line 26—This myth is known through the Eddic poem *Þrymskviða*. On the basis of this lay the Icelandic "rimes", *Þrymlur*, were composed about the year 1400; and both the ancient pagan poem and the *Þrymlur* form the foundation, according to Sophus Bugge and Moltke Moe's *Torsvisen i sin norske form* (in *Festskrift til Hs. Maj. Kong Oscar II ved Regjerings-Jubilæet 1897*), for a popular ballad which has been recorded in Norwegian, Swedish, and Danish versions. The Norwegian ballad is published in the article by Bugge and Moe named above, the Swedish in Arwidsson's *Svenska fornsånger* I, no. 1, and the Danish in S. Grundtvig's *Danmarks gamle Folkeviser* I, no. 1. The ballads show a close relationship to the Eddic myth; the names, however, have been considerably changed in the course of tradition. Thor is thus called "Torekall" (Norwegian), "Torkar", "Torer" (Swedish), "Tord af Hafsgård" (Danish); Loki (Laufey's son) is called "Låkjen" (Norwegian), "Locke Lewe" (Swedish), "Lokke Leimand" or "Lokke Læjermand" (Danish; he is here Thor's brother); Freyja is called "jungfru Frojenborg" (Swedish), "Freiensborg" (Danish); Thrym is called "Trolle-tram" (Swedish; cf. Old Norse *tramr*, "devil"), "Tossegreve" (Danish); and Asgard, "Åsgålen" in the Norwegian ballad, has become "Hafsgård" in the Danish. S. Bugge has found an echo

Notes

of the Eddic poem in an "Old Danish runic inscription in England," from about the year 1075; see *Aarbøger for nordisk oldkyndighed* 1899, p. 263 ff. The myth has been discussed by Axel Olrik in the article cited in the note to p. 65.

THE NECKLACE OF THE BRISINGS

Page 80, line 16—According to Sophus Bugge (*Beiträge zur Geschichte der deutschen Sprache* XII, p. 69 ff.), this myth was strongly influenced by an old German heroic legend localized in Breisgau (*Brisaha*) in Baden. *Brisinga-men* may be rendered as the "Necklace of the Brisings (the name of a people)". It is no doubt to be identified with the ornament *Brōsinga-mene* in the Anglo-Saxon epic of *Beowulf*, in which *Brōsinga* surely appears through an error in tradition instead of *Brisinga*. The ancient Northern peoples understood the name to mean the "gleaming ornament", no doubt connecting it with *brisingr*, "fire", in Modern Norwegian dialects *brising* "bonfire", "torch" (and *brisa*, "to shine", "to flame").

THE DEATH OF BALDER

Page 86, line 20—The first section is a summary of the Eddic poem *Vegtamskviða* or *Baldrs Draumar*. Vegtam means "the wanderer", more literally "one who is familiar with the way"; Valtam means "one who is familiar with battle". The last of the questions has to do with the same subject as Odin's last question in the verbal duels with Vafthrudnir (p. 102) and with king Heidrek (p. 143). In all three of these instances Odin reveals his identity through this question; and here, as in the two other cases, the query probably alludes to Balder's death. Accordingly Sophus Bugge (*Studier* I, p. 252 ff.) has taken the position that the maidens referred to are weeping for the death of Balder; if the "neckerchiefs" are taken to mean "sails", the signification may be this, that the waves, daughters of Ægir, hurl the blazing ship with Balder's body on board toward the heavens. As to the "mother of three Thursar", P. A. Munch points to Angerboda, who was the mother of Hel, Fenrir, and the Midgard Serpent.

The material in the following paragraphs of the section is based on Snorri's *Edda*, which in this case clearly has drawn on

Norse Mythology

poetic sources. The portion dealing with Balder's funeral is founded on a skaldic poem, Ulf Uggason's *Húsdrápa*, fragments of which still are extant. The remaining portions, dealing with Balder's death and Hermod's journey to Hell, presuppose Eddic poems, probably two in number, of which the strophe of Thokk alone remains.

On Hod, see p. 18. Mistletoe (*mistitteinn*) means literally the "plant mistletoe", which has had great importance in cult and magic over a wide area. The name of Balder's ship, Ringhorni, means "ring-prowed" (see Hj. Falk, *Altnordisches Seewesen* [in the periodical *Wörter und Sachen* IV, 1912] p. 38). Hyrrokkin is "one shrunken (*hrokkinn*) by fire (*hyrr*)". The Dwarf's name, Lit, is no doubt the common noun *litr*, "color", "complexion". Thokk is the word "thanks", here no doubt used ironically in the sense of "un-thanks", "ingratitude" (cf. S. Bugge, *Studier* I, p. 62 f.).

The myth of Balder is probably the most disputed of all the Norse myths. Among the suppositions which by this time have been pretty well discarded are that this myth is based on a myth of the seasons (Uhland, Simrock) and that it reflects a struggle between light and darkness conceived morally (N. F. S. Grundt-vig). A wholly one-sided theory built up on a separate portion of the myth is that of Frazer (*Balder the Beautiful* I–II, 1913) according to which Balder is made the personification of the mistle-toe-bearing oak, the soul or living principle of which is the mistle-toe itself. (Strongly influenced by Frazer is Henrik Schück's treatment of the myth in his *Studier i nordisk literatur - och religionshistoria* II, 1904.) A new foundation for the solution of the problem has been laid by Sophus Bugge; in his opinion there must exist an historical connection between the Balder-myth and Christianity (Balder=Christ). Kaarle Krohn (*Finnisch-ugrische Forschungen* V, 1905, p. 83 ff.) seeks confirmation of this view through an examination of connected traditions in the folklore of Finland: "The Eddic myth of Balder, as well as the section of the *Kalevala* dealing with Lemminkäinen's death, is nothing more or less than a Christian legend". A contrary posi-tion is taken by Gustav Neckel (*Die Überlieferungen vom Gotte Balder*, Dortmund, 1920), who maintains that the connection of the myth with Christianity is not immediate; according to his conception, Balder is to be linked with an Oriental god of fruit-fulness who belongs within the same religious and historical limits

·[322]

Notes

as Christianity. Neckel believes that the myth came to us by way of Thrace during the period of the great migrations. On another Norse form of the Balder-myth, see p. 94 ff.

ÆGIR'S BANQUET—THE CHASTISING OF LOKI

Page 94, line 5—The *Prose Edda* contains no record of Loki's scurrilities in the house of Ægir but does give, immediately after the story of Balder's death, an account of the vengeance of the gods upon Loki. The *Poetic Edda* is more explicit on the subject; it has an entire lay dealing with Loki's abusive speeches (*Lokasenna*, called in later manuscripts *Ægisdrekka*), and a prose appendix declaring expressly that Loki's punishment was reserved till that time. *Vǫluspá* too refers to the chastisement of Loki in a passage stating that he was bound with the entrails of Vali.

Lokasenna alludes to many matters not otherwise known; some of these things must no doubt be regarded as inventions of the poet. The accusation that Frigg had loved the brothers of Odin has to do with the same myth as that recorded in Snorri's *Heimskringla, Ynglinga Saga,* chapter 3. We read likewise in the *Ynglinga Saga,* chapter 4, that Njord had his own sister to wife while he was still one of the Vanir; among the Æsir, on the contrary, wedding with a sister was forbidden.

Besides much that is vague and obscure in *Lokasenna*, there is also much that is coarse, which however often has a boldly comic effect. We read of Freyja: *þegi þú, Freyja! þú ert fordœða, ok meine blandin mjǫk, síz þik at brœðr þínum stóðu blíð regin ok mundir þú þá, Freyja! frata.* Of Gefjon: *þegi þú, Gefjon! þess mun ek nú geta, er þik glapði at geði sveinn inn hviti, er þer sigli gaf, ok þú lagðir lær yfir.* Of Nojrd: *Hymis meyjar hǫfðu þik at hlandtrogi ok þér í munn migu.* To be accused of being a female animal or a woman was regarded as touching the honor of a man so closely that accusations of that sort were expressly forbidden by law.

OTHER NORSE MYTHS CONCERNING THE DEATH OF BALDER (IN SAXO)

Page 96, line 29—This story has throughout the characteristics of romantic medieval sagas. Saxo's Rinda is the Rind (earlier **Vrind*) of the *Eddas,* where however she is merely mentioned.

[323]

Norse Mythology

Rind was once actually worshipped as a goddess; on this point the ancient Swedish place name *Vrindavi* (near Norrköping), i. e., "Rind's sanctuary", bears witness (see E. Brate *Arkiv för nordisk filologi* XXIX, p. 109 ff.). (The opinion has been advanced that allusions to Odin and Rind occur in certain strophes of the Eddic poem *Hávamál*, where Odin tells the story of his unlucky courtship of "Billing's maiden"; yet the whole matter is uncertain.) Something more definite is to be learned from a statement of the Skald Kormak, who says, "Odin practised sorcery in order to win Rind." According to Saxo, magic runes were the means employed by Odin in the winning of Rind. An exhaustive literary and historical analysis of Saxo's saga of Balder is to be found in the work by Neckel cited in the note to p. 86.

THE DEATH OF KVASIR—SUTTUNG

Page 100, *line* 16—In accordance with the details of this myth, all of the poetic arts are called in the ancient poetic phraseology "Kvasir's Blood", "Drink of the Dwarfs", "Gilling's Ransom", "Odrœrir's (Son's or Bodn's) Contents", "Suttung's Mead", "Boat-Freight of the Dwarfs", "Nitbjorg's Liquor", "Odin's Booty", etc. In the *Hávamál* occur several strophes referring to the myth; thus we read (strophes 104–10): "I was a guest of the old Giant; little did I get there by holding my tongue; nay, I must needs use many words in Suttung's halls to gain my desire. Gunnlod of the golden chair gave me to drink of the precious mead; but ill did I reward her guileless love. I let Rati's mouth (the auger's bit) gnaw a passage for me through the stone; my life at stake I ventured through the hole, and round about me stood the Giants' roadways (the mountains). The beauteous maid (Gunnlod) served me well; for now Odrœrir is come into the light of day. Yet I fear I should not have escaped from the home of the Giants had not Gunnlod helped me, the kind young girl whom I embraced. The next day the Rime-Thursar came to the hall of the High One (Odin) to learn the High One's fate; they asked after Bolverk, whither he was gone, whether he had come back to the gods, or whether Suttung had done him to death. At that time Odin swore a false oath. Can his oaths still be believed? He beguiled Suttung of his mead and brought sorrow to his daughter." In another passage we read (strophe 13): "The herons of forgetfulness soar above the drinkers and steal away men's wits. With

Notes

the feathers of that bird was I spellbound in Gunnlod's home." Bolverk means "worker of misfortune". The name of Suttung is of uncertain origin. Odrœrir seems to signify "one who stirs up (sets in motion) the poetic faculties (óðr)". Bodn is no doubt the same word as Anglo-Saxon *byden*, "vat", "crock"; closely related would then be Modern Norwegian *buna* (from *buðna*), "tub". On these names see further, Hj. Lindroth *Maal og Minne* 1915, p. 174 ff. According to Sophus Bugge, (*Studier* I, p. 468 f.), Rati means "rat" (cf. the expression in the *Hávamál*, "Rati's mouth").

ODIN'S DEBATE WITH VAFTHRUDNIR

Page 102, *line* 9—This material forms the subject of the Eddic poem *Vafþrúðnismál*. The name of the Giant means "one who is skilled in answering intricate questions" (from *vefja*, "to weave", "to complicate" and *þrúð*-, "strength").

ODIN (GRIMNIR) AND GEIRRŒD

Page 104, *line* 31—This story is drawn from the Eddic poem *Grímnismál*. This lay and *Vafþrúðnismál* (note to p. 102) are among the chief sources of our knowledge of the ancient mythology; Snorri's *Edda* has borrowed extensively from both poems.

Of the homes of the gods, those of Ull and Frey, namely Ydalir and Alfheim, are mentioned in the same strophe, while a whole strophe is given to each of the others (and an entire series of strophes to Valhalla). From these circumstances certain scholars have reached the opinion that there was a close connection between Ull and Frey.

HARBARD AND THOR

Page 108, *line* 25—The source of this section is the Eddic poem *Hárbarðsljóð*. Scholars have differed as to who Harbard really was supposed to be; P. A. Munch held him to be a Giant, while others have thought of Loki or Odin. The latter supposition no doubt is the correct one; not only is Harbard (that is, the Graybeard) known as a name for Odin from *Grímnismál*, but his character as represented in *Hárbarðsljóð*—warlike and a lover of women, crafty and adept in magic—agrees fully with the myths that are characteristic of Odin. Doubtless it is the poet of *Hárbarðsljóð* who has originated this scene in which the god of craftiness, Odin, and the god of physical force, Thor, stand face to face. The allusions, too, are no doubt for the most part fictitious, for which reason it is not surprising that all the place names (Radseysund, etc.) and several of the personal names as well (Hildolf, Fjolvar, Lebard, Svarang) are otherwise wholly unknown. Fjorgyn is the mother of Thor; see p. 27 f.

RAGNAROK—THE TWILIGHT OF THE GODS

Page 112, *line* 17—"The Mighty One from above" is mentioned in only a single strophe of the *Vǫluspá* (according to many scholars, a later addition to the poem) and in one passage in the so-called *Shorter Vǫluspá* (inserted in the *Hyndluljóð*) which clearly presupposes the strophe in the *Vǫluspá*. The last mentioned passage runs as follows: "Then comes another, still more mighty; him I dare not mention by name; few now can look farther into the future than this, that Odin shall meet the Wolf." This notion of a god governing all things may very well go back to later pagan times, when Christian influences had begun to make themselves felt. As harmonizing with this view is probably to be understood what is told of several Icelanders: they believed only in the one god who had created the sun and the earth. Thus we read of Thorkel Mani, a grandson of the Icelandic pioneer Ingolf: when he was about to die, he caused himself to be carried out into the sunlight and there gave himself into the keeping of the god who had created the sun; he had also lived a righteous life, like that of the best of Christians. And Thorstein says of his father Ingemund, after the father has been murdered (*Vatnsdœla Saga* chapter 23): "He shall have his reward [be avenged] by him who has made the sun and all the earth, whoever he may be."

The account here given of Ragnarok and the regenerated universe follows in the main the narrative of Snorri. His story is built on still extant Eddic poems. The chief source is the *Vǫluspá*, but Snorri has used also—and indeed expressly cited—the *Vafþrúðnismál* and the *Grímnismál*. In addition he has relied on popular beliefs (Naglfar; Vidar's shoe) which came to him through oral tradition. These sources Snorri has subjected to a

Notes

process of revision. In certain points his narrative conflicts with the Eddic poems, for example in his mention of Manigarm (see note to p. 4). It is more significant, however, that Snorri refers to a place of punishment for evil men in the new world (the hall on the Strand of Corpses; cf. p. 38). This reference must be charged to Snorri alone. His source is the *Vǫluspá;* but there the place of punishment is mentioned *before* Ragnarok, and in general the description of the regenerated universe in this poem is devoted to presenting a state of eternal felicity which is to be enjoyed not only by the new race of gods but also by the offspring of Lif and Lifthrasir (the indications in the *Vafþrúðnismál* point in the same direction). There shall be a remedy for all evil, declares the *Vǫluspá;* for Balder shall return from Hell.

Snorri's *Edda* must therefore be regarded as a secondary source so far as it has a bearing in explaining the pagan ideas about Ragnarok. An investigation of this question must be based on the three Eddic poems referred to by Snorri, and in addition on various other sources: hints in several other Eddic poems (*Lokasenna*, the fettered Wolf, see p. 90; *Fáfnismál*, the battle on the fields of Vigrid [here called the island *Óskópnir*, that is, "the not yet created"]; etc.); Skaldic poems (*Eiríksmál*, cf. note to p. 49, Egil Skallagrimsson's *Sonatorrek*, *Hákonarmál*, and others); visible memorials (the Gosforth Cross in Cumberland [Vidar]; Runic crosses in Man, and the like).

All of these sources Axel Olrik has made use of in his exhaustive work, *Om Ragnarok* (*Aarbøger for nordisk oldkyndighed* 1902). Very properly Olrik assigns to the *Vǫluspá* a distinctive position determined by the very nature of the whole poem. *Vǫluspá*, one of the grandest of the Eddic poems, gives a summary view of the whole history of the universe and of the gods, from the first beginnings of things even to far intimations of the sequels to Ragnarok. The verses are put into the mouth of a sibyl or prophetess. She admonishes "all holy kindreds" to give ear while she recites to the Val-Father what has long since befallen and what is to befall in the future. She unfolds vision upon vision, a moving panorama of the origin of the universe, of the creation of the world, of the first epoch of the Æsir, of their golden age, of the great corruption (p. 49), of Balder's death, and of Loki's punishment, and finally of Ragnarok, of the ruin of one universe and the establishment of another. Certain motives appear—especially in the case of the *Vǫluspá* (from the very last

[327]

period of paganism)—which seem to be of Christian origin: the corruption of mankind (?), the Gjallar-Horn as a harbinger of Ragnarok, the darkening of the sun and the falling of the stars, the universal fires, the home of the blessed (on Gimle, see below), the coming of the "Mighty One" (see, however, the beginning of this note). Other Ragnarok-motives are also of Christian origin, according to Axel Olrik, but well known in the Viking age: Loki's release (on Loki = the Devil, see note to p. 25), the hosts of Muspell (see below), possibly also the return of Balder. Finally Olrik has elucidated the connections of the pagan motives outside the North: the swallowing of the sun by sun-wolves (very widespread), the Fimbul Winter (corresponding to something of the kind among the Persians), the sinking of the earth into the sea (Celtic also), the new race of the gods (Celtic), mankind surviving the winter (cf. Persian parallels). Of special significance is the circumstance that the fettered monster released at the last day can be traced to a centre of radiation in the south-east, in the Caucasus, where may be found a multitude of legends relating to giants or beasts held in bonds; in these regions earthquakes are numerous, wherein seems to lie a natural explanation of notions like those which in the North attached themselves to the figure of Loki. A continuation and conclusion for the article cited has been presented by Olrik in *Ragnarokforestillingernes udspring* (=*Danske studier* 1913).

The word Muspell is found in old German poetry dating from the earliest Christian times; here the term (*mûspilli, mûd-, mût-spelli*) is used with reference to the end of the world or a day of doom. The exact meaning is much debated. On the popular beliefs connected with the idea of Naglfar, the nail-ship, see K. Krohn, *Finnisch-ugrische Forschungen* XII, 1912, p. 154 ff., 317 ff. Rym (*Hrymr*) no doubt has something to do with the adjective *hrumr*, "decrepit". The name thus suggests the inclusion of the whole number of Giants, even to those infirm with age.—Surt (connected with *svartr*) indicates a Giant blackened with fire. In Iceland he has been localized in a mighty subterranean cavern or corridor called *Surtshellir*, in the county of Myra. Vigrid is the plain where men "ride to battle (*víg*)"; on another name for it, see above. Lif (the woman's name) means "life" and Lifthrasir (certainly a more correct form than *Leif-*), "he who holds fast to life". Hoddmimir means "Mimir of the treasure".—Gimle probably may be rendered "gem-lee" (*hlé*), according to Bugge

Notes

(*Studier* I, p. 416 f.) formed as a name for the heavenly Jerusalem, whose "light was like unto a stone most precious, even like a asper stone, clear as crystal"(Rev. 21. 11).

WAYLAND

Page 129, line 7—The narrative is drawn from the ancient Eddic poem *Vǫlundarkviða*. Beyond this the Norse legends have nothing to say about Wayland. The lay is very brief and has several omissions by reason of the poetic form in which it is couched; to understand it, these lacunae must be supplied from other ancient traditions. Thus a comparison with the well-known folk tales about swan maidens [1] makes it clear that Wayland and his brothers got the Valkyries into their power by taking the swan cloaks and hiding them; after the passage of seven years the Valkyries must have found their swan cloaks again while the brothers were absent in the chase, must at once have assumed their disguises and have flown away. It is evident also that Wayland must have had his own feather coat ready for a long time, but that he was not willing to make use of it before he had taken vengeance on Nidud.

The legend of Wayland has likewise been widespread in other Germanic countries, in which, however, it has in part been associated with other legendary cycles. Wayland's name in German is Wieland (Weland, Welant), and prolix stories about him are to be found in the great saga named after Dietrich of Bern, which is an Old Norse translation of Low German legends having to do with the Niflungs and with king Dietrich of Bern. According to this legend Velent (Wayland) is a son of the Giant Vadi and a grandson of Vilkin; he has learned the smith's handicraft from the smith Mimir and from certain Dwarfs in the land of the Huns. The apprentice soon excelled his masters, and therefore they sought his life; so he killed them, took their treasures, and carried these off to Denmark, where his father had once lived. He sailed down the river Weser on a hollow log, but was driven ashore in Jutland, where he drew upon himself the enmity of king Nidung of Thjod (Ty), who proceeded against him as in the narrative recited above. Everything in the *Dietrich's Saga*, however, is detailed with a greater number of accessory circumstances than in

[1] Cf. Helge Holmström, *Studier över svanjungfrumotivet i Volundarkvida och annorstädes* (Malmö, 1919).

the ancient lay, but also with definite marks of later additions. According to the saga it is Wayland's brother Egil, also called Olrunar-Egil, who provides him with the feather coat. The son of Wayland and Bodvild was the famous Vidga (Witich, Vidrik), one of the most celebrated champions of king Dietrich of Bern. Vidrik Verlandsson likewise often appears in the old heroic ballads. The Anglo-Saxons in England also knew legends about Wayland. Thus we read in *Deor's Lament*, a short lyrical-epic poem preserved in the Exeter book dating from the eleventh century, but obviously much older: "Wayland lived in exile; he suffered affliction in a den teeming with serpents,[1] and was alone with his sorrow and his longing throughout the winter's cold. Many were his pains after *Niðhad* had robbed his sinews of their power. *Beadohild* grieved less for her brothers' death than for her own shame". In the Anglo-Saxon poem *Waldhere*, Widia, the son of Wayland, is called *Nīðhādes mǣg*, that is, daughter's son to Nidud. In a document from the year 955 is mentioned *Wēlandes smiðÞe*, Wayland's smithy, and in a document from the year 903 reference is made to a place in the present Buckinghamshire called *Wēlandes stocc* (cf. Wayland's log, which in *Dietrich's Saga* is called *stokkr*). The Anglo-Saxons were in the habit of designating superior weapons and ornaments as "Wayland's handiwork" (*Wēlondes geweorc*), just as our own forefathers would say of an excellent smith, "He was a real Wayland at his craft" (*Vǫlundr at hagleik*). To this day legends are current in England having to do with Wayland Smith, and Walter Scott made use of him in his famous novel *Kenilworth*. Even in France people would speak of weapons from Galans' (Wayland's) smithy.

The linguistic interpretation of the name *Vǫlundr*, Anglo-Saxon *Wēland*, *Wēlond*, is uncertain; it appears impossible to explain it from *vél*, "art", "craft", "artifice". On the other hand, Sophus Bugge has probably found the correct meaning of *Slagfiðr* (= -*finnr*) in "the forging Finn" (from *slag*, "blow", "stroke of a hammer"). Nor are there any difficulties with the names *Niðuðr* and *Bǫðvildr*: from *nið*, "spite", "malice"; *hǫðr*, "battle"; *bǫð*, "battle" (Anglo-Saxon *beado*); *hildr*, "battle", "Valkyrie". Lodvi (*Hlǫvér*) has been understood to be equivalent to the name of the king of the Franks, Louis (Chlodewich); the interpretation of *Kiarr*, on the other hand, is still obscure.

[1] Cf. other interpretations of the Old English original.—Translator's note.

Notes

On this and related questions, see Sophus Bugge's article, *Det oldnorske Kvad om Volund (Vǫlundarkviða) og dets Forhold til engelske Sagn (Arkiv för nordisk filologi* XXVI, pp. 33–77). He discusses among other matters also a pictorial treatment of the legend of Wayland on an old English whalebone casket. [Translator's note.—The relations between Old Norse and Anglo-Saxon heroic material are discussed by W. W. Lawrence and W. H. Schofield in *Publications of the Modern Language Association of America*, vol. xvii (1902), pp. 247–95.] It should be added that the legend of Wayland shows a striking similarity to the ancient Greek myth of Daedalus, the inventor of the arts. Like Wayland, Daedalus is placed in durance for the purpose of forging treasures for a tyrant, and he makes his escape from prison by the same method, that of making wings and flying away. Even our forefathers were aware of the likeness; they designated the labyrinth which Daedalus built by the name of *Vǫlundarhús*. In the lameness of Wayland has been noticed a defect corresponding to that which the Greeks and the Romans attributed to Vulcan.

THE HJADNINGS

Page 130, *line* 22—The designation *Hjaðningar* is derived from the masculine name Hedin. The legend was generally known, and many poetic paraphrases owe their origin to it; thus the byrnie was called "Hedin's sark", battle was called the "storm of the Hjadnings", etc. In the ancient Skaldic poem *Ragnarsdrápa*, which according to Norse tradition was composed by Bragi Boddason in the ninth century, mention is made of the Battle of the Hjadnings in a manner that seems to agree in all important particulars with the form of the legend as it is detailed above after Snorri's *Edda*.—Notable deviations, on the other hand, are to be found in the much later work, *Sǫrla þáttr* (see p. 79), where the myth of the Necklace of the Brisings appears arbitrarily to have been connected with the Battle of the Hjadnings, as follows: Odin would consent to return the Necklace of the Brisings to Freyja only on the condition that she would cause two major kings with their armies to do battle against each other continuously until such time as a Christian dared to put an end to the strife. Not until after the period of Frodi the Peaceful did Freyja find an opportunity to fulfill the condition. Twenty-four years after the death of Frodi, a king of the Uplands named Sorli killed the Danish king Halfdan, but later entered into a compact of sworn brotherhood with his son Hogni. When Sorli afterward fell in the course of a warlike enterprise, Hogni became mighty and famous, twenty other kings acknowledging his rule. Rumors of his fame reached the powerful Hedin Hjarrandason, king of Serkland (Africa), who likewise held sway over twenty kings. Once upon a time Hedin met in a forest a beautiful woman who pretended to be the Valkyrie Gondul and who egged him on to rivalry with Hogni. (Gondul was probably none other than Freyja herself). Hedin set sail for Denmark; and, after having vied with Hogni in all manner of feats of prowess, formed an alliance of sworn brotherhood with him. Not long afterward, Hogni having sallied forth to war, Hedin remained behind and once more encountered Gondul; she gave him a magic potion which bereft him wholly of his senses. He allowed her to entice him to put Hogni's queen to death and to sail away with Hogni's daughter Hild. Off the island of Haey he met with head winds; and Hogni, who had set out in pursuit, overhauled him. Here the battle began—the account of it runs practically as in Snorri's *Edda*, with the exception that Hild sits quietly looking on and attempting no magic interference. The battle lasted for one hundred and forty-three years, until king Olaf Tryggvason landed on the island. One of his men, Ivar Ljomi, went ashore during the night and met Hedin, who told him of his sorrowful fate and asked him to put an end to the struggle by killing him and Hogni and all of their warriors. Ivar Ljomi consented to do so and thus succeeded in putting a stop to the Battle of the Hjadnings.

Saxo recounts the legend in a third form, principally drawn from Norse sources but in part from Danish traditions, as follows: The young king Hedin (*Hithinus*) of Norway gave aid to Frodi the Peaceful in his warfare against the Huns. He and Hild (*Hilda*), daughter of king Hogni of Jutland, loved each other without the knowledge of her father. Hogni and Hedin set out together on a campaign; but when the war with the Huns was over, Hogni learned of the understanding between Hedin and Hild, and evil tongues even made their relations unlawful. Hogni, believing the reports, attacked Hedin but was defeated. Afterward Frodi sat in judgment between them; Hedin got a favorable decision and wedded Hild. Hogni notwithstanding continued to demand his daughter's return, and Frodi at length bade him determine the matter in single combat. Hogni being

Notes

the stronger, Hedin suffered defeat; but Hogni took pity on him and spared his life. Seven years later they met once again at Hedinsey, resumed their combat, and killed each other. But Hild, longing for her husband, woke the dead to life by means of incantations, and so the struggle continued without ceasing.

The narrative in Snorri's *Edda* represents the legend in its oldest and purest form. Yet Saxo, on the basis of Danish traditions, has no doubt preserved the more original localization, at Hiddensee (*Hithinsø*) near Rygen. Hogni and Hedin are mentioned together in the Anglo-Saxon poem *Widsith*, which enumerates Germanic tribes with their kings during the period of the great migration: "Hagena ruled over the Holm-Rugians and Heoden over the Glommas." The Holm-Rugians are the people whom Jordanes (6th century) mentions as the *Ulmerigi* living near the mouth of the Vistula, and the Glommas must be a neighboring people to the Rugians. It is thus evident that the legend of Hogni and Hedin originally belonged locally south of the Baltic, in regions lying near *Hithinsø*, and that the story must be very ancient. Further proof appears in the fact that something corresponding to the Hjadnings appears in Old English poems (*Heodeningas*). Not before the Viking Age can the Battle of the Hjadnings have been localized in the Orkneys (*Háey*, that is, the "high isle", now known as Hoy, the highest island in the group). This western theatre of events also is to be found in the popular ballad *Hildinakvadet*, which deals with the same happenings, and which during the eighteenth century was recorded in writing in Shetland; the language in it is Shetland-Norse, otherwise called "Norn" (that is, *norræna*), which became extinct at the time mentioned. The ballad has been edited and published by Marius Hægstad (*Hildinakvadet*, Christiania, 1900). *Dáinsleif* means literally "Dain's remnant"; Dain is mentioned in the *Vǫluspá* as one of the Dwarfs. Otherwise *dáinn* means "one who is dead".

The latest and most exhaustive treatment of the legend is that of B. Symons, to be found in the introduction to his edition of the Middle High German poem *Kudrun* (2nd ed., Halle 1914). This poem has incorporated materials which at a comparatively late date were borrowed from Denmark.

THE LEGEND OF TYRFING

Page 147, line 16—The legends of Tyrfing and the kindred of Arngrim form the contents of the *Hervarar Saga*, or *Hervor's*

Norse Mythology

Saga, a "saga of antiquity" belonging to the thirteenth century; it contains, however, a rich supply of poetic fragments which serve to carry the legends back to a much earlier period. These lays deal chiefly with the combat on the island of Samsey, with Heidrek's and Gestumblindi's riddling match, and with the strife between Angantyr and Lod. The saga has come down to us in various redactions, which differ not a little from one another, particularly as regards the homes of the persons concerned in the action. Of greatest importance are the two old manuscripts, the *Hauksbók* [H] and the *Gammel kongelig samling 2845, 4to* [R], which Sophus Bugge edited and published in *Norrøne Skrifter af sagnhistorisk Indhold*, 3dje hefte, 1873, in which, however, lacunae have to some degree had to be supplied by means of later paper manuscripts. The narrative as given above follows "H", the most complete manuscript; yet the story of Heidrek's boar has been drawn in part from "R". According to "H", Arngrim is son to a daughter of Starkad Aludreng (cf. p. 221), and Bolm is here localized in Halogaland (in reality it is a place in Småland, the island of Bolm in Lake Bolmen). According to "R", Sigrlami, king of Russia, gets Tyrfing from the Dwarfs, Sigrlami's descent from Odin not being mentioned in this source; Sigrlami gives the sword to Arngrim, his ranking captain, who is married to his daughter Eyfura. Of the combat on the island of Samsey there is an account also in *Qrvar-Odd's Saga* (see p. 236). Saxo too knows this legend; in his version Arngrim fights against the Finns in order to win the friendship of Frodi the Peaceful; he succeeds in his purpose and weds Eyfura (*Ofura*), who is here presented as the daughter of Frodi. In another passage Saxo refers to a certain Gestumblindi (*Gestiblindus*) as king of the Goths, though without mentioning the riddling match. Arngrim, Eyfura, and their sons are mentioned also in the Eddic poem *Hyndluljóð* ("to the eastward in Bolm"). As late as the seventeenth century legends relating to the combat of the Vikings are said to have been current on the island of Samsø.

The saga may be divided in several sections, which group themselves about the fragmentary lays discussed above. The first section contains the narrative of the battle of Samsey and of Hervor's incantations at her father's barrow; both accounts are based on sundry verses. The next section contains the history of Heidrek, in which only the story of the riddling match is couched in verse. It forms a transition to the last section, on the

Notes

battle between Angantyr and Lod, which also rests on a series of verses (called by recent scholars the "Lay Of the Battle With the Huns"). Yet the entire group of legends seems not from the first to have formed a complete whole. The legends of the sons of Arngrim, of the battle of Samsey, and of the life of Hervor depict the Viking Age; the scene is the Baltic and its littoral; the events are not historical. On the other hand, the place names in the last section of the saga appear to point to times and localities totally different. Heidrek, we read, ruled over Reidgotaland, which in the verses goes by the name of *Goðþjóð*. The neighboring kingdom is Hunaland, from which it is separated by the frontier forest Dark Wood (*Myrkviðr*). When Lod sets forth to demand his patrimony, he rides toward the west to meet Angantyr; and when Hervor is preparing to defend her stronghold against the Huns, she looks for their coming from the south. Hunaland was thus thought of as lying to the south-east of Gotaland, and the Goths and Huns in question must have belonged to the time of the great migrations. Indications leading toward the south-east are also to be found in the name *Danparstaðir*, the first element of which word is the ancient name for the Dnieper River (Danapris), and likewise in the name *Harfaðafjǫll*, which must be the Germanic name for the Carpathians. As to the details there is little unity among scholars. See on this matter Otto von Friesen's last article, *Rökstenen* (Stockholm, 1920), p. 108 ff., which lists much important older literature. O. von Friesen (who to a great extent follows Gudmund Schütte's article *Anganty-kvadets Geografi* in *Arkiv för nordisk filologi* XXI, p. 30 ff.) thinks of the Goths of the *Hervarar Saga* as living in the valley of the Vistula, and thus finds points of agreement with the Anglo-Saxon poem *Widsith:* the scop Widsith visits Wyrmhere (i. e., Ormar) while the army of the Rædas (cf. the name Reidgotaland) in the forests of the Vistula are defending their ancient domains against Atli's men (i. e., the Huns, see p. 184 ff.). According to von Friesen's view we have to do with a struggle between the Huns and a Gothic (Ostrogothic) kingdom north of the Carpathians not mentioned by the older historians. According to earlier scholars (Heinzel, *Über die Hervarar-Sage*, in *Sitzungsberichte der Akademie der Wissenschaften in Wien; Philosophisch-historische Classe* 114, 1887) we have to do with the Battle of the Catalaunian Plains.—The later narrators and scribes who dealt with the legend were apparently at a loss to fix the locality of events dating from so remote a period. Many of the place names occurring in the last section of the saga were unfamiliar to them, and therefore they fixed upon wholly erroneous localities. At a relatively late period Reidgotaland was understood to be the main land of Denmark, for which reason one version of the saga says that Reidgotaland "now is called Jutland". Through this reasoning Danparstad also came to be looked for in Denmark, and from this name was thus formed "Danp", who in the Eddic poem *Rigsþula* and in Snorri is mentioned among the earliest Danish kings. According to certain German scholars (Heusler and Ranisch, *Eddica minora*, Dortmund 1903, p. VII ff.) the "Lay of the Battle with the Huns" dates from the time of the composition of the Eddic poems, while according to Finnur Jónsson (*Litteratur-historie* 2 II, 1, p. 142) it belongs to a materially later date.

The riddling match in the central section of the saga reminds very much of the Eddic poem *Vafþrúðnismál* (p. 100), which no doubt served as a model; the decisive riddle is the same in both poems.

The saga thus consists of a series of mutually independent legends which have been unified by the aid of the Tyrfing motive; similar motives are employed in the Volsung Cycle,—the sword Gram and the treasure of Andvari. This unification is certainly older than the complete saga as we have it, since Tyrfing is to be found in all of the older poetic fragments employed in the composition of the saga. A fixed point for the dating of this agglutination of materials appears in the words of Hervor (in one of the verses) to the effect that she would rather possess Tyrfing than rule over "all Norway"; this phrase points to a period antedating the union of the Norwegian kingdoms into one. In this connection reference may be made once more to the riddle poem, which appears to presuppose *Vafþrúðnismál*.

THE LEGENDS OF THE VOLSUNGS—HELGI HJORVARDSSON

Page 151, line 16—These legends have been narrated here in accordance with the Eddic poem *Helgakviða Hjǫrvardssonar*. The section dealing with Rimgerd, the verse form of which is different from that otherwise employed in the Helgi lay, was at first probably an independent poem.—Cf. S. Bugge, *Helge-Digtene i den ældre Edda*, Copenhagen 1896, p. 218 ff.

Notes

VOLSUNG—SIGGEIR—SIGMUND—SINFJOTLI

Page 159, line 3—This narrative is not to be found in the Eddic poems but in the so-called *Vǫlsunga Saga* (dating from the 13th century), which contains circumstantial accounts of the legends of the Volsungs and which no doubt is to be regarded as a prose redaction of ancient lays. Certain it is that the story of Signy is to be traced to a poetic source; a small verse of this poem, narrating how Sigmund and Sinfjotli shore the stone in two, has found its way into the saga. The presupposed lay of Signy seems to have borrowed various motives from the Eddic poems dealing with Gudrun (note to p. 187). The stories of Sigi and Volsung, on the other hand, appear to be based on prose legends. On the legend of Sigi, Sophus Bugge has published various conjectures; see *Arkiv för nordisk filologi* XVII, p. 41 ff. The name Volsung (*Vǫlsungr*) is by virtue of its form originally a family name which a later tradition has misunderstood to be a true masculine given name. That this is the case may be seen from the Anglo-Saxon poem *Beowulf*, in which Sigmund is called *Wælses eafera*, that is, Volsi's son or scion. The actual progenitor thus would appear to have been "Volsi" Anglo-Saxon *Wæls* (possibly related to the Gothic adjective *walis*, "genuine", "chosen"). The meaning of the name *Sinfjotli* is uncertain. It has been used as a man's name in Norway, just as the corresponding Old High German *Sintarfizilo* in Germany. A shorter form of the name is the Anglo-Saxon *Fitela*, which occurs in *Beowulf;* there we read that *Sigemund Wælsing* with his sister's son Fitela performed many valiant deeds and brought many giants to earth. In Danish popular ballads Sinfjotli's name appears as *Sven Felding*.

HELGI HUNDINGSBANE

Page 165, line 2—The story of Helgi Hundingsbane is told in the two Eddic lays *Helgakviða Hundingsbana in Fyrra* and *Helgakviða Hundingsbana Ǫnnur* (and also in the *Vǫlsunga Saga*). The first-named lay deals at large with Helgi's birth, with the weaving of the Norns, with the journey to Logafjall, with Gudmund's and Sinfjotli's flyting at Svarinshaug, and with the battle of Frekastein; the second has to do with Helgi's visiting of Hunding, with his discourse with Sigrun at Brunavag, with the battle of Frekastein, with Helgi's death and his meeting with Sigrun in the burial mound.

Norse Mythology

The reincarnation of Helgi and Sigrun as Helgi Haddingjaskati and Kara is mentioned in a prose appendix to *Helgakviða Hundingsbana*. Here reference is made also to a lay, *Káruljóð*, which is said to have been concerned with Helgi and Kara, but which is no longer extant (cf. also the note to p. 245). Helgi Haddingjaskati's name occurs furthermore in the genealogical treatise *Fundinn Noregr*, where we read that Hadding, son of Raum, and grandson of Nor, was king of Haddingjadal (Hallingdal) and Telemark; his son was Hadding, who was the father of Hadding, who was the father of Hogni the Red, after whom again ruled three men of the name of Hadding; to the retinue of one of these belonged Helgi Haddingjaskati.

Saxo too has a Helgi Hundingsbane; here, however, he is identified with Helgi Halfdansson, father of Rolf Kraki (p. 215). That this was the actual historical relationship, S. Bugge has sought to prove in his book on the Helgi lays (see note to p. 151).

SINFJOTLI

Page 166, *line* 13—The legend of Sinfjotli's death is related in the *Vǫlsunga Saga* and in the *Poetic Edda;* not, however, in the form of a lay, but very briefly in prose. The ferryman who disappeared with the body of Sinfjotli was no doubt Odin himself; in this manner he meant to make sure of the doughty hero for himself; otherwise the dead man might have come under the domain of Hel, since he had not fallen in battle.

THE DEATH OF SIGMUND

Page 168, *line* 23—The *Poetic Edda* relates only that Sigmund fell and that Hjordis was wedded to Alf, son of Hjalprek; the whole story is to be found in the *Vǫlsunga Saga*, but there are besides certain references in various Eddic lays. In the *Prose Edda*, Hjalprek is king of *Þjóð*, that is, Ty in Jutland; *Nornagests þáttr*, on the other hand, makes him king of Frankland (p. 238). In this source Lyngvi's two brothers are mentioned by name, as Alf and Heming.

The old one-eyed man who caused the death of Sigmund was Odin. It was possible for him to carry Sigmund away with him to be made a Hero in Valhalla, now that a still more remarkable champion was soon to be born of the same race.

Notes

SIGURD FAFNIRSBANE

Page 175, line 3—The foregoing story is told in Eddic lays (*Grípisspá, Reginsmál*, and *Fáfnismál*), in the *Prose Edda* and in the *Vǫlsunga Saga;* the fullest account is found in the saga, and the briefest in the *Prose Edda*. Several unimportant discrepancies appear here and there. Besides, *Nornagests þáttr* (note to p. 239) gives the narrative in summary.

According to information in the *Prose Edda*, the skalds were accustomed on the basis of these legends to give to gold the designations "Oter's penalty", "the Æsir's ransom", "Fafnir's lair", "the ore of Gnita Heath", "Grani's burden". These kennings and others like them drawn from the same legends occur in great numbers in ancient skaldic poems.—*Hrotti* has some connection with the Anglo-Saxon sword name *Hrunting* in *Beowulf*.

THE NIFLUNGS—THE SLAYING OF SIGURD

Page 184, line 14—This narrative is related rather briefly in the *Prose Edda*, but completely in a series of Eddic poems (*Sigrdrifumál, Sigurðarkviða in Skamma*, the fragmentary *Sigurðarkviða, Helreið Brynhildar*, and *Guðrúnarkviða* I), and in the *Vǫlsunga Saga*, which is based on these lays. On the inward connection between the saga and its sources reference may be made to an article by Andreas Heusler (*Die Lieder der Lücke im Codex Regius*) in *Germanistische Abhandlungen Hermann Paul dargebracht*, 1902. Here also is to be found an excellent characterization of the various Sigurd lays; these are not contemporaneous, but represent the literary taste and the varying views of the legendary material in different ages.

In the section of *Sigrdrifumál* dealing with the runes we find traces both of the runic magic of real life and of legendary notions as to the origin of the runes; see on this point, M. Olsen, *Norges Indskrifter med de ældre Runer* III, p. 128 ff.—Arvak and Alsvin are the horses of the sun.

Sigurd Fafnirsbane is sometimes called in Northern legends Sigurd Svein. In the Danish popular ballads his name has become Sivard Snarensvend, and we read of him there that he won proud Brynhild of the Glass Mountain. Brynhild's bower with its ring of fire (*vafrlogi*) has thus been changed into one of the numerous glass mountains, known from folk tales, in which are lodged men and women who have been entranced but who by some means or other regain their liberty. To Fafnir correspond the fabled serpents (*lindormer*) of the tales, fearful, gigantic, magical reptiles.

The story of Sigurd's meeting with Sigrdrifa is taken from the *Sigrdrifumál*, and what follows, up to the quarrel of the queens, from the *Vǫlsunga Saga*. This saga also contains the story of his meeting with the Valkyrie on Mount Hindarfjall; but here the Valkyrie is Brynhild herself, and Sigurd plights his troth with her on the mountain itself. But in this way the saga comes to have two meetings and two betrothals between them, and in so far must be in error. How the *Poetic Edda*, according to which Sigrdrifa and Brynhild are not one and the same person, originally recounted the first meeting between Sigurd and Brynhild we cannot learn directly, since several leaves which followed the *Sigrdrifumál* are missing from the manuscript. In all probability, however, the *Vǫlsunga Saga* is based on an Eddic poem which must have told the story of the meeting at Heimir's dwelling; and for that matter, extant Eddic lays contain allusions to such a meeting. Snorri's *Edda* has no account whatever of Sigurd's visiting of Heimir; here the Valkyrie is called Hild and is identified with Brynhild. No mention is made of Sigurd's plighting his troth with her, and hence it is not necessary for Grimhild to give him a drink of forgetfulness. When in the semblance of Gunnar he rides through the circle of fire to Brynhild, he gives her the ring of Andvari as a morning gift and gets another ring from her instead. When the queens later quarrel at the river, it is Brynhild's own ring that Gudrun exhibits. In the *Vǫlsunga Saga* and in Snorri's *Edda* we thus appear to have two different forms of the legend, of which the first represents Sigurd and Brynhild as betrothed before the arrival of the hero at the court of Gjuki, a situation which the second fails to record. Which of the two is the original it is not easy to determine. If the saga recounts the earlier form of the legend, it is certain that, besides the error in the account of the two meetings and of the repeated betrothal, it has still another error, namely the representation of Aslaug as the fruit of Sigurd's and Brynhild's union, inasmuch as this state of affairs would be directly opposed to the situation as presented in the Eddic lays. The version of the saga has been followed in our rendering of the legend, since Snorri's *Edda*, as regards this story, is very brief, passing most cursorily over these phases of Sigurd's life; the *Edda* does, however, mention Aslaug as a daughter of Sigurd.

Notes

ATLI

Page 187, line 15—The story of Atli is narrated at length in Snorri's *Edda* and in the *Vǫlsunga Saga*, which here draws on Eddic poems that are still known; and these lays—*Guðrúnarkviða II*, *Atlakviða*, and *Atlamál in Grœnlenzku*—are thus the real sources. Smaller individual episodes, not included in our summary, are to be found in *Guðrúnarkviða III* and in *Oddrúnargrátr*.

In *Guðrúnarkviða II*, Gudrun bemoans her fate to king Thjodrek (Theodoric), who after the loss of all his men was staying at the court of Atli. She tells him the story of Sigurd's death, of her sojourn with Thora, daughter of Hakon, and of their weaving there a tapestry on which were depicted the deeds of Sigurd and the Gjukungs; she tells how Grimhild brought her the drink of forgetfulness and induced her to wed Atli; the drink was cold and bitter; within the horn were dim, blood-red runes, and in the drink were mingled many simples, burned acorns, soot from the hearth, the entrails of sacrificial beasts, the sodden liver of a swine; this drink deadened her griefs.

In *Guðrúnarkviða III*, Atli's serving woman Herkja accuses Gudrun of being too intimate with Thjodrek; but Gudrun proves the accusation false by picking up unhurt an amulet from the bottom of a kettle filled with boiling water, while Herkja, in trying to do the same thing, scalds herself, and suffers drowning in a morass. This is a relatively late legend, lacking all marks of antiquity.

Oddrúnargrátr, the *Lament of Oddrun*, contains the lament of Oddrun, Atli's sister, because she was not the wedded bride of Gunnar, whom she loved.

Atlakviða, one of the very oldest of the Eddic lays, deals with Atli's treachery and Gudrun's revenge. The same story is told much more circumstantially in a much later poem, *Atlamál*, the *Greenland Ballad of Atli*. The second title indicates the place of origin of the lay; there are besides various features in the poem itself which point to Greenland (for instance, Kostbera's dreaming of a polar bear, *hvítabjǫrn*).

In *Nornagests þáttr* (note to p. 239) the story is told of Gest's playing on the harp in Olaf Tryggvason's hall, on which occasion he finally played a piece of music called *Gunnarsslagr*, the name indicating a dance tune (Gunnar's harping in the den of serpents), and not a poem. As the title of a poem *Gunnarsslagr* belongs to a

Norse Mythology

very late period: there is a poem of that title which demonstrably was written by the Icelandic clergyman Gunnar Pálsson (died 1793), but which in the early part of the nineteenth century was erroneously included in various editions of the Eddic poems (cf. S. Bugge's edition of the *Edda*, p. xlix).

Atli, who is called king of the Huns, is the transformation in heroic legend of Attila, king of the Huns. The historian of the Goths, Jordanes, repeats a story borrowed from an earlier writer to the effect that Attila died of a hemorrhage the night after his wedding with *Ildico* (453). In all likelihood this was the name of a Germanic woman, originally *Hildico*, which may be presumed to be a Gothic diminutive of the name "Hild". On the basis of the compounding element "hild" the historic name of Attila's wife has been identified with the Kriemhild of heroic poetry (see p. 193), a name which again according to its form corresponds to the Grimhild of the Northern legends; in the North the wife of Sigurd and Atli has been endowed with a new name, Gudrun, and the name Grimhild has been transferred to Gudrun's mother. We are enabled to follow the development of the Atli-legend some steps farther through testimony of later writers to the effect that Atli was killed during the night by Ildico. No historical source, however, has anything to say of Attila's being wedded to a Germanic princess.—In the Eddic poems Gunnar is commonly called the king of the Goths, yet in one single passage (*Atlakviða* 18) the king of the Burgundians; the latter represents the original tradition, and it is as king of the Burgundians that he appears in German poetry. His name is also a matter of historical record. In the year 437, a Burgundian king named *Gundicarius* with his men was slaughtered by the Huns, who on this occasion, however, were not under the command of Attila. This event, occurring on the banks of the Rhine, the makers of the legend have seized upon and transferred to another time and another place,—king Attila's court in Hungary. In a Burgundian legal code dating from the 6th century the names *Gibica*, *Godomar*, *Gislaharius*, and *Gundaharius* (i. e., *Gundicarius*) are recorded as the names of earlier Burgundian kings. In these forms we recognize the names of Gjuki, Guttorm, and Gunnar, and besides, Giselher, who according to German story is one of the brothers. No trace, on the other hand, is to be found of Hogni's name; for that matter he is not among the Germans the brother of Gunnar, but his vassal, and this probably represents

Notes

the original situation. The legends thus appear to have drawn their subjects from historical events but to have treated these events in accordance with the laws governing legendary composition.

JORMUNREK

Page 189, line 28—This legend is narrated in the old Eddic poems *Guðrúnarhvǫt* (Gudrun's Inciting) and *Hamðismál;* from a Low German poem on the death of Jormunrek, appearing in a pamphlet dating from the 16th century (see B. Sijmons, *Zeitschrift für deutsche Philologie* 38, p. 145 ff.), inferences lead to a very ancient German heroic poem which must have been identical in its main features with the *Hamðismál*. Many poetic paraphrases have been derived from the legends dealing with the sons of Jonaker; the byrnie is called "Hamdir's sark" and "Sorli's garment", and stones are called "the grief of Jonaker's sons". The *Ragnarsdrápa*, attributed to the Skald Bragi the Old, also contains the story of Hamdir's and Sorli's attack on Jormunrek. Saxo too (who here rehearses a Norse legend) knows this king but calls him *Jarmerik* and makes him ruler of Denmark and Sweden. He mentions the evil counselor Bikki and tells how the king in jealousy causes his son Broder (not Randver) to be hanged and his fair wife Svanhilda to be trampled to death by horses. He was later attacked by her "Hellespontine" brothers, who had secured the aid of a witch named Gudrun; but Odin was the real cause of the downfall of the brothers through his teaching Jarmerik's men to make use of stones when they found that their weapons would not bite.

In Jormunrek we recognize an historical personage, the famous Gothic king Ermanaric (Anglo-Saxon *Eormenric*), who in the middle of the 4th century ruled over Ostrogoths, Visigoths, Gepidæ, Slavs, Antes, and Wends, from the Baltic to the Black Sea. The contemporary Roman historian Ammianus Marcellinus narrates that he killed himself (in the year 375) from fear of the Huns, against whom for a time he had striven to defend himself. According to the account of the later Gothic writer Jordanes, on the other hand, we read that he was grievously wounded by two brothers of the tribe of the "Rosomones", Sarus and Ammius, whose sister Sunilda he had caused to be torn by wild horses; he afterward died at an advanced age from his wounds and from grieving over the attack of the Huns. The names of these brothers and the sister clearly correspond to Sorli, Hamdir, and Svanhild. Jordanes, however, makes no mention of Ermanaric's being wedded to Sunilda, nor does he associate these events with any other legendary cycle.

ASLAUG

Page 192, *line* 2—This legend, not found in the Eddic poems, provides the connecting link between the Volsungs and Ragnar Lodbrok. Various great families traced their descent from Ragnar Lodbrok, and through Aslaug these families became descendants of the hero of heroes, Sigurd Fafnirsbane.—At Spangereid there was recorded in the 17th century a legend about a little girl named "Oddlau" (also written, in Latin, "Otlougam vel Aatlougam") or Kraka, who had drifted ashore there in "Guldvig", and after whom the brook Kråkebekken is supposed to have its name; see Moltke Moe, in *Norges Land og Folk*, X, 1, p. 489. The legend forms the basis of a (lost) Norwegian ballad, from which one or two Danish ballads have been derived. The supposition has been put forward that "Oddlau" is the same as Oddlaug. There seems to be no reasonable doubt that "Oddlau" is an inexact rendering of a spoken form Atlau or Atlu; the name Aslaug has the form Atlu at the present time in the locality to which the legend has long been ascribed (cf. K. Liestøl, *Maal og Minne* 1917, p. 105 f.).

GERMAN LEGENDS DEALING WITH SIEGFRIED AND THE NIBELUNGS

Page 197, *line* 5—"Nibelungs" is at the beginning of the *Nibelungenlied* the name of the people of king Nibelung, whom Siegfried conquered; in the latter part of the poem, the term is used as another name for the Burgundians. It is derived from the German word *Nebel* (hence, "child of darkness") and no doubt originally designated the subterranean owners of the hoard. Its being used for the royal house of the Burgundians probably is due to an erroneous deduction from the poetic formula, "the hoard of the Nibelungs", by which term the last owners of the treasure were thought to be indicated.—*Blödel* or *Blödelin* is Attila's brother *Bleda*.

The legend of Siegfried is known also from the poem entitled

Notes

Hörnen Seyfrid. This is extant only in a very late redaction, printed in the 16th century, but it points none the less to a very ancient legendary original, so far as the youth of the hero is concerned. It has several details strikingly similar to those of the Northern legends. Siegfried is apprenticed to a smith, whose anvil he cleaves in twain. He kills a dragon and burns it on a bonfire with many other serpents. Their scales melt with the heat and flow away like a brook; he bathes in it, and his skin becomes hard as horn. This poem mentions king *Gibich* (Gjuki), who is not referred to in the *Nibelungenlied.* Siegfried wins Gibich's daughter *Kriemhild* on emerging the victor from an encounter with still another dragon, which had carried her off; but he is killed by his brothers-in-law, who envy him his fame. Their names are *Gunther, Hagen,* and *Gernot.* It is Hagen who commits the murder.

Finally, the German legend has been preserved in a Norse work, *Dietrich of Bern's Saga (Þiðriks Saga).* Written in Norway during the 13th century, it contains a series of loosely connected legends, taken down "as German men have told it". The story of Sigurd's youth is here narrated in fairly marked agreement with *Hörnen Seyfrid* and the Eddic lays; the story of his later life and the last battle of the Nibelungs, on the other hand, agrees more fully with the *Nibelungenlied.* The names have German forms; Sigurd is called both *Sigurðr* and *Sigfrøðr* (the latter is the equivalent of "Siegfried" and not of "Sigurd"); the mother of the king is named *Oda,* the daughter *Grimhild;* the brothers are *Gunnar, Guttorm, Gernoz,* and *Gisler. Hogni* is their half brother. The basis of the saga is to be found in Low German legends told by German merchants in Norway.

THE DEVELOPMENT OF THE LEGENDARY CYCLE OF THE VOLSUNGS

Page 203, line 30—Memories of the Volsung legends have furthermore been preserved in popular ballads in Norway, the Faroe Islands, and Denmark, and in pictorial records in Norway and Sweden. On the door of Hyllestad church in Setesdal are to be found carved inscriptions setting forth the contents of *Reginsmál, Fáfnismál,* and the narrative of Gunnar in the serpents' den. The contents of the two poems named are likewise depicted on the portals of the church of Vegusdal (Aust-Agder). From the

Norse Mythology

church at Lardal, Vestfold, no doubt came a door bearing pictorial representations of the following subjects: Oter's ransom, Regin forging the sword, and the slaying of Fafnir. On a plank from a church door at Austad (Setesdal) may be seen certain scenes from *Atlakviða:* the cutting out of Hogni's heart, and Gunnar in the den of serpents. A similar plank from the church at Opdal (Numedal) bears a representation of the death of Gunnar; the same subject appears on a chair from Hove in Telemark (originally belonging to the church at Hitterdal) and on a baptismal font from the church at Norum (Bohuslen). On another chair, in the church at Hitterdal, may be seen "Gunnar and Sigurd, bearing the ring of Andvari and riding to meet Brynhild through the wall of flame" (L. Dietrichson, *De norske stavkirker*, Christiania 1892, p. 75 f.; cf. K. Liestøl, *Maal og Minne*, 1917, p. 98). In Sweden pictures of Sigurd and of Regin are cut in stone on the runic monuments of *Ramsundberget* and *Göks-stenen*.

On the development of this legendary cycle, particularly in Germany, see Andreas Heusler, *Nibelungensage und Nibelungenlied*, Dortmund 1921.

HADDING

Page 211, *line* 19—According to the investigations of Axel Olrik (*Kilderne til Sakses oldhistorie* II, Copenhagen 1894, p. 1 ff.), the basis of Saxo's story was no doubt furnished by some Norse saga of antiquity (cf. p. 124), which again was probably embellished with certain legendary features (the journey to the nether world; the ride on Sleipnir in the company of Odin) but which clearly had for hero a Viking king. In all probability Hadding is to be thought of (as was the case with Ragnar Lodbrok, p. 245) as an historical personage. By reason of the similarity in names it has been conjectured that he is to be identified with the great Viking chieftain Hasting,[1] who during the second half of the ninth century harried France. Olrik characterizes Hadding's saga as a "literary treatment of a religious problem (faith in Giants as against faith in the Æsir), like *Orvarr-Odd's Saga* and *Fridthjof's Saga*." "The crowing of the cock beyond Hell-Gate portends the victory of life over death; and it is this passage particularly that has borne the saga down through the Christian era."

[1] Hadding and Hasting cannot be the same name linguistically. Hasting is commonly identified with the Northern name *Hásteinn.*

Notes

Hadding's and Ragnhild's antiphonal chant is borrowed from a poem celebrating the deities Njord and Skadi (see p. 14). Vagnhofdi, Haflidi (Saxo's "Haphlius") and Hardgreip ("Harthgrepa") are mentioned in doggerel name-verses in Snorri's *Edda*.

The genealogical tables referring to the Haddings are those mentioned in the note to p. 165.

FRODI THE PEACEFUL AND HIS MILL

Page 215, *line* 19—"In Northern legendary literature are two kings named Frodi, to each of whom the Peace of Frodi is indiscriminately referred. One of these holds a place at the head of the Scyldings and is distinguished particularly for his wealth; he grinds gold from a mill. The other comes later in the descent of the same royal family; the legends emphasize especially his legal codes and the wide extent of his realm. The Icelanders distinguish between them by calling the first Peace-Frodi, the second Frodi the Peaceable (in Danish he is known as *Frode den fredgode:* Frodi, friend of peace).

"In legendary tradition these two figures are constantly contending for the position of the true king of the Peace of Frodi. The Icelanders obviously choose the first, ascribing to him expressly the Peace of Frodi and as well the legend of lawful security; in accordance with this view *Fróði hinn friðsami* is assigned to a relatively low station. The sagas of the Norwegian littoral (as given by Saxo) have on the contrary declared just as expressly for the other king Frodi, and have made the first into a Viking king. Danish tradition, finally, has altogether obliterated the first king Frodi and knows only the second, *hin frithgothæ*.

"We can not do away with either of the kings Frodi; both are rulers of the golden age. It follows of necessity—there is but one golden age—that the two Frodis in reality are one and the same." (Axel Olrik, *Danmarks heltedigtning* I, p. 278 f.; the legend of Grotti is exhaustively treated in the same connection.)

It is in the aforesaid sagas of the Norwegian coast that we find the legend of Erik of Rennesey. From a saga of antiquity dealing with Erik (no doubt from the eleventh century) Saxo borrowed the circumstantial account which here is presented in an abbreviated form. In Norse sources Erik the Eloquent is mentioned in *Flateyjarbók* I, 25 and in Snorri's *Edda* I, 522; but these sources give no narrative account of him. Saxo tells that the first Frodi strewed his food with finely ground gold. This detail clearly has some connection with the legend of Fenja and Menja, which is not to be found in Saxo.

The entire Grotti Song, one of the most superb lays of antiquity (doubtless dating from the tenth century), has come down to us in Snorri's *Edda;* the legend must have been well known, since gold is frequently referred to by the skalds as "Frodi's meal" or as the "Grist of Frodi's bondwomen."

The maelstrom in the Pentland Firth is in the old language called *Svelgr (Orkneyinga Saga)*, a word still preserved in the form, "the Swelki". In the Orkneys reminiscences still linger of the two bondwomen who turned the mill, there known as Grotti-Fenni and Grotti-Menni. The legend which explains how the sea became salt has borrowed motives from the widespread folk tale of the Wishing Mill (cf., for example, Asbjørnsen and Moe, *Norske folkeeventyr*, no. 50).

HELGI AND ROLF KRAKI

Page 221, line 2—Legends dealing with the Danish kings of the Skjoldung family are extant in various literary forms, of which the most important are the following:

A. *Other than Norse.* 1. The Anglo-Saxon heroic poems *Beowulf* and *Widsith:* Roar, son of Halfdan, and his brother's son Rolf, son of Helgi, hold rule contemporaneously and engage in warfare against a people whose boundaries adjoin those of Denmark to the south, the Heathobards; there are portents of approaching divisions within the royal house. These are without doubt historical personages who flourished about the year 500.

2. The Danish lay *Bjarkamál*, probably from about the year 900, which Axel Olrik has reconstructed principally on the basis of Saxo's Latin account in prose. It deals—in antiphonal strophes assigned by turn to Hjalti and to (Bodvar) Bjarki—with the last fight of Rolf's champions at Leire; it mentions only these two of Rolf's warriors by name. This "old" *Bjarkamál*, which forms the point of departure for new legendary creation, was widely known. We find echoes of it, for example, in Sighvat's hereditary lay in honor of Saint Olaf. It is most famous from its connection with the battle of Stiklestad, as told in the *Sagas of the Kings:* Thormod Kolbrunarskald before the battle chants the *Bjarkamál* for the king and his host.

Notes

3. Danish legends in Saxo. Here the story of the childhood of Helgi and Roar is to be found in another passage than that detailed above, which is based on Norse sources (see under B below). Saxo identifies Helgi with Helgi Hundingsbane (as do various later scholars; cf. note to p. 165). He is acquainted with the legend of Yrsa, but gives her mother's name as Thora. He recounts Rolf's story at great length.

B. *Norse.* 1. The later *Bjarkamál*, probably dating from the twelfth century, of which only scattered strophes have been preserved.

2. The lost *Skjǫldunga Saga* (ca. 1200) which we know from the Icelander Arngrim Jónsson's Latin summary of about the year 1600, and from Snorri's *Edda.*

3. *Hrólfs Saga Kraka*, the extant version of which dates from the fourteenth century but which builds upon ancient sources and which contains, among other things, a prose rendering of the "old" *Bjarkamál.* See, on all of these sources, Axel Olrik's admirable discussion in *Danmarks heltedigtning* I.

In our foregoing narrative the Norse sources have been followed, particularly *Rolf's Saga* (B 3). The story of Vogg (whom Saxo calls Viggo) and of the incursion upon Uppsala is taken from Snorri's *Edda.*

Rolf was one of the most famous kings of antiquity. His memory was honored by the drinking of his skoal at solemn ceremonies (*Heimskringla* I, 68); and Olaf the Saint once said that if he were to be likened to any one of the ancient pagan kings, it must be Rolf Kraki (*Flateyjarbók* II, 134).—From Rolf's history were drawn various kennings for gold, such as the "seed of the Plains of Fyri" and "Kraki's sowing".

The stories of Helgi, of Roar, and of Rolf Kraki have, as is well known, been given poetic treatment by Oehlenschläger in his *Helge, Hroars Saga,* and *Hrolf Krake.*

STARKAD THE OLD

Page 234, line 26—Starkad is mentioned in a number of the ancient sources, both Danish and Norse; but in no one of them is there a connected account of his life such as we have narrated in the foregoing passage. The story of his sojourn with Horsehair-Grani, with Vikar, and with the kings of Uppsala is to be found in the unhistoric *Gautrek's Saga,* a saga of antiquity from the 14th

Norse Mythology

century; this saga contains the poem *Vikarsbalk*, which is attributed to Starkad (it was probably composed in the 12th century in the neighborhood of Bergen). Items of information as to Starkad's descent are given not only in *Gautrek's Saga* but also in the induction to *Half's Saga*.—Concerning Starkad's part in the battle between Hugleik and Haki there is a recital in Snorri's *Ynglinga Saga*, which here builds upon the no longer extant *Skjǫldunga Saga* (from about the year 1200). The same work forms the basis for the account of his deeds in the Battle of Bravalla, which occurs in the so-called *Sǫgubrot* (*Fornaldar Sǫgur* I, 363 ff.). Finally we hear of his combat with Sigurd Fafnirsbane in *Nornagests þáttr* (note to p. 239). Various minor notices of Starkad and references to his battles are to be found scattered about in other pieces of Norse literature.

The chief source of the legends dealing with Starkad, however, is Saxo's *History of Denmark*, where Starkad's deeds bulk large, particularly in the sections having to do with Frodi and Ingjald. Here is his proper place, in the company of the original Heathobard kings Frodi and Ingjald, the enemies of the Danish Scyldings (in later Danish tradition incorporated in the royal succession); he was no doubt at first to be identified with that "old spear-champion" who, at the wedding of Ingjald with a Danish princess, incited men to a breach of the peace (as the story runs in the Anglo-Saxon heroic poem *Beowulf*). In harmony with this view, Sophus Bugge has explained the name *Starkaðr* or *Stǫrkuðr* as *Stark-hǫðr*, that is, "the strong Heath(obard); still the word *hǫðr* ("battle") was during prehistoric times frequently used in the composition of masculine names, and consequently the foregoing explanation is by no means certainly right. In Danish heroic literature of the 10th century Starkad holds a prominent place. We know in Saxo's Latin rendering the *Lay of Ingjald* (from ca. 950: Starkad eggs the effeminate Ingjald to action and to revenge for his father's death) and the *Lay of Helga* (somewhat later: on Starkad in the house of the goldsmith). Moreover, there existed in Denmark, about the year 1000, accounts in prose of Starkad's combat with Angantyr and his brothers. The more extensive elaboration of the legends of Starkad, however, has taken place on Norwegian soil, and the development has proceeded through the following works: 1) The *Lay of Bravalla*, composed, according to S. Bugge and Olrik, by a man from Telemark in the year 1066; 2) Starkad's *Death Lay*, from the closing years of the

Notes

11th century, composed likewise probably by a man of Telemark, since the lay indicates a Telemark point of view (Starkad once comes off badly from an encounter with the smiths of Telemark); besides, Olrik has supposed 3) a Norwegian lay dealing with the youthful prowess of Starkad (the "Youthful Lay"). (As number 4 in the series of Norwegian Starkad poems we find the aforesaid *Vikarsbalk* which, in contradistinction to the three others, has been preserved in its original linguistic form.) It was in Norway, during the 11th and 12th centuries, that Starkad's life as a Viking and his dastard's deeds came to be a dominating interest in poetic invention. The Norwegian elaborations of the legends found their way in large measure into Saxo's *History of Denmark*, in which older Danish verse and story and later Norwegian legend have taken a place side by side. On the course of this development, reference may be made to Axel Olrik's exhaustive discussion in *Danmarks heltedigtning* II (Starkad the Elder and the later succession of the Skjoldungs).

Of peculiar details found in Saxo, the following are worthy of special mention: Saxo fixes Starkad's birthplace far to the east, which according to Olrik implies Jotunheim; it is to be remembered that Starkad, as presented in Norwegian legend, was of Giant race—*Áludrengr*, his father's surname, may possibly refer to what was originally a Water-Troll, a Water-Sprite (cf. Modern Norwegian *ála*, meaning a "deep channel in a stream")[1]—and it is therefore natural that Thor became his enemy. Furthermore Saxo localizes Haki's combat with Hugleik in Iceland.

In the Icelandic *Skáldatal* Starkad is mentioned as a skald. This is not surprising, since several Starkad lays have been attributed to him directly. In a similar way the Icelanders reckon Ragnar Lodbrok among the skalds by reason of the poem *Krákumál* (note to p. 251). From Starkad the metrical form *Starkaðarlag* has its name.

Among other reminiscences of Starkad of more recent date may be mentioned Starkad's tooth. It was one of the molars knocked from Starkad's mouth by Sigurd Fafnirsbane, and it weighed,

---

[1] In late Icelandic manuscripts of *Hervarar Saga* (from the 17th century) Starkad is said to have dwelt *við Áluforsa*. Herewith is probably indicated Ulefoss in Holla, Telemark (S. Bugge, *Norsk Sagafortælling og Sagaskrivning i Irland*, Christiania, 1901–08, p. 127; cf. *Norske Gaardsnavne* VII, p. 172 f.).

Norse Mythology

according to *Nornagests þáttr*, six pennyweight [1]—"it now hangs fastened to the bell rope in Lund". It was no doubt this same tooth of Starkad's, six inches in length, that the German knight Heinrich Æmeltorp is supposed to have carried with him in the year 1253 from Denmark to Germany and there to have exhibited as a curiosity (See *Ryd Årbok*). Furthermore, several local legends have been connected with Starkad. According to Saxo, he lies buried at Roljung (near Rönneå in the extreme south of Halland, north-east of Kullen), at the place where he slew Angantyr.

As to the birth of Vikar, *Half's Saga* has an account differing from that in *Gautrek's Saga*. Vikar's father had two wives, Signy and Geirhild, who agreed so ill that he found it impossible to keep more than one of them. The one who brewed the best beer against his homecoming from war he would permit to remain; the other he would put away. Signy called upon Freyja for aid; Geirhild called upon Odin. Odin spat in her brew, but demanded in recompense what was between her and the vat. She promised to fulfill his demand; the ale turned out to be excellent, and the king kept her, but said: "With my mind's eye I can already see your son swinging from a gallows, a sacrifice to Odin." Not long afterward she gave birth to Vikar.

The legend of Hagbard, which is loosely joined to the legends of Starkad, was in ancient times and still is commonly known throughout the North. From the north of Norway and down into Denmark many places are pointed out as the dwelling of Signy. Saxo, who gives a circumstantial version of the story, localizes the events in Zealand, where popular belief still finds the home of Sigar and Signy in the neighborhood of Sigersted. The Icelandic *Landnámabók* relates that Sigar was supposed to have lived at Steig on the island of Engeløy in Halogaland; according to another source (*Flateyjarbók* I, 25) he was a son of a daughter of Grjotgard, king of Møre, and the son of a brother of Siggeir, the enemy of the Volsungs (p. 152). At Engeløy men still point out Signy's bower, her well, and the like. The legend has also been attached to Dragsmark in Bohuslen, to Sigersvoll at Lista, to Urnes in Sogn. The legend of Hagbard has supplied many items to the phraseology of poetry; thus the gallows in one passage is called "Sigar's horse", and in another passage "the cool

[1] In the Norwegian text: *ører.*—Translator's note.

Notes

steed of Signy's lover". On the relation between the ancient
story of Hagbard and Signy and the ballad derived from it, see
Axel Olrik, *Folkelige Afhandlinger* (1919), p. 96 ff.

ORVAR-ODD

Page 237, line 11—The stories of Ketil Hæng, Grim Loddinkinn, and Orvar-Odd are told in three sagas of antiquity (*fornaldarsǫgur,* cf. note to p. 147), highly romantic, and filled with
monotonous accounts of combats with Giants and Vikings. *Orvar-Odd's Saga,* the oldest of these, was probably written down in
the 13th century; the two others are no doubt from the early
part of the 14th century. Ketil Hæng and Grim Loddinkinn, the
ancestors of the Rafnista family, are mentioned in the *Landnámabók* and in *Egil's Saga* as historical personages. It is worth
noting that the death of the Russian-Varangian ruler Oleg is told
in the same manner as that of Orvar-Odd. Berrjod is situated
not in Jæren but in Sokndal, Dalene. Of the horse Faxi a
reminiscence is supposed to have survived down to recent times
in "Faxatiorn" (Faxi's lake), mentioned in Arni Magnusson's
correspondence with Torfæus, as edited by Kålund (Copenhagen,
1916), pp. 49, 293.

Orvar-Odd was reputed to have been twelve yards in height.
To him also legend has thus attributed superhuman height,
strength, and age. Similar tales are told of Starkad. Of Sigurd
Fafnirsbane the *Vǫlsunga Saga* relates that when he rode through
the tallest field of rye, the highest ear reached only up to the fer-
rule of his sword. Such exaggerated stories of the legendary
heroes of old are common to all peoples. Traces of superstitions
of the same kind are to be found among the ancient Greeks and
Romans. Even in our own day the belief is widespread that the
champions of antiquity were much taller and stronger than the
men of later times.

NORNA-GEST

Page 239, line 3—The story of Norna-Gest is narrated in
Nornagests þáttr, which was written by an Icelander about the
year 1300 and later incorporated as an episode of *Olaf Tryggvason's Saga* in the *Flatey Book*. It gives a brief summary of the
narratives dealing with the life and death of Sigurd Fafnirsbane,

Norse Mythology

reciting in its course several of the ancient poems. The accounts of the prophecies of the Norns recall to mind the Greek myth of Meleager.

ASMUND KEMPIBANE

Page 242, line 13—The legend is related here as told in *Ásmundar Saga Kappabana* (ca. 1300). It has several somewhat less original features that bear witness of the influence of other legends; the fateful sword is reminiscent of Tyrfing, and king Budli's testing the swords brings to mind Sigurd Fafnirsbane's similar test. Attention must also be called to the names Alius and Olius, which have a late, non-Northern tinge. Finally, it is worth noticing that there are contradictions within the saga itself: Olius foretells that the sword is to cause the death of two sons of the king's daughter, but in the event it appears that the prophecy strikes Hildebrand alone. The kernel of the saga must nevertheless be ancient; not only is the legend found in a closely related traditional Danish form in Saxo, but the central motive may be recognized in the ancient South-Germanic literature dealing with Hildebrand, one of the retainers of Dietrich of Bern.

In Saxo the legend takes the following shape: A Swede, the warlike Gunnar, made an incursion into Norway in the course of which he pillaged Jæren in a fearful manner. The Norwegian king Regnald placed his daughter Drota in hiding in a subterranean cavern, where he also concealed certain precious swords, while he himself sallied forth against the Vikings. The king was slain, and Gunnar discovered Drota's hiding place and carried her away; but he failed to find the swords. They got a son, who was named Hildiger and who at an early age developed such violent traits of character that his father at last was compelled to send him into exile. The Danish champion Borkar killed Gunnar and thus avenged the death of Regnald; he took Drota to wife and with her had a son named Halfdan, who came to be a very brave man. Borkar fell in battle, and Halfdan on the same occasion received a gash across the mouth that never quite healed and that left his features badly disfigured. Nevertheless he paid court to a princess named Guritha; and when she turned him away, he vowed to do such mighty deeds that she would no more think of his appearance. Having received from his mother the splendid swords Lysing and Hviting, he took service as a warrior among the "Ruthenians" (Russians), who at the

Notes

time were engaged in warfare with king Alf (*Alverus*) in Sweden. Hildiger was one of the combatants in the Swedish army. He had slain many men of the enemy and had challenged many more. Halfdan now stepped forward; but Hildiger recognized his brother, and without making himself known refused to fight against him. Halfdan then challenged another of the Swedes and laid him low; the next day he despatched two men, and continued in his course until on the eighth day he slew eleven. Hildiger could no longer refuse to go out against him, but Hildiger too received a mortal stroke. Yet before he died he revealed their kinship through the singing of a lay; he declared also that all his deeds of prowess would be found depicted on his shield, but in the center of the targe was the image of his only son, whom he had slain with his own hand. Thus he ended his life, and Halfdan returned to Denmark. In the meantime a rumor had spread abroad that Halfdan was dead, and Guritha was about to be wedded to a Saxon noble named Sigvard. Halfdan, however, came home in such good season that he was able to kill the Saxon and wed Guritha himself. Their son was the famous Harold Hilditonn.

In Saxo, as it thus appears, Regnald corresponds to Budli of the saga, Drota to Hild, Gunnar to Helgi, Hildiger to Hildebrand, Borkar to Aki, Halfdan to Asmund, and Guritha to Æsa; the last named princess has in each of the sources a father named Alf. Though the names differ, there is much to indicate that we have to do with one and the same legend. The combat of the brothers is presented in the same way in both passages; the number of the Berserks who fall on the last day, for example, is eleven. The verses quoted by Saxo agree in part verbally with those cited in the saga; Hildebrand's shield is mentioned in both poems, and likewise the slaying of the son, in spite of the fact that Saxo in his narrative makes no mention of this detail. One remarkable point of identity between Saxo and the verses of the saga (but not of the prose narrative of the saga) is that the verse has the name Drott instead of Hild. Here Saxo's account is more primitive than that of the saga. One important name, meanwhile, the saga has preserved the more faithfully, that of Hildebrand.

Hildebrand must be the German hero of the same name who is well known from the *Nibelungenlied* (see p. 196). He was Dietrich of Bern's armorer and dwelt with his overlord at the court of Etzel, king of the Huns. In the extant fragment of the re-

Norse Mythology

markable ancient German poem, the *Hildebrandslied* (dating from the eighth century), Hildebrand's story runs as follows: Having been granted a furlough by Dietrich for the purpose of visiting his home, he met on the journey his own son Hadubrand, whom he had last seen as a small boy. Each gave the other his name; but Hadubrand, thinking that the old man was twitting him in claiming to be his father, engaged in combat with him. Since the poem is not extant in its entirety, the outcome of the duel can only be surmised. According to *Dietrich's Saga*, which rests on late German narratives, Hildebrand worsted his son (who is here called Alebrand) but did not kill him, and the two journeyed home together. Both Saxo and the saga mentioned above, on the other hand, declare that Hildebrand killed his only son; so it seems likely that the original legend (and the *Hildebrandslied* probably as well) gave a more tragic ending to the combat. No struggle between Hildebrand and a half brother of his is known to German legend, and this story therefore seems to have originated in the North in a period when the memory of the true circumstances had grown faint; this situation would also account for the difference as to the outcome of the combat. Some dim recollection of Hildebrand's having killed his only son nevertheless continued to survive; it is recorded in Saxo without connection with the rest of the narrative, while the saga bears witness to a most unfortunate attempt at motivation of the deed in question.

ROMUND GREIPSSON

Page 245, line 6—The story of Romund is told in a highly romantic saga (*Hrómundar Saga Greipssonar*), in which, however, old legends have been incorporated. Helgi the Brave is to be identified with Helgi Haddingjaskati, and the Troll woman Kara is his beloved, the Valkyrie Kara; they were the subject of a lost poem, the *Káruljóð* (see note to p. 165). Another legendary feature as well, belonging to the Eddic lays, has found its way into this saga. In *Helgakviða Hundingsbana Qnnur* we read that Helgi Hundingsbane was a foster son of Hagal and that he was saved from the designs of king Hunding by his foster father's setting him to work grinding at the mill in woman's clothing. The saga thus seems to be a product in part of ancient legendary motives and in part of stories of adventure of a type that was very popular in later times. The *Landnámabók* mentions a cer-

Notes

tain Romund Greipsson as having lived in Telemark; he is said to have been the ancestor of Ingolf and Leif, the first settlers in Iceland.

The *Sturlunga Saga* (Kålund's edition, I, 22) informs us that Rolf of Skalmarnes, in the course of a festival at Reykjahólar in Iceland (in the year 1119) recited a saga "of Rongvid the Viking and of Olaf, king of warriors, of the robbing of Thrain's mound, and of Romund Greipsson, and in it there were many verses. The same saga was (later) recounted for the amusement of king Sverri, and he said that these lying sagas were the most entertaining. Yet men have been able to trace their origin back to Romund Greipsson. Rolf himself composed this saga." The brief list of contents shows clearly that the saga told by Rolf was the one detailed above. But the saga cannot have been committed to writing so early, and its present shape cannot be the original; proof hereof is to be found in the fact that the saga as we know it contains no verse.

RAGNAR LODBROK AND HIS SONS

Page 251, line 24—Ragnar Lodbrok and his sons form the subject of two Icelandic sagas, *Saga af Ragnari Konungi Loðbrók ok Sonum Hans*, which has connections with the *Vǫlsunga Saga*, and *þáttr af Ragnars Sonum*. The last named is derived, like the Latin excerpt in the Icelander Arngrim Jónsson's *Rerum Danicarum Fragmenta* (ca. 1600), from a lost saga of the Danish kings, the *Skjǫldunga Saga*. Mention may be made besides of Ragnar's death lay, *Krákumál* (from the twelfth century). Saxo too has (in Book IX) many and in part divergent accounts of Ragnar. He gives Ragnar no less than ten sons, among them one named Ubbi. The Icelandic sources make especially prominent Ragnar's two marriages and what is connected with these, and also his unfortunate incursion into England; they attribute to his sons the famous deeds. Saxo, on the other hand, presents Ragnar too as a formidable Viking and a great conqueror.

As Axel Olrik has demonstrated, Saxo derives his history of Ragnar in great part from Norse legends. This is the case, for example, with the story of Ragnar's first wife, Lathgertha, in which Saxo follows a local legend from the neighborhood of Trondhjem. It runs, in brief, thus: Frœ, king of Sweden, to be identified with the god Frey, has slain the Norwegian king Sivard,

[357]

the father of Ragnar's father, and has carried off women belonging to the royal house. Ragnar takes vengeance, and in the struggle against Frœ receives aid from sundry Norwegian women; at their head marches Lathgertha, a maiden used to warfare, with her hair hanging down about her shoulders. Later he goes alone to her dwelling in "Gœlerdal" (Guldal); a bear and a dog stand bound outside the door; he knocks down the one and splits open the muzzle of the other. Then he enters the house and gets the maiden herself "as a reward for the dangers he had run."

In connection with the story of Jormunrek reference has been made to the disposition on the part of the makers of legend to connect originally distinct legends into a legendary cycle (see p. 190 and p. 199 f.). Like Jormunrek, Ragnar too has in this way found a place, by means of his marriage, in the great legendary cycle dealing with the Volsungs. Ragnar's death in the serpents' den had so definite a similarity to details in the legends of the Volsungs that it was able to carry over with it the combat with the serpent; Ragnar thus has features in common both with the Gjukung Gunnar and with Sigurd Fafnirsbane.

The legends of Ragnar and of the sons of Lodbrok have their basis in great measure in historical events. These events, however, have in the Icelandic saga been embellished with romantic motives of purely literary invention; *Ragnar's Saga* is thus far from being actual history. The historical foundation must be sought in the works of foreign writers, in French and English chronicles. We read in contemporary Frankish annals that a certain Ragnar in the year 845 sailed up the Seine as far as Paris, which he pillaged, and that another chieftain named Bjorn (called by a later writer *Bier ferreae costae*, i. e., Bjorn Ironside) by way of the same vein penetrated far into the country and remained in France for the space of several years. In English annals we read that an army under the command of the brothers Halfdan, Ingvar, and Ubbi in 855 made an inroad upon England. In 866 Ingvar and Ubbi came back once more, and in 867 they defeated two Northumbrian kings near York; both kings, of whom the one was named Ella, fell in the battle. The brothers remained in the land several years, and in 870 killed the East-Anglian king Edmund. Ingvar died soon afterward, but the army carried on its warfare in England for some years, until Ubbi was slain. The sources give no indication, however, that the incursion of 866 was due to any desire of the brothers to avenge their father. A certain Sigfred,

Notes

brother to a Danish king Halfdan, is mentioned in an entry
under the year 873. There is no evidence in any of the contemporary sources that these brothers were sons of the Ragnar
first mentioned or of any other man whatsoever bearing this
name. The Norman historian William of Jumièges (ca. 1070) is
the first writer to call the aforesaid *Bier ferreae costae* a son of
"king *Lothroc*" (he does not call him *Ragnar* Lodbrok); and
English sources of the twelfth century are the first to name
Ingvar and Ubbi as the sons of *Lodebroch.* (From the close of the
same century dates a runic inscription in the very ancient burial
mound at Maeshowe in the Orkneys, reading as follows: *sia
hǫuhr uar laþin hælr loþbrokar synir hœnar þœir uǫro huater;*
that is, "this mound was raised before Lodbrok's; her sons they
were bold." According to Sophus Bugge we are not permitted,
with Munch and G. Storm, to assume from *hœnar* that *loþbrokar*
here is a woman's name; *hœnar* is used because *loþbrokar* is
grammatically feminine; cf., in rustic Norwegian dialects, "ho"
as used of "ei kjempa".) The name Ragnar Lodbrok occurs for
the first time in Danish sources in a chronicle dating from about
the year 1150, and in Icelandic for the first time in Ari Frodi
(about 1130). Whether any of the brothers really made expeditions into the Mediterranean and conquered Luna (in Tuscany) is
likewise uncertain; this story was originally told of Bjorn Ironside
by William of Jumièges; but this writer is most untrustworthy in
dealing with the history of the Viking expeditions. Certain it is,
at any rate, that they never captured Vivilsborg (i. e., Wiflisburg
or Avenches in Switzerland). *Nornagests þáttr* also has an account of their conquest of these two towns; here the old man who
dissuades them from proceeding against Rome is called *Sónes;*
according to S. Bugge, this is an alien name, probably Romance
in origin, and the legend dealing with this expedition therefore in all probability found its way from without into the
North.

Cf. Johannes Steenstrup, *Normannerne* I (1876), pp. 81–127;
Gustav Storm, *Kritiske Bidrag til Vikingetidens Historie* (1878),
pp. 35–132; Axel Olrik, *Kilderne til Sakses oldhistorie* II (1894),
pp. 102–33, with which see *Aarbøger for nordisk oldkyndighed*
1894, pp. 94–96, 147 ff. (Arngrim Jónsson); S. Bugge, *Bidrag til
den ældste Skaldedigtnings Historie* (1894).

Norse Mythology

HJORLEIF AND HALF

Page 256, *line* 20—The source of this narrative is the historico-legendary (Icelandic) *Hálfs Saga*, which probably was composed about the year 1300 or somewhat earlier, but based on older legendary materials. The kernel of it is an ancient account of Half and his champions; even in as old a work as the skaldic poem *Ynglingatal* (ninth century) allusion is made in a poetic paraphrase to the arson practised against Half. The story of Half and Half's Champions has clearly been influenced by the saga of Rolf Kraki (p. 215). Furthermore, there are episodes in *Hálf's Saga* that have the character of folk tale, and there are definite marks of ancient genealogical records; it may be mentioned, for example, that In-Stein is referred to in the genealogical Eddic poem *Hyndluljóð* as a son of Alf the Old and as the father of that Ottar who is the real subject of the lay. Cf. A Le Roy Andrews's introduction to his edition of *Hálfs Saga ok Hálfsrekka* (*Altnordische Saga-Bibliothek*, vol. 14), Halle 1909. Half's Champions bore a high reputation in ancient times, and several of the great families of Iceland traced their descent to Half and to his men.

It is not certain whether the legend of Half was originally Norwegian. It is worth noting that *Hálfr* according to its form may be the same name as *Hapuwulafᴙ* ("battle wolf"), which is found on a Swedish runic stone of the seventh century (Stentoften, Blekinge); this stone also bears a masculine name *Haeruwulafᴙ* ("sword wolf"), which contains the same components as *Hjǫrr*, *Hjǫrleifr* and which, syllable for syllable, corresponds to *Hjǫrolfr*.

FRIDTHJOF

Page 263, *line* 32—*Friðþjófs Saga* is one of the later sagas of antiquity (p. 124), built on a love motive. One of its marked traits is the almost complete freedom from supernatural features, the artistic composition, and the ethical idea that runs like a red thread through the whole. It is Icelandic and probably was composed about the year 1300 (or possibly earlier). The story is no doubt to be regarded as a product of free invention; at any rate, no demonstrable historical basis is to be discovered in it. See Hj. Falk, *Arkiv för nordisk filologi* VI (1890), p. 60 ff. The very name *Friðþjófr*, that is, "thief of peace", is proof that

Notes

the bearer of the name is no historic personage. On the basis of the connected narrative of the saga, the name has been independently compounded after the model of other names in *þjófr* (*Valþjófr*, *Geirþjófr*, etc.); but in these older names the element *þjófr* hardly means "thief"; it is rather an adaptation of the Anglo-Saxon *þēow* and the Old German *dio* ("thrall"), a compounding element in various personal names. See S. Bugge, *Arkiv* VI, p. 224 ff. Systrand (in old Norwegian sources "*Systrǫnd*", while the saga, no doubt less correctly, has *Syrstrǫnd*) is still used as a name for Leikanger parish.—Framnes must be sought at Vangsnes.

The story of Fridthjof's father Thorstein Vikingsson is told in a separate saga, filled with romantic features. It tells of Thorstein's origin (his remote ancestor was king Halogi of Halogaland), of his strife and later friendship with king Beli of Sogn, and of their conquest of the Orkneys and their appointment of a Viking named Angantyr as earl.

OF TEMPLES, OF SACRIFICES, AND OF DIVINATION

Page 276, *line* 11—Further reference may be made to R. Keyser, *Nordmændenes Religionsforfatning i Hedendommen*, Christiania 1847 (=*Samlede Afhandlinger*, Christiania 1868, pp. 249–399); K. Maurer, *Die Bekehrung des Norwegischen Stammes zum Christenthume* II, München 1856, pp. 188–238; Henry Petersen, *Om Nordboernes Gudedyrkelse og Gudetro i Hedenold*, Copenhagen 1876; cf., in addition, the handbooks of mythology listed in the bibliography. One specific phase of the worship of the gods, the sacrificial banquet, has been exhaustively treated by Maurice Cahen, in his *Études sur le vocabulaire religieux du vieux-scandinave. La libation*, Paris 1921.

INDEX

Key to symbols not found in the English alphabet (approximate equivalents):

Æ=AE; æ=ae.   Q=O; ǫ=o.   Ø=OE; ø, œ=oe.
ð=d.   Þ=TH; þ=th.

Foreign symbols carrying separate marks of accentuation are entered in the index as if unaccented; thus, Ö=O; å=a; ē=e, etc.

[363]

Index

Index

Index

Index

Index

Index

Index

Index

Index

Index

Index

Index

Index

Index

Index

Index

Index

Index

Index

[382]

Index

Index

Index

Index

Index

Index

Index

Index

Index

Index

PUBLICATIONS OF

THE AMERICAN-SCANDINAVIAN FOUNDATION

Committee on Publications

WILLIAM WITHERLE LAWRENCE, Professor of English in Columbia University, *Chairman*

HANNA ASTRUP LARSEN, Editor *The American-Scandinavian Review*, *Secretary*

JOHN A. GADE, author of *Charles the XII*

CHARLES S. PETERSON, Publisher, Chicago

HENRY GODDARD LEACH, Editor *The Forum*

JAMES CREESE, Secretary of the Foundation

SCANDINAVIAN CLASSICS

I. *Comedies by Holberg: Jeppe of the Hill, the Political Tinker, Erasmus Montanus*

Translated by OSCAR JAMES CAMPBELL, JR., and FREDERIC SCHENCK *$2.00*

II. *Poems by Tegnér: The Children of the Lord's Supper and Frithiof's Saga*

Translated by HENRY WADSWORTH LONGFELLOW and W. LEWERY BLACKLEY *$2.00*

III. *Poems and Songs by Björnstjerne Björnson*

Translated in the original meters, with an Introduction and Notes, by ARTHUR HUBBELL PALMER *$2.00*

IV. *Master Olof, by August Strindberg*

An historical play, translated, with an Introduction, by EDWIN BJÖRKMAN   *$2.00*

V. *The Prose Edda, by Snorri Sturluson*

Translated from the old Icelandic, with an Introduction and Notes, by ARTHUR GILCHRIST BRODEUR   *$2.00*

VI. *Modern Icelandic Plays, by Jóhan Sigurjónsson: Eyvind of the Hills and The Hraun Farm*

Translated by HENNINGE KROHN SCHANCHE   *$2.00*

VII. *Marie Grubbe: A Lady of the Seventeenth Century, by J. P. Jacobsen*

An historical romance, translated, with an Introduction, by HANNA ASTRUP LARSEN

VIII. *Arnljot Gelline, by Björnstjerne Björnson*

A Norse Epic, translated by WILLIAM MORTON PAYNE   *$2.00*

IX. *Anthology of Swedish Lyrics, from 1750 to 1915*

Selections from the greatest of Swedish lyrics, translated by CHARLES WHARTON STORK

X & XI. *Gösta Berling's Saga, by Selma Lagerlöf*

The English translation by LILLIE TUDEER, completed and carefully edited. Two volumes

XII. *Sara Videbeck (Det går an), and The Chapel, by C. J. L. Almquist*

A sentimental journey with a practical ending, and the tale of a curate, translated, with an Introduction, by ADOLPH BURNETT BENSON   *$2.00*

XIII. *Niels Lyhne, by J. P. Jacobsen*

A psychological novel, translated, with an Introduction, by HANNA ASTRUP LARSEN   *$2.00*

XIV. *The Family at Gilje: A Domestic Story of the Forties, by Jonas Lie*

Translated by SAMUEL COFFIN EASTMAN, with an Introduction by JULIUS EMIL OLSON *$2.00*

XV & XVI. *The Charles Men, by Verner von Heidenstam*

Tales from the exploits of Charles XII, translated by CHARLES WHARTON STORK, with an Introduction by FREDRIK BÖÖK. Two volumes *$4.00*

XVII. *Early Plays: Catiline, The Warrior's Barrow, Olaf Liljekrans, by Henrik Ibsen*

Translated by ANDERS ORBECK *$2.00*

XVIII. *The Book About Little Brother: A Story of Married Life, by Gustaf af Geijerstam*

Translated, with an Introduction, by EDWIN BJÖRKMAN *$2.00*

XIX. *A Book of Danish Verse*

Selections from the works of Danish Poets from Oehlenschläger to Johannes V. Jensen. Translated in the original meters by S. FOSTER DAMON and ROBERT SILLIMAN HILLYER. Selected and annotated by OLUF FRIIS *$2.00*

XX. *Per Hallström: Selected Short Stories*

A collection of tales by Sweden's great master of the short story. Translated, with an Introduction, by F. J. FIELDEN *$2.00*

XXI & XXII. *The Poetic Edda*

A complete metrical version of the Poetic or Elder Edda, including the Lays of the Gods and the Lays of the Heroes, translated, with a General Introduction and Notes, by HENRY ADAMS BELLOWS. Two volumes bound as one *$4.00*

XXIII. *America of the Fifties: Letters of Fredrika Bremer*

The journal of an American tour, illustrated with sketches by the author. The translation of Mary Howitt, revised and edited, with an Introduction, by ADOLPH BURNETT BENSON *$2.00*

XXIV. *Norwegian Fairy Tales*

Translated by HELEN and JOHN GADE, from the Collection of Asbjörnsen and Moe. Drawings by KITTELSEN and WEREN-SKIOLD $2.00

XXV. *The Swedes and Their Chieftains, by Verner von Heidenstam*

Stories of Sweden's great men from the coming of the Swedes to the beginning of the present century of peace. Translated from the Swedish by CHARLES WHARTON STORK. Illustrated

$2.50

XXVI. *Hans Christian Andersen, by Himself: The True Story of My Life*

The autobiography of the world's most beloved story-writer. The original edition in the contemporary translation of MARY HOWITT. Illustrated $2.50

XXVII. *Norse Mythology: Legends of Gods and Heroes by Peter Andreas Munch in the Revision of Magnus Olsen*

An authoritative book brought up to date. English version by SIGURD BERNHARD HUSTVEDT $2.50

SCANDINAVIAN MONOGRAPHS

I. *The Voyages of the Norsemen to America*

A complete exposition, with illustrations and maps, by WILLIAM HOVGAARD $7.50

II. *Ballad Criticism in Scandinavia and Great Britain During the Eighteenth Century*

A comparative study, by SIGURD BERNHARD HUSTVEDT

$5.00

III. *The King's Mirror*

A famous treatise, translated from the Norwegian of the thirteenth century, with an Historical Introduction, by LAURENCE MARCELLUS LARSON $5.00

IV. *The Heroic Legends of Denmark*

Revised and expanded for this edition by the author, the late AXEL OLRIK, in collaboration with the translator, LEE M. HOLLANDER $5.00

V. *Scandinavian Art: A Survey of Swedish Art, by Carl G. Laurin; Danish Art in the Nineteenth Century, by Emil Hannover; Modern Norwegian Art, by Jens Thiis; Introduction by Christian Brinton*

The first comprehensive discussion of the artistic production of the three Northern nations; in one volume of 660 pages with 375 illustrations $8.00

THE
AMERICAN-SCANDINAVIAN REVIEW

An Illustrated Magazine, presenting the progress of life and literature in Sweden, Denmark, and Norway
$3.00 a year

For information regarding the above publication address the

SECRETARY OF THE AMERICAN-SCANDINAVIAN
FOUNDATION
25 West 45th Street, New York City

www.ingramcontent.com/pod-product-compliance
Lightning Source LLC
Chambersburg PA
CBHW020833030726
47496CB00001B/214